Great Leaders

Biographies of Abraham Lincoln, Winston Churchill, George Washington, Ulysses S. Grant, and Napoleon Bonaparte

By
Simon Johnson

engaging in the rendering of legal, financial, medical or professional advice. The content within this book has been derived from various sources. Please consult a licensed professional before attempting any techniques outlined in this book.

By reading this document, the reader agrees that under no circumstances is the author responsible for any losses, direct or indirect, that are incurred as a result of the use of the information contained within this document, including, but not limited to, errors, omissions, or inaccuracies.

Bundle Book

Abraham Lincoln

Table of Contents

Introduction

On the evening of April 14, 1865, a crowd rushed then-president Abraham Lincoln from Ford's Theatre to the Peterson's house. Doctors arrived at the house as fast as they could. Unfortunately, there was nothing they could do. The next morning, at 7:22, President Abraham Lincoln passed away.

When a person hears about Lincoln, one of their first thoughts goes back to this fateful night. Most people know that actor John Wilkes Booth assassinated Abraham Lincoln, but people don't often think about why this became one of America's widely told stories about our 16th president. On the surface, Booth and his conspirators planned to kill Lincoln because of his role in ending slavery. But there is so much more to the story than what's on the surface. When it comes to the truth of the matter, it all goes back to what a great leader Abraham Lincoln was. From his first steps in politics as a young man in Illinois to one of the best presidents of the United States, Lincoln held strong beliefs. He remained calm in times of crisis and buried his emotions and worries so others could fight a good battle.

Before you can learn what a fierce leader Lincoln was, you need to get an idea of how this came to be. Chapter 1 will do exactly this for you. You will get a glimpse into Lincoln's childhood. You will see how the people of Lincoln's life and events that occurred paved the way for his views on politics and slavery.

Chapter 2 will further this insight through a brief look at Lincoln's early adulthood. This chapter focuses on how Lincoln started to develop as a leader as a dedicated worker and member of the New Salem, Illinois, debate club. Chapter 2 shows a sharp turning point in Lincoln's life, one that made him believe the institution of slavery had to be stopped.

Chapter 3 takes a look at Lincoln's early political career. Starting with winning a seat in the Illinois House of Representatives in the 1834 election, Lincoln quickly proved he had what it took to be a successful politician. On top of this, Lincoln used this time to strengthen his leadership skills.

Chapter 4 discusses Lincoln's career as a lawyer. During his first session in Congress, Lincoln started to teach himself about politics and American law. He wanted to know everything he could about these topics, which only gave him more ambition to become a lawyer. It was also during this time that Lincoln started to focus on courting, marriage, and raising a family.

Chapter 5 gives you a glimpse of Lincoln's road to the White House. Several years before his 1860 Presidential election,

Lincoln found it necessary to protect the country from becoming a stronger slave nation.

Chapter 6 discusses Lincoln as a presidential leader. From the time he took the oath, Lincoln knew that he could change the course of American history. Southern states had already started to secede from the Union, which Lincoln vowed to preserve.

Chapter 7 looks at Lincoln as a leader for the Union Army. Throughout his presidency, America was divided, and the Civil War waged on. Lincoln put all of his leadership skills to the test as the Commander in Chief of the United States Army.

There are many characteristics that made Abraham Lincoln a great leader. It is essential to remember, however, that many of these features grew with him. As a child, he was quiet with low expectations. He didn't believe he could look beyond the world he knew, which was farm and family life. But as Lincoln stepped out into the world and truly started to realize what he was capable of, he shook the world. He became one of the most popular United States presidents and is known as the man who helped free the slaves. This book will show you a part of this journey. It will show you how he strengthened his leadership abilities to become The Great Emancipator.

Chapter 1: Early Life

Abraham Lincoln saw the Earth's sunshine for the first time on February 12, 1809. He joined his father, Thomas Lincoln, mother, Nancy Hanks Lincoln, and sister, Sarah (who was called Sally), in a one-room cabin on the outskirts of Hodgenville, Kentucky. Lincoln always saw his father as a tough man and knew that his father did everything to provide for his family. While Lincoln struggled with his father, he adored his mother. Besides taking care of her family, Nancy spent her days teaching her children. She believed education was the foundation for a successful life. Even though schools were scarce and the family often moved, Nancy made sure her children received an education.

The Molding of Lincoln's Views on Slavery

Thomas's views on slavery had a profound influence on Lincoln. He often heard about slavery from his parents, as they were part of an abolitionist group. At such a young age, however, Lincoln struggled to understand the slavery debate. The first time Lincoln started to understand the slavery debate was when he saw a slave auction. At the time, his family was visiting a city to gather their winter supplies. As the family walked down the dirt road, Lincoln saw people being auctioned off for work. Although he didn't fully comprehend the event, he knew it enraged his parents and saw fear in the faces of the slaves. While the Lincoln family didn't stay in the area long, as neither Thomas or Nancy wanted their children to see such horrors, Lincoln never forgot this event.

It wasn't long after this that Thomas decided to move his family from Kentucky to Indiana. While there were many reasons for this uprooting, one of the main reasons was slavery. Kentucky had been a slave state since the early 1790s, and Thomas could no longer live in a state that supported the institution (Abraham Lincoln's Childhood: Growing Up to Be President, 2013). It didn't take a lot to convince Nancy, as she felt the same way as her husband. Further, she didn't want her children to grow up supporting slavery.

While most people feel the move helped Lincoln shape his opinion that slavery was wrong, it taught him much more. Moving taught Lincoln that you want to flee from slavery. Leaving Kentucky showed Lincoln that you need to be willing to do whatever you can to get away from the institution of slavery. Moreover, it showed a young Lincoln that putting yourself through hardship is better than living in a state that allows slavery.

Once the family settled in Indiana, they were all put to work trying to make the overgrown land of weeds and trees a home. Lincoln helped his parents clear the bushes, trees, and build a small log home. After the family had a roof over their heads, Thomas and his son went to work clearing land for a field, which they plowed the following season. The family lived miles away from any other civilization, including neighbors. If they needed supplies from the store, the trip would take days to a week by horse.

Not long after the family moved, Nancy learned of a one-room schoolhouse about nine miles away. This schoolhouse became the first time Lincoln and Sally received public education. The children spent a total of five to six hours going back and forth between school every day. While this wasn't ideal, it was what the family could do to give their children an education. Even though the school wasn't open long, the education Lincoln received help mold him into the man he would become. He understood the importance of education, which is a feeling that followed him into the White House.

Lincoln's World Shifts

In 1818, Nancy became ill with "milk sickness," which took her life. The loss of Nancy brought more stress and emotional pain to her husband. Not only did he have to spend his days in the field and hunting, but he now had to care for his two young children solely. Sally, who was about 11, quickly learned how to cook the meals and take care of the household chores. She tended to her brother and did whatever she could to fill the hole their mother left.

While Lincoln and his sister did their best to care for themselves and the house, Thomas knew that he needed to find a new wife. Leaving his children in the log cabin, he traveled back to Kentucky, where he searched for a wife. At first, it didn't seem like their father would be gone for so long, but they soon started to run out of food and began to feel abandoned. Their closest neighbors would check on them, noting they were filthy and skinny. By this time, the children had little to eat but dried berries and whatever food people brought for them.

The Influence of Lincoln's Stepmother

Six months after leaving, Tom returned with his new wife, Sarah Johnston, and her three children. Lincoln reminisced on meeting Sarah for the first time later in his life. He stated he had longed for a woman's care and compassion for so long he couldn't help but rush into Sarah's arms and give her a warm embrace. Sarah returned the affection and immediately started to clean up the children and the home. She got Tom to put in wood floors and learned about Lincoln and Sally's interests.

As a child, Lincoln craved learning but was unable to attend school. While Tom didn't see education as a waste, it wasn't high on his list. He needed his son to help him with the outdoor chores. But, Lincoln was interested in learning how to read. He would often become frustrated with the outdoor work, grab a book, and find a quiet place to build his reading skills.

Sarah, who couldn't read or write herself, admired Lincoln for his efforts and showed him the six books she had brought with her. A few of these books were *Life of Washington* by Parson Weem, *Aesop's Fables* by Aesop, and *The Pilgrim's Progress* by John Bunyan. They weren't the most comfortable books for Lincoln to learn from, but with the added help of a new country school, he was able to learn how to read and write. Unfortunately, the school closed three years after opening, but it established one more step toward Lincoln's leadership skills.

Developing His Mind

At the age of 15, Lincoln only had about a full year of education. The schools near the Lincoln home rarely stayed open long, and when they did, Lincoln often had to stay home to help his father on the farm. This is around the time Lincoln started to find ways to focus on reading and growing his mind over his farm chores. Of course, catching his son reading when he was supposed to be working did not sit well with

Thomas. The differing beliefs on the importance of education began to drive a larger wedge between Lincoln and his father.

At this time, Thomas' health started to deteriorate. He was going blind and began to rely on Lincoln for income. Lincoln had to tend to his family's chores and find work outside of the home. Lincoln was not like his father, however. He was more academic and didn't have a lot of physical strength. Because of this, Thomas viewed his son as lazy and was often dissatisfied with Lincoln's work.

The wedge only grew deeper when Lincoln began working for neighbors. As a young man, he wanted to get out on his own but struggled because he had to give his father all the money he earned. At the time, Indiana state law forbade children to keep their earnings; they had to give all their money to their fathers. Lincoln wanted to keep the money for himself as he started to see it as a way out.

Lincoln wanted more for himself. He had a taste of socializing with peers and academics when he attended schools. He wanted that again. He enjoyed telling people stories and started to become known for his joke-telling. Lincoln also realized he was comfortable talking in front of other people. Public speaking didn't seem to bother him as much as it did others.

Through his education and socializing, Lincoln's confidence began to blossom. He began to realize what he could accomplish if he put his mind to it. He learned there was more for him than farming. He could be a teacher, lawyer, or anything else. He could go to college if he could ever pay his way. The more Lincoln developed his mind, the more he realized what the world has to offer.

Chapter 2: Lincoln Out on His Own

Thomas uprooted his family again when Lincoln was about 20 years old. They moved from Indiana to Macon County, Illinois (Abraham Lincoln's Childhood: Growing Up to Be President, 2013). The main reason for the move was that Thomas' cousins told him the land was better for farming there. While Lincoln followed, he would not continue to live with the family. About a year later, Lincoln moved to New Salem, Illinois where he started to pursue other interests.

Lincoln worked at a variety of jobs such as a store clerk and boatman. He found work whenever and wherever he could. Because Lincoln no longer had family holding him down, he often took jobs that involved travel. In 1831, Lincoln joined John Hanks and John Johnston on a job. Their mission was to bring a load of cargo from Illinois to New Orleans. This was Lincoln's second trip to Louisiana. He made the same voyage a couple of years prior. This trip, however, became one that set the mold for Lincoln's views on slavery.

Lincoln's New Orleans Trip

Lincoln, Johnston, and Hanks received the job offer to bring Denton Offutt's general store cargo from New Salem to New

Orleans. Lincoln had the task of the clerk, which put him in the leadership role. Offutt felt that the steamboat would be an excellent way to bring the cargo down by following the Mississippi River. Lincoln, who made that trip on a flat raft before, agreed.

The men started in April 1831 and finally arrived at their destination in July. While the journey went smoothly, the three men witnessed the real conditions of slavery almost immediately after stepping onto land. As they were walking around New Orleans, Lincoln and Hanks saw the horrors of slavery. They saw slaves who were beaten, chained, and maltreated. Neither man could believe what they were witnessing. While Hanks was able to compose himself a bit better, Lincoln struggled with the sights, sounds, and smells. Later in life, Hanks would tell people this was the moment that defined Lincoln's views on slavery. Lincoln, who enjoyed a good conversation and often had something to say, become silent. His manner became solemn as he wanted to help the slaves but knew he could not interfere (Experiences with Slavery, n.d.). Unfortunately, this would not be Lincoln's last experience with slavery on the trip.

A few days later, while walking around the town Lincoln noticed a young girl being auctioned off. The auctioneer had told the men who were interested in bidding to examine her thoroughly. Lincoln watched in disbelief as he saw grown men touching every part of this girl's body. They discussed how well she would work on their plantation or what issues she had and how this would interfere with her work. Lincoln became thoroughly disgusted with this event. He could no longer stand the sight of slavery. According to several biographies, it was this event that sets the tone of hate against the institution of slavery for Abraham Lincoln. In 1865, John Hanks recounted this moment in Lincoln's life. Before they left the scene, Lincoln said to Hanks and Johnston, "By God, boys, let's get away from this. If ever I get a chance to hit that thing (slavery), I'll hit it hard." (Experiences with Slavery, n.d.).

Lincoln's Early Days of Leadership

When Lincoln returned to New Salem, the scenes of slavery were still fresh in his mind. No matter how hard he tried, he could not erase what he saw or heard. Lincoln's heart still ached -- he compassionate individual who believed people should be treated fairly, which was a characteristic Nancy and Sarah built in him.

Many historians feel that Lincoln's real-life experience of slavery is what started to pave his path for his law and political career. It was during this time Lincoln began to openly discuss his views on the issue. He felt that slavery needed to be abolished at all costs. The more Lincoln spoke at public events, the more he started to debate. It didn't take long for people to take notice of Lincoln's intelligence and natural speaking ability. He was a keen debater and not afraid to stand on his own. Lincoln knew what he felt, and no one was going to change his beliefs.

Lincoln joined a debate club in New Salem. He soon became one of the most persuasive debaters, causing him to reach the status of a leader in the community. He quickly grew into this role and soon found himself discussing politics with some of New Salem's leading politicians. At first, Lincoln was not thrilled about the notion of politics. It was never something he envisioned for himself. Although he was a great public speaker, Lincoln never felt he could persuade people toward his beliefs. After all, this was not a part of his personality.

It wasn't just his gift for debating that brought out Lincoln's leadership skills. Since coming back from New Orleans, Lincoln dedicated himself to Denton Offutt's general store. People were quick to notice how efficiently Lincoln worked and how well he treated every customer. Lincoln also extended his abilities to helping at the sawmill when they needed extra hands.

For the first time in his life, Lincoln felt as if he truly belonged. He enjoyed social outings, even if it was going to the debate club. The more Lincoln felt people believed in him, the more he started to believe in himself.

Chapter 3: Early Political Career

A few months after he joined the debate club, Lincoln started to look into politics. He made his first public political announcement in the spring in 1832 for the Illinois House of Representatives. Although he lost this election, it wouldn't keep him from aiming higher in the next political election.

Illinois State Legislature

Lincoln decided to run for Illinois State Legislature in 1834. After the announcement, people who knew Lincoln were thrilled. They knew he would become a successful legislator. Lincoln didn't fully agree with his supporters, however. While he appreciated their support, he didn't feel he was fit for office. Personally, Lincoln decided to get into politics to satisfy what he jokingly called his "national debt."

During this campaign, Lincoln didn't use the same strategy he used during the 1832 campaign. Instead of giving speeches, he used the benefits of his job as a land surveyor to walk around the state and meet as many citizens as possible. He discussed their beliefs rather than focusing on his views. For many citizens of Illinois, Lincoln made them feel that they mattered when it came to the government.

Lincoln's new political strategy worked as he won a seat in the House of Representatives in 1834 with 1,376 votes. As a member of the Whig Party, Lincoln's first session started in December 1834 and ended in February 1835. During the first session, Lincoln sat back and observed the discussions of the House of Representatives. He watched how politicians reacted to each other, especially when they didn't have the same views. It didn't take long for several legislators to find Lincoln had more to offer than he was giving.

When Lincoln spoke, he did so with confidence and authority. Other legislators would stop and listen to the new attendee. Although Lincoln had only one year of official schooling in his life, many people felt he was highly educated. He knew the language of the American laws, which made him an easy target to draft bills.

As Lincoln started to become comfortable in his role, he spoke powerfully about his beliefs, which included abolition and women's suffrage. Other members of the House of Representatives quickly realized Lincoln stood for equality. Gender, ethnicity, and skin color of skin didn't matter to Lincoln. What mattered was how people treated each other. Lincoln believed to gain equality in the United States, it had to start at the governmental level.

During Lincoln's first session, he became good friends with John Todd Stuart, an Illinois lawyer and Representative with Lincoln. Abraham Lincoln wanted to learn as much as he could about laws and politics, and Stuart has an excellent library for this task. Lincoln also started spending his time at auctions, which often sold the type of books Lincoln needed.

Lincoln Becomes a Whig Leader

When Lincoln ran for Illinois State Legislature in 1836, he received the highest number of voters over all other candidates. It was during this session that Lincoln took the reins of the Whig Party and became a leader. Because Lincoln was the second youngest legislator in his district, his role as the floor leader was rare. This role was generally reserved for one of the older legislators who held more experience. Through his continued self education and speeches, legislators felt he was the most qualified for the role.

His role as a leader is one that Lincoln preserved with dignity, but also maintained a persona that helped other legislators feel comfortable. As a leader, Lincoln understood that everyone on the team should be able to say what they believe. He never allowed the power he held as the Whig floor leader to control other legislators. After all, the state of Illinois was in desperate need of all the brainpower it could get from legislators as the economy was in a bad state. The Governor of Illinois became so worried about the economy that he called for legislators to hold a special meeting to discuss internal improvements.

In 1836, the Illinois legislators approved the plan for the Illinois and Michigan Canal. This canal would connect the Chicago and Illinois rivers to the Mississippi River and Lake Michigan. The proposal the legislators approved, which Lincoln favored, called for $500,000 loan. At the time, the economic state for both Illinois and Michigan allowed for this type of financing.

Unfortunately, the Illinois and Michigan Canal plan was on hold because of the Panic of 1837. The Panic of 1837 was a financial crisis that lasted until 1843 (Abraham Lincoln, Banking and the Panic of 1837 in Illinois, n.d.). Unemployment went up as wages went down. Both businesses and banks started to collapse. The panic affected Lincoln as a political leader in two ways. First, he wanted to do what he could to help his Illinois district. Once the panic started, employees working on the canal were laid off. Further, Michigan and Illinois would struggle to pay off their debt, and several roads and canals were unfinished.

Although Lincoln and other legislators tried, there was very little they could do to help the internal improvements. Even so, this didn't mean that Lincoln didn't come up with possibilities to improve the situation. The first option Lincoln brought forth to the legislative committee was that the state would buy land from the federal government at a reduced rate. Illinois would then take this land and sell it to settlers for a profit. While the committee praised Lincoln for the idea, the federal government declined. The other purpose was they would set up a new state tax. Anyone who owned highly valuable land would have to pay more in state taxes. The committee declined this idea. Unable to help improve Illinois' financial conditions, the state could no longer make any internal improvements until the 1840s.

Lincoln Supports Moving the Capital of Illinois

During the 1830s, Illinois was growing with new settlers from the East Coast. Most were moving to areas in central and northern parts of the state. This soon became a problem for the citizens of Illinois because the state seat was located in the southern end of the state. Lincoln, who was a strategic thinker, quickly noted that the capitol building needed to be moved from Vandalia, where it was located, to Springfield. He felt this would be the best location because the population was growing rapidly. Furthermore, Springfield was located in central Illinois, which meant people could easily reach the capital no matter where they settled. When Lincoln proposed this move to the committee, he received little support.

After Lincoln's proposal, legislators who were opposed to this idea started to work on dividing Sangamon County, where Springfield is located, in an attempt to weaken its delegator influence. If the county was separated, it wouldn't have as much power, and Springfield would have no chance of becoming the state capital. This plan did not work as Lincoln's leadership skills were stronger. He was able to get the bill approved and sent through the state legislature. The law did not expressly state the capitol building would be built in Springfield, however. The compromise among the committee members was that the capitol building would be built in the city that came up with two acres of land and $50,000. But everyone knew that Springfield was the only city that could meet these requirements. Because of this, the bill was tabled twice.

During the next session, Lincoln was able to secure more support for the bill. While some legislators requested reconsideration over the requirements, when it was put to the vote, that was not approved. Finally, the law was put to a vote with a list of locations. With Lincoln's additional supporters in the state legislature, Springfield was chosen as the location for the capitol.

Lincoln and the Debate on Abolition

The debate on abolition was a part of Lincoln's whole life. Not only were his parents, including his stepmother, abolitionists, but it had been a social debate since the creation of the United States of America. Through his studies, Lincoln learned that the Founding Fathers, specifically the author of the Declaration of Independence, Thomas Jefferson, tried to start a plan of abolition throughout his political career. This knowledge put a different spin on slavery in abolition for Lincoln. While Jefferson was a slaveholder, he also knew that the institution was not to last long on American soil. Unfortunately, decades later, the institution was still standing strong in many American states. This realization gave Lincoln more determination to do what he could to find an end to slavery, even if he would have to help develop an abolition plan just like Thomas Jefferson tried to do.

At the same time, Lincoln knew that he had to be careful when it came to the topic of abolition. Since the founding of the country, the anti-slavery literature was growing, and slaveholding states were becoming aggressive. They were establishing tighter laws to help keep their slaves under control. Even in the 1830s, Lincoln knew that someone with political authority bringing out terms for abolition would be met with a very hostile crowd.

The time to fight for abolition during Lincoln's third session in the state legislature occurred in the wrong moment. By this time, Lincoln was on a number of committees, more than the average legislator, and focusing the majority of his time on a new location for the Illinois state capital. Because of this, when members of Congress voted that Illinois did not support abolitionist societies and that it is every state's right to decide if they will be free or slaveholding, Lincoln voted against this bill but could not spend time arguing against it.

This doesn't mean that Lincoln wouldn't reopen the issues later. After the state capital bill was set, Lincoln turned his attention to the abolition bill. To try to get the bill back on the table for a re-discussion and vote, Lincoln sent around a written petition that allowed other legislators to sign in support. He argued that the institution of slavery was created in bad taste and stands for injustice of human beings. He also, however, didn't stand with the side of abolitionists groups either. Lincoln admitted that the issue of slavery would be able to see a close soon and easier if the groups wouldn't specifically talk about the evils of slavery. As a leader, Lincoln understood that people become defensive when they felt they were being attacked by someone else. Therefore, he believed if abolitionists handled the issue of slavery without attacking slaveholding states and slave owners, the issue would be put to rest.

Throughout the abolition discussion, Lincoln believed it was unconstitutional for Congress to abolish slavery for any state. It was the people of that state who needed to call for abolition. If they did not do this, then Congress could not step in. For

Lincoln, this was a defining moment in his political career. He held this position on abolition until a couple of years into his presidency.

Illinois State Bank

Abraham Lincoln was a strong supporter of the banking system. During his third Representative term, Lincoln was trying to help the economy of his state and bring forth a better banking system. For Lincoln and other Representatives who were on his side, this was a struggle because then-President Andrew Jackson had damaged the internal banking system. On top of this, banks started to struggle in the Panic of 1837, and many were closing their doors. One of these banks was the Illinois State Bank.

Lincoln had a different idea when it came to the Illinois State Bank—he believed that it could help the economy. The trick is, the legislators had to find the right way to go about this. Even when the Illinois State Bank joined other banks and suspended special payments, Lincoln continued to support the bank. Lincoln's efforts to help the bank would not bring the bank on better terms with the legislature as many were still skeptical about the banking system. Even though Lincoln started to focus on other matters by 1840, he continued to support the bank. During his speeches, he would often tell his audience that the war against the banking institutions needed to come to a close for the economy to get stronger.

Lincoln and Congress During the 1840s

Throughout the 1830s, Lincoln had gained a lot of support from other people, in and outside of Congress. While he took a bit of a backseat in the late 1830s and early 1840s, his wife, Mary Todd Lincoln, pushed him to run for the United States House of Representatives in 1846. After campaigning for Henry Clay a few years before, Lincoln ran a successful campaign and was elected into Congress.

Lincoln's leadership skills had only grown over the last decade, which made him more confident when he took his seat. But the United States House of Representatives was different than the state legislature. Other than the change of duties, Lincoln was the bottom Congressman. Other members of Congress didn't believe Lincoln was a powerful leader. But Lincoln knew he was and he was not afraid to show his leadership skills to anyone on the Congressional floor.

Unfortunately, Lincoln's views did not match up with everyone else's. He was open and honest about what he thought, what would work, and what wouldn't. If Lincoln didn't agree with what people had to say, he would challenge their views. He even challenged the views of the president when it came to the Mexican-American War, which he did not support. For some Congressional leaders, this made Lincoln stand out and they began to discuss this freshman House member.

Still a member of the Whig party, Lincoln made many Democrats angry by not supporting President Polk and the Mexican-American War. This anger only escalated when Lincoln successfully petitioned Congress to change the wording of a bill that detailed the Mexican-American as a "war unnecessarily and unconstitutionally begun by the president of the United States" (Glass, 2016).

As Lincoln continued to speak out about the war, he started to damage his political reputation. While most political leaders would take a backseat to keep their reputation to a higher standard, Lincoln refused to do this. Instead, he continued to stand up for his beliefs. Nonetheless, Lincoln would eventually step down from the United States House of Representatives after his good friend and legal partner, William Herndon, warned Lincoln about the damage he could continue to do to himself.

In 1848, Lincoln stayed in the political field, but he didn't run for reelection. Instead, he put his support into campaigning for Zachary Taylor. After Taylor won the election, he offered Lincoln a position for governorship of a small piece of Oregon Territory. Lincoln knew that taking this offer would damage his reputation even further, especially with his own state of

Illinois. Lincoln declined Taylor's offer and went back to his home in Springfield, Illinois with his wife and children.

Chapter 4: Lincoln the Lawyer

Research on Lincoln's days as a lawyer has become a popular topic for historians over the past few decades. One of the main reasons for this is it gives us more insight into Lincoln's personality and his skills as a leader. Lincoln was not only a self-taught lawyer, but he was a successful lawyer.

Lincoln started working toward his career in law in the mid-1830s when he became friends with John Stuart. While meeting with legislators during the day, Lincoln read books on law at night. At first, Lincoln had no interest in obtaining a license to practice law, which Illinois required. But Lincoln soon changed his mind and started learning about the legal practice through books and by talking with Stuart, who owned a law practice. In the fall of 1836, Lincoln made a trip to meet with the Illinois Supreme Court, which approved Lincoln's legal license. On March 1, 1837, Lincoln took the oath to support the Illinois and the United States Constitution.

Like most lawyers of his time, Lincoln used this job to give him the upper hand in the political field. Not only did the knowledge of laws give politicians a stronger understanding of their political job, but it also gave Lincoln a way to gain supporters.

Many people felt Lincoln's price for his services was fair. He started by charging his clients about $5. By the time he left for his presidency in 1861, Lincoln was closer to the $20 range. While this was thought to be expensive for a lawyer, many people felt Lincoln was worth it.

While Lincoln became an exceptional lawyer, he did not establish his own practice. He always had a legal partner but his partners weren't always around to take cases. For instance, Stuart was Lincoln's first legal partner, but he was more interested in his political career than taking cases. Immediately after receiving his license and taking the oath, Lincoln took major step by taking on the majority of cases in Stuart's law firm. Lincoln's other law partners during his more than 20-year career as a lawyer were Stephen T. Logan and William H. Herndon.

Like most of the career paths Lincoln took, he became his own type of lawyer. Lincoln was always honest about who he was and his skills, which often came to the surface whether he was speaking publicly or taking legal cases. Because of this, Lincoln continued to enhance his leadership skills throughout his legal career, which lasted until he moved into the White House.

One of Lincoln's great leadership abilities as a lawyer was simplifying his cases. He took some of the most complex cases and rationalized them into a few key points. Lincoln did this without the use of legal research. Of course, he continued to read and educate himself as this was his way. When it came to his cases, he read through all of the information and created logical arguments with clarity and ease. Lincoln also had a gift that allowed him to think rationally on the spot. He was rarely caught off guard by the opposing attorney in his cases.

Lincoln was naturally persuasive. This part of his personality would shine when he was speaking to a crowd or in the courtroom. He observed the body language of the juries and used the information he gained from this to persuade them to his side.

Lincoln often changed his prices depending on his client. He also did pro bono work. Lincoln understood the financial struggles people faced, especially when he first started, and the economy went into a recession. He understood that sometimes people didn't have the means to pay him financially, but this didn't mean they didn't have the right to a lawyer. At the same time, he would charge some clients more. This was the case when it came to the Illinois Central Railroad. For this case, Lincoln charged his highest rate in his legal career: $5,000.

As a lawyer, Lincoln took on any case brought to his desk and was often called a "Jack of all trades." It didn't matter if the cases were civil or criminal. He defended murders, freedmen, and the railroad. Some of his most notable cases are The Almanac Trial, The Matson Trial, and Illinois Central RR vs. County of McLean.

The Almanac Trial

The Almanac Trial is thought to be Abraham Lincoln's most famous case. It is said that Lincoln used the Old Farmer's Almanac to win his case. In reality, no one truly knows if Lincoln actually used The Old Farmer's Almanac. What people do know is Lincoln was a very skillful lawyer, and this is one case that proves it.

In this case, Lincoln defended William "Duff" Armstrong, a man accused of murdering James Preston Metzker. On the night of August 29, 1857, just a few minutes after midnight, Armstrong hit Metzker with what they called a slung-shot (a leather thong with a weight tied at the end of it). The only witness, Charles Allen, stated he saw the murder occur about 150 feet away from where he was standing at the time (Hale, 2019).

When Lincoln took on Armstrong's case, he refused to take payment because Lincoln had been friends with Armstrong's father, who passed away a few months before the trial. Another reason Lincoln didn't charge Armstrong is because he wanted to help the family. He took pity on Armstrong, who he didn't believe was a murderer, and he took pity on

Armstrong's mother as well. This is another example of one of Lincoln's leadership skills that's often overlooked. No matter what legal case Lincoln focused on or what was going on in his political career, he observed and thought of every situation individually. He understood the laws of cause and effect, and he also understood that everyone is their own person and each event was its own.

The Old Farmer's Almanac came into the story when Lincoln was asking Charles Allen questions. One of the questions Lincoln asked was how he knew it was Armstrong who killed Metzker. Allen famously stated, "By the light of the moon" (Hale, 2019). In response, Lincoln brought out *The Old Farmer's Almanac* and showed the jury this would not be possible because the moon, which was low on the horizon and in its first quarter, would not be able to produce enough light for Allen to see 150 feet away.

It was this that won the case for Lincoln. The jury agreed that with the moon at the position it was at the time of the murder, there was no way Allen could be certain it was Armstrong who killed Metzker. Armstrong was acquitted on the murder charges.

The Matson Trial

The Almanac Trial is one of Lincoln's most famous cases, and the Matson Slave Trial is one of his most important. This trial became a turning point for local free African Americans. Lincoln defended a slave owner, Robert Matson, during the trial in which the freedman and foreman for Matson, Anthony Bryant, fought for his family. While Bryant was free, his wife and children were still enslaved. After moving with Matson from Kentucky, a slave state, to Illinois, a free state, Matson's Caucasian housekeeper told Bryant's wife that her children were going to be sold in the south. Soon after this, one of Bryant's children was sent back to Kentucky. Fearing for his children, Bryant contacted abolitionists in the area who sent him to Hiram Rutherford and Gideon Ashmore. Because Illinois was a free state, Rutherford and Ashmore told Bryant to take Matson to court to get his family freed.

At first, Rutherford asked Lincoln to defend Bryant, but Lincoln had already chosen to defend Matson. Prior to Matson moving to Illinois, he signed documentation that he would free all his slaves in Illinois within a year of arrival. Lincoln tried to use this defense, but it didn't hold up in court because the Bryant family had been living in Illinois for two years. Because of this, Lincoln lost the case.

Many people feel that Lincoln's defense of a slave owner is ironic because of his view of slavery and later ending slavery in America. What this trial truly shows is Abraham Lincoln's leadership skills. First, he stood true to his rules of taking any case that came to his desk. Matson came to Lincoln before

Rutherford. Second, Lincoln put his emotions about the case aside and did what he could to defend his client. Lincoln never changed his mind about the horrors of slavery. During the trial, he still despised the institution of slavery. The bottom line for the Matson trial is Lincoln believed Matson had rights and it was his responsibility to defend Matson's rights.

Illinois Central Railroad vs. County of McLean

It is no surprise that Lincoln defended the Illinois Central Railroad during his time as a lawyer. As a young man who had just moved away from home years before, he worked on the railroad. The railroad was his longest career besides his political career. Like many of his jobs, he showed high potential and leadership. So when the railroad needed someone to defend them against McLean County in Illinois, Lincoln was its first choice. The railroad kept Lincoln employed as its lawyer until he left for the White House.

The Illinois Central Railroad vs. County of McLean is also known as the "McLean County Tax Case" (Gantt, 2019). Tax officials in McLean County stated that the railroad had to pay Illinois a charter tax for each county in which they were building. McLean County sent a nearly $500 bill to the railroad, which refused to pay. The railroad stated that its charter made no mention of such tax.

Lincoln and two other lawyers, Mason Brayman and Asahel Gridley, lost the first trial case. Gridley left the case, so Brayman, Lincoln, and another lawyer, James Joy, appealed the case and took it to the Supreme Court of Illinois. The first time they did this was in 1854. Lincoln appealed the case to the Supreme Court of Illinois again in 1856, this time by himself.

Lincoln won the case for the railroad in 1856, for which he sent them a bill of $5,000 for his services. This was an unusually high price for a lawyer, but the railroad case was rather complex and took years to win. But the railroad refused to pay Lincoln and told him to take them to court. If he won, they would pay the bill and request his services for their other trials. If they won, he would waive the bill. Lincoln agreed and took the railroad to court.

In the first trial, Lincoln won by default because the railroad didn't have a lawyer. For the second trial, the railroad had found an attorney while Lincoln represented himself. At the end of the trial, Lincoln was awarded the $5,000. He was also given the task of representing the Illinois Railroad in several cases throughout the next few years.

Today, many people question why the Illinois Railroad continued to use Lincoln as its attorney after he sued them for his bill. While we can never know the real reason for this, many historians speculate it is because Lincoln was the best lawyer of his political party. He was often asked to take on some of the toughest cases and would do so with ease. Other people feel it is because he always maintained a relaxed composure and worked hard to defend his clients. Further, during the time of the lawsuit, Lincoln was the special advisor to the Illinois governor, which put him on a higher rank than many other lawyers.

Lincoln continued to practice law until his presidency. He never truly gave up practicing law as he always planned to return to Illinois and continue to work with Herndon. The last time Lincoln saw Herndon before he left for Washington. He pointed to the sign with Herndon's and Lincoln's names on it and told Herndon not to change that sign. Lincoln stated, "If I live I'm coming back sometime, and then we'll go right on practising law as if nothing had ever happened" (Abraham Lincoln's Law Office in Springfield, Illinois, n.d.).

Chapter 5: Road to the White House

In ways, Lincoln's road to the White House happened unexpectedly. But once it started, he put everything he could into ensuring his presidency. Abraham Lincoln's road to the White House started in 1854 when his rival, Stephen A. Douglas, sent a bill through Congress asking to reopen the land from the Louisiana Purchase. Douglas felt these states should be able to choose to allow slavery. This bill became known as the Kansas-Nebraska Act and put a spin on the political parties. Before long, Lincoln and many other Whig Party members were politically homeless. Douglas, who was a Democrat, felt he should join the Republican Party because it could give him more pull. Once Lincoln heard about this, he quickly switched his political party from Whig, which started on its decline, to Republican. He wanted to do whatever he could to stop Douglas from establishing himself in a stronger political level.

Lincoln-Douglas Debates

Once Lincoln became a Republican, he quickly started targeting Douglas for a Senate seat in 1858. The men went through a series of debates, which are now known as the Lincoln-Douglas Debates. Altogether, the men engaged in seven debates, mainly focusing on the issue of slavery.

While the men discussed many issues within these debates, the main issue was slavery. Douglas was supportive of the institution whereas Lincoln had despised the institution since he was a young man. Although Lincoln believed every state had their rights, Lincoln felt the slavery extension into the Louisiana Territories had been settled during the Missouri Compromise. After the Mexican-American War, new territory was added to the United States, which brought the issue of slavery into question again. This led to the Missouri Compromise of 1850, which is one reason the Civil War held off as long as it did. This compromise provided a temporary solution to the growing aggressive slavery debate. But the question of extending slavery into the territories was once again on the table because of Douglas' Kansas-Nebraska Act.

The Republican Party was formed because of the Kansas-Nebraska Act. This party was meant to help keep slavery away from the American territories, which is why Douglas wanted to become the Republican leader. If he could get the political party to switch opinions on slavery, he would be able to push the Kansas-Nebraska Act through. This would not be an easy step for Douglas, especially with the Dred Scott Decision of 1857. The end result of this case told both Congress and the legislature of the territories that they had no right to exclude slavery from a territory. With this ruling, the Republican

Party's view against slavery became more intense. It continued to divide the Republican and Democratic parties.

As a leader, Lincoln understood the dangers of the political parties and that the American Union being separated on the issue of slavery would result in a war. As Lincoln stated during his speech when he announced his run for the Republic Senate seat, "A house divided against itself cannot stand...this government cannot endure permanently half slave and half free," (Lincoln-Douglas debates, n.d.). After stating these words, Lincoln openly challenged Douglas to a series of debates about the subject. Lincoln believed by doing this, they would be able to inform the people the truth about the slavery issue and the people would be able to decide what they wanted. Douglas agreed and then the two men set a schedule for their debates around Illinois.

The location of the debates were as follows:

- Ottawa - August 21
- Freeport - August 27
- Jonesboro - September 15
- Charleston - September 18
- Galesburg - October 7
- Quincy - October 13
- Alton - October 15

Each debate was to be three hours long (Lincoln-Douglas

debates, n.d.). Lincoln spent most of his time focusing on the moral sins of slavery. He would often ask Douglas specific questions to get a rise out of him. Douglas, on the other hand, would often attack Lincoln and supported the racial inequality that came with the institution of slavery. He approved of the disruption within the Union. When it came to support, the Southern states started to become irritated by Douglas' responses to Lincoln and his praise for inequality. Many slave states felt that Douglas didn't understand what slavery meant to them, but Douglas continued to hold the support of the Democratic Party.

In the end, Douglas defeated Lincoln by a few votes. When it came to their reputation, Lincoln succeeded in building his backup. He now had a stronger support system than previously. Moreover, the Republican Party held Lincoln in his esteem as their spokesperson because of his eloquent public speaking. Douglas, on the other hand, saw his system of support diminish.

This was not the last time the Lincoln-Douglas debates would be used in a campaign. When Lincoln and Douglas ran for the presidency in 1860, these debates were printed. They were then passed around and used in a way to persuade a person to vote for Lincoln or Douglas. Both men also used these debates throughout their speeches in order to gain supporters.

At the end of the 1858 election, an editorial column written by

Jeriah Bonham for the Illinois Gazette gave his prediction for how the presidential campaign of 1860 would play out. He wrote that Stephen Douglas would become the leading candidate for the Democratic Party and gain the pro-slavery supporters. Bonham further discussed how Abraham Lincoln would become the lead candidate for the Republican Party and gain support among the abolitionists.

The Presidential Campaign of 1860

After losing the Senate seat to Douglas, Lincoln mainly focused on his law practice. That was until people started to discuss the presidential election. The Democratic candidates were: Stephen Douglas, Robert Hunter, Andrew Johnson, Joseph Lane, James Guthrie, and Daniel Dickson. In the first voting poll held at the Democratic convention, Stephen Douglas took the lead, be needed to secure more than 50 more votes to win to become the Democratic candidate for the presidency. In the second poll, Stephen Douglas was nominated. He became the official Democratic candidate for the presidency.

The Republicans met for their convention around the same time as the Democrats. The candidates looking to receive the Republican nomination for president were: Simon Cameron, Salmon P. Chase, Edward Bates, Abraham Lincoln, William Seward, Benjamin Wade, John McLean, and William L.

Dayton. Lincoln won the votes and became the official Republican candidate.

Besides the Republicans and Democrats, there were two other political parties in the running. The Constitutional Union Party, whose candidate was John Bell and the Southern Democratic Party candidate, who was John C. Breckinridge (United States presidential election of 1860, n.d.).

Before the 1860 campaign for the presidency began, the political parties were in an internal war over the issue of slavery. For instance, the Southern Democratic Party organized because they didn't agree with the Democratic Party's stance on slavery. Prior to the Southern Democratic Party, the Republican Party formed in response to what Stephen Douglas was trying to do when it came to placing slavery in the territories. When it came to the Constitutional Union Party, they did what they could to ignore the issue of slavery. Because of this, this party mainly appealed to the border states, as they too did what they could to ignore the issue of slavery.

When it came to the debates, the candidates were mainly split. Lincoln and Douglas remained in the Northern states where they debated between each other just as they had two years earlier. Bell and Breckinridge remained in the Southern states, where they debated between each other. The division of candidates further divided the United States.

Lincoln's Role in the Campaign

In reality, 1859 named Lincoln as a possible option for the Republican presidential nomination. While he was popular among the Republicans, most people were not willing to say that Lincoln would gain the Republican nomination. But there were a lot of events that transpired between the fall of 1859 and early 1860 that caused many people to feel that Lincoln was the ideal candidate.

One of the main steps Lincoln took toward winning the Republican candidacy was speaking at Henry Ward Beecher's Brooklyn church. While Lincoln was unsure speaking about politics and slavery at a church was model, his law partner, Herndon, advised him to go. Herndon told Lincoln this could be a great way to get into the running for president. Herndon's advice proved to be correct. Once Lincoln spoke at the Brooklyn church, he was requested for speaking engagements all around the Midwest and New England.

While Lincoln was better prepared and effective with some speeches over others, he gained more voters as time went on. He impressed reporters and leading political figures in various states. By the time the Republicans met for their convention, most people felt that Lincoln was the best choice.

Once Lincoln received the nomination, he immediately made changes in his life so he could focus on winning the presidency. First, he stopped practicing law so he could focus on running his campaign from his home in Springfield. He spent his days meeting with politicians, supporters, and possible interests. He would go out of his way to make sure supporters were taken care of, and his wife, Mary, went out of her way to ensure people knew her husband was the best choice.

When it came to the soon-to-be First Lady of the United States, Mary Lincoln knew the power of politics and was one of Lincoln's biggest supporters. Not only because he was her husband, but because of the status it would bring her family. Unlike Lincoln, who grew up poor, Mary Todd Lincoln grew up on a plantation run by slaves. This was often a point brought up by the Democratic Party and other people who tried to tarnish Lincoln's growing popularity. But with his strong leadership skills, Lincoln handled these comments and questions with ease. He handled them in a persuasive way that proved to people anyone can put the issue of slavery to rest through doing what his wife did–get out of that type of lifestyle.

One of Lincoln's great leadership abilities was realizing the damage disunity can do within a group. When he was in the running for the presidency, his main concern was keeping the Republicans united. There was a lot of division around them from the states to the Democratic Party. Lincoln knew that if the Republican Party was able to stay united, they would have a better chance at winning. Therefore, in his speeches, he advised Republicans to not discuss points where they could disagree. He warned them what a disagreement within their party could do.

When it came to adding more supporters, Lincoln followed the same strategy he had since his second time running for Illinois Legislature: He went out and met with people. He would shake their hands and talk to them about what they felt the president should focus on. As a leader, Lincoln knew the importance of making sure everyone felt they were heard. Unfortunately, it was also around this time that Lincoln started to learn how many people didn't support him. Although he was able to persuade hundreds of people, there were still thousands who didn't want to spend any time on him. Of course, Lincoln handled these situations with ease and understanding. He knew that great leaders were able to handle criticisms just as well as they could handle compliments.

The Election of 1860

By the time election night rolled around, people knew it was going to be a close race between Democratic candidate Stephen Douglas and Republican candidate Abraham Lincoln. There was a lot of worry and fear traveling through

America at what would happen to the country in the future. To many people, including Lincoln, it didn't matter who was elected as war was coming. Several slaveholding states had already made one thing clear: if Abraham Lincoln became president, they would secede from the Union. They would form their own country and no longer be a part of the United States of America.

While this realization bothered Lincoln, it didn't keep him from withdrawing his nomination or make him want to lose. Lincoln wanted to win the presidency. He knew he had to in order to restore unity among the United States. In fact, this was Abraham Lincoln's main goal as president. It wasn't to bring an end to slavery, it was to keep the United States together, just as the Founding Fathers had created it.

The election of 1860 has gone down in the history books as one of the most intense elections. When it came to the evening of Tuesday, November 6, 1860, everyone was waiting for the election results. America had gone through a tense political time during the campaign of 1860 and most people realized when the results were read, the fate of the states would be made as well. Many people knew the importance of this election so nearly 82 percent of American citizens cast their vote. To this date, this is known as the highest voter turnout in American history.

When it came down to the candidates, Stephen Douglas secured 30 percent of the popular vote, but only 12 electoral votes. Breckinridge secured about 18 percent of the popular vote and 72 electoral votes. Bell gained a little under 13 percent of the popular vote and 39 electoral votes. Abraham Lincoln took the lead in both the popular and electoral votes in comparison to the other candidates. He received close to 40 percent of the popular vote and 180 electoral votes (United States presidential election of 1860, n.d.).

Chapter 6: Lincoln the President

The election of 1860 was one of the many stops on the road to the American Civil War. From the time Lincoln was nominated as the Republican candidate for the presidency, he spent a lot of time discussing how he did not want to take away the rights of any state, including their decision to have slavery. But he was also open and honest about his distaste for the institution of slavery. This contradiction is often one of the most highly debated topics when it comes to Abraham Lincoln, but it is one that would be solved throughout his presidency.

The Beginning of Secession

Abraham Lincoln was never truly allowed to celebrate his presidency. Immediately after the election, he decided to head to Washington to take care of official business. Further, slaveholding states were quick to discuss how they were going to leave the Union. Every one of them wanted to leave by the time Lincoln officially became president in March 1861.

Soon after Lincoln's win, then-President Buchanan tried to tell the slaveholding states that it was illegal to secede from the Union, but he also told the governmental leaders that they could not resist if a state tried to secede. Because Lincoln still had a few months before he would officially become president, he had no power. There was no way he could try to save the Union before the first state seceded. But this didn't keep Lincoln from doing what he did best: try to give people advice in order to save the Union.

Abraham Lincoln knew he had to walk a fine line as he was trying to keep the slaveholding states within the Union. Lincoln had to keep the Republicans on his side as this was his political party. They saw Lincoln as the man who was going to end the institution of slavery in the United States. While Lincoln always wanted to see slavery end, he knew he could speak to the slaveholding states in a way that wouldn't make them feel attacked. He had to speak to them soothingly, yet with authority. As Lincoln continued to debate how he should address the crowds, he came to realize the best step he could take was to remain silent. He felt that anything he said or tried to say would be twisted by the slaveholding states. They were angry and didn't want to recognize Abraham Lincoln as their president.

About a month later, Lincoln received a note from a southern supporter who was a merchant. He told Lincoln to try to reach out to the southern states through a politician the slaveholding states supported. Lincoln knew of one man who would be best for this job, Senator Lyman Trumbull. Lincoln wrote what he wanted to say and sent it to Trumbull, who weaved it into his public address. At the time, very few people knew that Lincoln was behind part of the speech. Even so, the Southern states completely ignored the advice and continued to focus on secession.

By December 1860, Lincoln was spending most of his time in Washington. Congress developed a couple of committees to help ease the tension of secession in any way possible and Lincoln was working closely with them. At this time, Lincoln had started negotiations with Congress and the individual states. He knew that issues like slavery could find a compromise as this is what had happened in the past.

As Congress and Lincoln were working hard to ease the impending crisis, South Carolina became the first state to adopt an ordinance of secession on December 20. Hearing that news, Lincoln knew that immediately after taking the oath and walking into the presidential office, he would spend every waking hour trying to save the union.

The closer it got to Lincoln's Inauguration, the more slaveholding states seceded. By February, the list had grown to include Mississippi, Alabama, Georgia, Florida, Texas, and Louisiana. Following secession, the states decided to call themselves the Confederate States of America. They then appointed Jefferson Davis as their president and extended invitations to other states to join their Confederacy. At the time, North Carolina, Tennessee, Kentucky, Delaware, Maryland, Virginia, Missouri, and Arkansas all declined the offer and remained in the Union.

Not Giving Up Yet

Even after seven states seceded from the Union within 40 days, Lincoln and Congress continued to find a solution to save the Union. By this time, they all had created this goal in mind. Everyone who listened and worked with Lincoln knew he was willing to allow slavery to continue as long as the slaveholding states returned to the Union. This would remain Lincoln's main concern throughout the Civil War.

One of the steps Congress took to try to preserve the Union was holding a Peace Conference with the Confederate States. About 131 delegates from more than 20 states went to meet with officials of the Confederacy and asked them to come up with a constitutional amendment that would tell the delegates what the states wanted if they were to join the Union again. After the Confederacy sent the document to Congress, it was immediately rejected.

Another step that Congress took was the Corwin Amendment, which was never officially decided on. This amendment would shield slaveholding states from having to follow the parts of the law that discussed the abolition of slavery. The amendment made it through Congress, which sent to the states for ratification. But this occurred a few days before the outbreak of the Civil War.

Lincoln Officially Moves to Washington

Lincoln decided to make his final move to Washington, D.C. on February 11, 1861. He had decided that Mary and the children would join him later, once everything was a bit more settled in Washington. Before the outbreak of the Civil War, Lincoln believed that they would be able to find a solution and the Confederate States of America would be eliminated quickly.

When Lincoln took the train to Washington, he decided he was going to create a special trip. He wanted to try to reach out to as many people as he could between leaving Illinois and reaching the White House. He decided to make several stops along a two-week journey. It was during this trip that people started to learn of reports of people wanting to assassinate Lincoln. Officials quickly worked to try to find if any conspirators were trying to sabotage Lincoln's train route. Not only did Lincoln receive some of the first Secret Service Agents, but his schedule was randomly changed in order to throw anyone off who might try to harm Lincoln. Once Lincoln reached Washington near the end of February, he was placed in a disguise so people wouldn't recognize him.

Abraham Lincoln wasted no time getting to work on completing his Cabinet and taking care of other official business. One of the first things Lincoln did was to meet with

Republican leaders. He wanted to get their thoughts on the secession situation and any changes they would like to see. Like a good leader, Lincoln never promised that any of the changes would be made, but he did tell them that he heard them, understood, and he would do what he could to make it happen. For many Republican leaders, this was a positive step for the new president. Very few presidents before Lincoln took the time to meet with political officials and talk to them about what type of changes they would like to see happen. Not only did Lincoln do this to keep on the good side of the Republican Party, but because he felt it was necessary. Lincoln believed in unity, whether it was between the president and political leaders or the states.

Lincoln's Officials

When Abraham Lincoln announced to his wife that he had won the presidency, he immediately started listing people he would like to see in his Cabinet. As a great leader, Lincoln understood that he needed to find a good blend of people who would listen to him, help him, and challenge him. Another reason Lincoln was highly cautious of who he chose was he needed to make certain that the Republican Party remained united. This was more necessary now that Lincoln knew secession was about to occur.

One of the tricks Lincoln used when selecting his

administration was to look beyond the Republican Party. He even looked at people who had once been his rivals within the Republican Party because he knew they would make good leaders, would be honest with him, and they'd be willing to do what they could to keep the Union together.

There was another important factor when it came to picking his Cabinet members. Lincoln needed to make certain they did not want to see slavery expanded into the territories. He had to get members who were all on the same page when it came to this situation because America and the political parties were already divided enough when it came to slavery. Lincoln knew if there was any type of division like this within his Cabinet, he would not be able to save the Union.

The process of choosing his officials took months. In fact, Lincoln was completing his Cabinet selection when he arrived in Washington near the end of February. Once he arrived, this was one of the first actions he took.

Lincoln filled his first Cabinet spot, Secretary of State, in December 1860. He knew he needed someone who was popular among his political party as this was customary for the senior membership position. It didn't take Lincoln and his vice president, Hannibal Hamlin, to decide who to offer this spot to—it was William Seward. As was the way the offer worked, Hamlin was the one who needed to offer the position to Seward, who immediately accepted. When the announcement came that Seward was Lincoln's Secretary of State, many people within the Republican Party were shocked. The two men hadn't always gotten along. But this didn't matter to Lincoln as he couldn't imagine another man in that position.

The second Cabinet spot to be filled was the Secretary of the Treasury. When Lincoln chose the man for this position, he looked for someone who was willing to abolish slavery quickly and at any cost. He knew that someone like this was needed in his Cabinet to ensure everything on the abolitionist side ran as smoothly as possible. Lincoln knew he had to do his best to maintain a neutral stand between the free and slaveholding states if he wanted to preserve the Union. Therefore, he needed a few Cabinet members who would give a push toward ending the institution of slavery. Lincoln decided the best person for this job was none other than William Seward's political rival, Salmon P. Chase.

Many people questioned Lincoln's choice of Chase because of his well-known domineering personality and the fact he and Seward couldn't stand each other. Chase, however, had a strong relationship with the abolitionists. Despite this, Seward immediately went to Lincoln and told him he was making a mistake. Seward, along with many other Republicans, was certain Chase could hurt their chances of gaining any Confederate states back into the Union. Lincoln stood by his decision. He even stood by Chase despite Chase running against him in the 1864 election, and Chase's attempts to sabotage Lincoln's reputation and campaign. Lincoln was determined to keep Chase on board despite the opposition. It was Chase who would eventually choose the leave the Cabinet after Lincoln became president for a second term in 1864. Lincoln would then elect William P. Fessenden, who was the Chairman of the Senate Finance Committee. Fessenden only stayed a few months in this role due to his health and stress of the job. After Fessenden resigned, Lincoln brought in Hugh McCulloch, who ran the Office of the Comptroller of the Currency.

The Secretary of War was the third Cabinet position Lincoln filled. His first choice was Simon Cameron, who was another Republican that many people didn't care for. Once again, Seward and others question Lincoln on his choice. They worried about Cameron's corrupt manner, but Lincoln was focused on his public speaking skills. Lincoln also chose Cameron because he was one of the most influential politicians in Pennsylvania. Unfortunately, once the Civil War broke out, Cameron quickly proved to be the wrong choice for the Secretary of War position. Lincoln would remove him in 1862 and place Edwin Stanton into the position. Stanton proved to be a much better choice and worked well with Lincoln. During the course of the war, Stanton and Lincoln formed a very close bond and would often be on the battlegrounds together making sure the troops were being taken care of as best as possible.

Edward Bates became the first Attorney General. Bates was from a border state, which was a positive for Lincoln. He knew he needed representation from around the Union and border states were often overlooked. Therefore, including Bates and a few other Cabinet members from other border states would help representation in those areas. James Speed would receive the title of Attorney General after Bates resigned in 1864.

Montgomery Blair became the first Postmaster General in Lincoln's Cabinet. Lincoln chose Blair because of his connection to border state Democrats, and he was a strong abolitionist. Unfortunately, Blair and his family started to be seen as a threat to the Northern and Border states during the Civil War. After Lincoln dismissed Blair, he appointed William Dennison.

Gideon Welles became Secretary of the Navy in 1861 and held the position until 1865. Welles was brought to Lincoln's attention by his vice president. After hearing about Welles' service in the Navy and under President Polk, Lincoln felt he was the best choice as well.

The first Secretary of the Interior position went to Caleb Blood Smith. Lincoln had known Smith for years and felt that he would be good for the position because of the work he put into Lincoln's campaigns. While he wasn't the best man for the position, Smith did what he could until bad health forced him to resign in 1862. Lincoln then appointed John Palmer Usher.

Lincoln's First Inauguration

Abraham Lincoln's first inauguration took place on March 4, 1861. While Lincoln went through the customs that many other presidents did, there was a lot of anxiety when it came to his inauguration. Lincoln had already been the target of a few assassination attempts and people worried about how many would try to assassinate the president as he delivered his inauguration speech. The stress that many of Lincoln's bodyguards and administrative members faced that day was described by the man who had to do most of the work, Lieutenant-General Winfield Scott. Later, he described his emotions about the day by stating is was "the most critical and hazardous event with which I have ever been connected" (Abraham Lincoln's First Inauguration, 2019). The atmosphere of that day was so intense that Scott feared for his own life. Prior to the inauguration, Scott had received many threats stating he would see his death if he tried to protect the president that day.

While nearly everyone else was on guard that day, Lincoln

remained calm and collected. He tried to keep everyone's spirits up by telling stories and jokes. This was a part of himself that Lincoln would hold onto dearly for the next few years. He knew, as he would tell many of his friends, that the more he was able to lighten the mood when the Union was at such a dark place, the better he felt that they would all be able to pull through.

As people listened to Lincoln's speech, he gave his promises to the country. He talked about how he wanted to secure the Union and bring back the states that had seceded. He didn't want the United States to divide because of his election; he wanted the states to come together and become closer than before. He also talked about slavery and how he did not want to use any type of force to see an end to the institution. In fact, Lincoln stated that if the states that had seceded came back into the Union, he would not take away their slavery. He would let the people of that state decide what was best. He wanted to establish a compromise and promised to do so in a way that wouldn't drive away the Northern states or further push away the Southern states.

Domestic Issues Within the War

One of the biggest factors a lot of people don't realize when they learn about Lincoln's presidency and the Civil War is that Lincoln still had other domestic issues to attend to besides the war. Although the war was always considered to be the primary focus among Lincoln and his Cabinet members, Lincoln had to make sure other pieces of the country were running smoothly as well.

How to Fund the War?

Once the Battle of Fort Sumter began, Lincoln had to sit down with his Secretary of Treasury and figure out how they were going to fund the war. They knew they would need thousands of soldiers. They were looking at close to 500,000 soldiers to win the war. While training all these men was one problem, another problem was making sure they received clothing, food, and all other necessities for a war. Because the Civil War had already begun, Lincoln and Chase had to quickly come up with a solution, which included taxation.

Lincoln came up with the idea of taxing because this was one way the Revolutionary War was paid for. Lincoln believed that most people would be supportive of raising certain taxes because the Union citizens were supportive of the war. Lincoln knew he needed to come up with the best solution, which meant he not only had to focus on the Union troops, but also the civilians.

Confederate Sympathizers

Confederate sympathizers became a problem immediately after the Civil War started. Lincoln knew this was one area he needed to act quickly on because sympathizers often became spies and could easily cause more damage to the Union troops and states than anything else. Therefore, Lincoln quickly suspended habeas corpus and agreed to place all Confederate sympathizers they could round up into prisons. This wasn't one of Lincoln's favorite decisions, however, he knew it was necessary if he wanted to protect the Union states and army.

Approval of New Union States

While Lincoln quickly had a plan for any Confederate States that wanted to rejoin the Union, he also needed a plan for any new states that wanted to join the Union. One of these states was West Virginia, which had split from the state of Virginia. This admission occurred near the beginning of the Civil War.

The next state to be admitted into the Union was the Nevada territory in 1864. Not too long after this, several other territories, such as Colorado and Nebraska, began to take the necessary steps to join the Union.

With the approval of new states, Lincoln started to feel that the Union could win the Civil War after all. At the beginning of the war, the Union troops struggled. Then they suffered through Gettysburg, which is considered to be the biggest loss of the Civil War. As a leader, however, Lincoln always did his best to remain as positive as he could. This meant that he would look for a reason to smile or find a reason to make someone laugh during the toughest of times. It also meant that he would appreciate the positives, such as a new state joining the Union.

Chapter 7: The Civil War and Lincoln

The first gunshot that officially launched America and the Confederate states into the Civil War occurred on April 12, 1861, at Fort Sumter. From that moment, Lincoln had to change the direction of his leadership. As the commander-in-chief, he held in the highest position in the United States Army. In fact, it would be this role that would define his presidency. While many people feel this way because the Civil War lasted throughout Lincoln's presidency, the real reason was Lincoln's leadership skills.

Lincoln's Internal Leadership in the Civil War

Looking at the course of American history, no president became so heavily involved in war than Abraham Lincoln. He felt that it was not only his role to support the Union soldiers in any way possible, but also felt it was his obligation. One of the hidden characteristics of Lincoln is that he took responsibility when it came to the Civil War. Not just because he was America's leader, but because of his self blame.

The Confederate States were open and honest about why they succeeded from the Union—they wanted to preserve slavery. They believed Lincoln had no right to take away their constitutional right to hold slaves, which is a belief the president also held. Although Lincoln never supported slavery, he knew that it was not in his power to tell individual states what they could and could not do. After all, this is one reason George Washington, John Adams, Thomas Jefferson, and other Founding Fathers fought for independence. But Lincoln also knew it was his duty to preserve the Union, and he was going to do this at any cost.

One of the differences between Lincoln and other leaders is that Lincoln preferred to take action over what was happening instead of simply laying out policies and demanding everyone follow them. Lincoln didn't believe this type of leadership worked out well because it didn't give people a stable sense of trust. It gave people a dictatorship, which is something that Lincoln did not support. While he knew he had to speak with authority, he also knew that most people reacted to compassion more than demands. So he often stated that he didn't control situations that happened, instead, they controlled him. This was one of the biggest factors that helped Lincoln become such a great leader during the Civil War.

Another reason Lincoln became a great leader was that he had the ability to hide his true feelings yet state them in a way that allowed people to feel connected to him. Lincoln was a very soft-spoken man who cared deeply. Although this side of Lincoln was often overshadowed by his stories and jokes, the people who knew him best understood this factor. This part of his personality would lead a lot of people to become acquainted and proud of their president. This brought a special light into a dark time within the Union.

Lincoln was not afraid to experiment and often did during the Civil War. He helped war generals come up with different strategies to try in order to gain the upper hand when it came to the Confederacy. Lincoln was also known to send generals suggestions from Washington. The generals never had to take Lincoln's advice, but they sometimes did because they believed it would work.

Another benefit Lincoln had when it came to his leadership skills and the Civil War was his previous war training. Lincoln had signed himself up to be a part of the Black Hawk War as a young man. While he never had to officially fight in battle, he did go through training and learned the basics of the American Army through this war. This helped Lincoln when it came to the Civil War. While he understood this was different territory, he also knew that his previous knowledge could give him the upper hand at times.

Finally, Lincoln turned to people he admired for guidance and help. Many of his friends became involved in the Civil War, especially his political friends he had known for decades. This not only allowed Lincoln to trust the people he sent to manage the front lines but also helped everyone when it came to communication. If people knew Lincoln, they were more willing to communicate. This is another reason Lincoln spent so much time on the military camps. He wanted to make certain that all his troop leaders, along with the troops, knew him well. While he spent most of his time with troop leaders, he was often caught walking around the camp meeting with the Union troops and thanking them for their service. On top of this, he often gave them a speech, similar to what he had done during the Battle of Gettysburg.

The Early War

One of Lincoln's biggest fears when it came to the Civil War, especially during the first couple of years, was that more states would join the Confederacy. After the Battle at Fort Sumter, Lincoln felt that the Union's numbers were good, especially when it came to the number of states within the Union vs. the number of states within the Confederacy. As time went on, however, more states started to look at becoming a member of the Confederate states. This was especially worrisome when it came to the border states, such as Kentucky and Maryland. The Union had to keep Maryland because of its location. When it came to Kentucky, the main worry was its size.

Fort Sumter

After taking the oath and leaving the crowd stunned by his persuasive speech, Lincoln learned that the tensions between the Confederate States and Union were mounting. Within a few hours after his inauguration, Lincoln was told that they had to resupply Fort Sumter. Lincoln, who struggled with depression throughout his life, became quiet at this announcement. To him, it was taking America one step closer into war. It also caused a problem within the promises he had already made to the Union in his inauguration speech. He promised the Southern states he would not use any type of force. Yet, he promised the Northern states that they would keep Fort Sumter, which was located in South Carolina, and he would protect that location and the Northern states. Lincoln was torn over what to do and found several members of his Cabinet to discuss the matter with. Lincoln was not sure a decision could be made immediately. Lincoln was a leader who would often think of all possibilities before making a decision. He wanted to ensure that the decision he made was the right choice. While this often limited mistakes on Lincoln's part, it also caused tension between Lincoln and members of his Cabinet. There are times, especially during war, where decisions need to be made quickly. While this wasn't Lincoln's strongest characteristic, it was one he would become attached to for many decisions within the Civil War.

After hearing about Sumter, Lincoln and his Cabinet would continue to watch the location closely. A few days after Lincoln's inauguration, General Winfield Scott warned Lincoln about the conditions surrounding Sumter. He told Lincoln that they didn't have time to train enough men to place around the fort to protect it. While Secretary of War Welles disagreed with Scott, the mention of bringing 25,000 men into Fort Sumter was in question. The biggest problem was that these men would need months of training and they didn't have the months to dedicate to the training.

Lincoln was told that a decision had to be made when it came to Fort Sumter. Lincoln's first step with this was to reach out to his Cabinet members and ask them to write their decision on whether they should resupply Fort Sumter. Only one member of his Cabinet agreed to this. Again, no decision came out of this discussion.

A couple of days later, the question came up again, this time with a little more urgency. Now, Welles was telling Lincoln that they needed to take care of Fort Sumter and Fort Pickens. Lincoln finally made the decision to resupply both forts. While Fort Sumter was ready to go, Fort Pickens would take a few days longer. By now, it was April 10 and the Confederate officials were meeting to discuss their next move. At the same time, South Carolina Governor was receiving notice that the forts were going to be resupplied.

Two days later, on April 12, 1861, the first shots that officially started the Civil War occurred on Fort Sumter. All the intervening the Union was about to do would arrive too late. The next day, troops surrendered at Fort Sumter, allowing the Confederacy to take over the fort. News of this occurrence brought Lincoln to a standing halt. His worst fears had come true. The United States of American was now in a Civil War with the Confederate states.

The Fort Sumter attack would define Lincoln in many ways for the rest of his life. First, many people who knew him well say he sank into a major depression, one which he remained in throughout the Civil War. Since he was a child, Lincoln struggled with mental illness. Many historians believe it was due to his mother's death and the poor relationship he had with his father. Whatever the reasons were, the Civil War has a profound impact on Lincoln's mental health. But he continued to do what he could to lift everyone's spirits because he knew this would be one factor that would get the Union through the Civil War.

Another way Fort Sumter defined Lincoln was with his presidency. The Civil War officially started on April 12, 1861, just a little over a month after Lincoln's first inauguration. The War would wage on until April 9, 1865, just a few days before Lincoln would pass away from a gunshot wound. Lincoln would not only spend all but a little over a month in a war during his time as president, but also the rest of his life. In fact, Lincoln would never be allowed to see the remaining pieces that needed to be finished to put the Civil War to rest.

The attack on Fort Sumter also brought Lincoln's leadership abilities into focus. Once he heard about the first shots, Lincoln knew he had to work at a faster pace and maintain focus as a leader. As he was focusing on his presidential duties in Washington, he also had to focus on the Union troops who would be stationed around American during the Civil War.

Battle of Bull Run

The Battle of Bull Run is known as the first major battle in the Civil War. At the time, both Lincoln and many Union soldiers thought that the war would quickly end. In fact, they didn't believe there would be a lot of battles in the Civil War. They were still pretty confident that the Confederate states would come to a compromise with Lincoln and the United States government and rejoin the Union.

At the beginning of the war, Lincoln wanted to make sure that the plans for battle were very precise. When it came to the Battle of Bull Run, the Union troops and generals involved spent a lot of time focusing on the strategy. Lincoln helped with this through his telegrams and other means.

Unfortunately, the Battle of Bull Run did not go as planned for the Union Troops. They were unable to secure a quick victory, which made many people realize that the Civil War could last much longer than expected.

It was this battle that also put Lincoln on his toes about finding more troops. While he did this after Fort Sumter, the Battle of Bull Run made him realize he couldn't wait to ask for more people to join the United States Army. Therefore, Lincoln start to go to work finding ways to recruit people.

Although both sides made mistakes when it came to the Battle of Bull Run, the Union Army took a larger hit and lost the battle. Of course, Lincoln did what he could and brought something positive to this great loss. He discussed all of the mistakes the troops made during the battle and help the Union generals find a way to take note of these mistakes and learn from them so they wouldn't make the same mistake again.

The Year of 1862

Even though the bloodiest battle of the Civil War happened during 1863, the Civil War took a drastic turn in 1862. It is this year that is considered to be one of the toughest and bloodiest years of the Civil War.

One of the most devastating realizations to occur during the Civil War was the amount of lives that were lost. The number of battles that took place during 1862, including the Battle of

Shiloh, started to bring into focus of the number of lives lost. About 13,000 people lost their lives during this battle on the Union side. The Confederate side didn't fare any better as they lost of 10,000 soldiers. When these numbers started rolling in, Lincoln was devastated. He couldn't imagine such as loss from his own country, even in the Confederate states.

It was during 1862 that Lincoln put another one of his strengths as a leader to use—when people are grieving, grieve with them. Of course, Lincoln was grieving for many reasons in 1862, including the loss of so many people. Therefore, if wasn't hard for Lincoln to put this leadership quality into practice. Lincoln wanted to make sure that people not only saw him a strong leader, which is why he always maintained his composure and controlled his emotions, but also a leader people could connect with.

Another leadership factor Lincoln worked on during 1862 was building strong alliances. While Lincoln had always strived to do this, he understood that it was just as important during tough times. In fact, it could become more important. Even if he had built a relationship with someone before the start of the Civil War, Lincoln wanted to work on tightening this bond and he felt it would help keep the unity within the Union and the Union Army.

Sometimes Lincoln's leadership skills were tested. In 1862, Lincoln was trying to keep up with everything going on during the Civil War. At the same time, there were problems within his Cabinet. Not all of Lincoln's Cabinet members got along, and he hoped that they would. In fact, there were a couple of Cabinet members who were starting to cause more issues than the Union could afford at that time.

Along with the trouble within his Cabinet, which did get resolved over the course of a few months, Lincoln was struggling to reach a connection with George McClellan. McClellan was leading the Union Army through a few battles during 1862. When Lincoln went to visit him on numerous occasions, he would always receive hostility from the soldier. This never bothered Lincoln, in fact, he would often go out of his way in order to ensure McClellan felt respected but it was bothering other people in the Lincoln administration. However, Lincoln would assure them that there was nothing to worry about when it came to McClellan. He stated that there were other factors to consider when someone was being hostile and rude during the Civil War.

No matter what McClellan did, Lincoln continued to put forth his best efforts to be kind to the soldiers. He would also spend time discussing various strategies with McClellan. Of course, this didn't sit well with the soldiers at first. By the middle of 1862, after McClellan had suffered a few loses, he started to think differently about Lincoln. The president was surprised when McClellan sat down to talk to Lincoln when he came to visit one day to discuss strategies. Instead of talking to McClellan about how he had been acting, Lincoln let the situation go. He decided to focus on the present and the future. After all, as Lincoln believed, there was nothing anyone could do to change the past. They could, however, take what they learned from the past and put it toward developing a better future.

The Emancipation Proclamation

Historians often debate the true value of the Emancipation Proclamation as it pertains to the Civil War. In reality, many people feel that the Emancipation Proclamation didn't free anyone. In a way, it freed very few slaves. One reason for this is because the Emancipation Proclamation was created as a war measure. After nearly two years in battle and losing more people than Lincoln cared to think of, he knew he needed to do something drastic. But his hands were tied because he had no control over the Confederacy. One of his last efforts in trying to bring the Confederate states back into the Union was the Emancipation Proclamation.

The announcement of the Emancipation Proclamation occurred in September 1862. Lincoln spent three months working on the proclamation and often questioned whether he should release it. He talked to many members within his Cabinet and other people he trusted about the document before he officially made the announcement. As he made the announcement, he told people that slaves who were part of the rebellion states would be freed in 100 days.

One of the biggest reasons Lincoln made the announcement was simply that he wanted to give the Confederate states one more chance to come back to the Union and keep their slaveholding status. None of them followed through with this. Therefore, on January 1, 1863, Abraham Lincoln sent out the official Emancipation Proclamation, which declared all slaves in rebellion states free.

The reality of the situation was that slaves still weren't officially free. With lack of control, Lincoln couldn't make anyone in rebel states give up their right to own slaves. Also it was used as a military measure, so other steps within Congress still had to be taken in order to officially end slavery. What Lincoln really did was make a promise to the slaves that they would officially be free after the Civil War. While many slaves are known to have left their plantations on January 1, many others remained because people understood Lincoln had no control.

Gettysburg Address

Nearly everyone knows the first line of the Gettysburg Address. This is definitely Lincoln's most popular speech of his political career. Lincoln delivered his famous speech on

November 19, 1863, when the site of the Gettysburg battlefield received its dedication of the Soldiers' National Cemetery. While many people know of this address, very few people understand all the lessons in leadership Lincoln fit into this brief address.

One of the first leadership lessons the Gettysburg Address taught us is that words do matter. If you use powerful words, you will be able to get people to remember what you said. They might not remember every single word, but they will remember the powerful words you used.

Another lesson is that leaders need to acknowledge the cost of what happens. In the speech, Lincoln doesn't allow people to think that the thousands of men who died in that battle are going to be forgotten. He stated that people will remember them because of their courage and the steps they took to try to win. They will be remembered for their bravery as they fought to preserve the Union. Lincoln said they will go down in history for everything they did on this battlefield.

Throughout the Gettysburg Address, Lincoln never wrote or said the word "I." This is because another great lesson to take from Lincoln through the address is to look beyond yourself. People often get caught up in the world and focus on themselves. It's one of the most common characteristics within humans, and Lincoln understood this. Therefore, when he focused on his leadership, he made sure that people understood everyone was part of a team.

Finally, another great lesson to take from the Gettysburg Address is to think about the message that's being delivered and the structure. This address is one of the best-known addresses ever stated in American history and it is only four paragraphs long. Moreover, it probably didn't take any more than five minutes for Lincoln to deliver it. Not only did he make sure to keep the message short, he also focused on structure. Lincoln started with universal truths and ended with the direct situation of that time.

Abraham Lincoln and the 13th Amendment

If it wasn't for the 13th Amendment, Lincoln would have never known that slavery was forever abolished in the United States and the Civil War was coming to a close before he passed away. In order to keep his promise to the slaves that they would be forever free, Lincoln had to ensure abolition became more official. If the 13th Amendment didn't pass, slavery would have continued in the United States. The Civil War would have had a different ending, one in which the Confederate states could have kept the Union divided.

Therefore, the 13th Amendment meant more than ending the institution of slavery. It meant that Lincoln would make his other goal. He would be able to bring the Union back together. While John Wilkes Booth would shoot and kill Lincoln before he could officially see this moment, he did know that it was in the near future. He just had to work out the fine details with his Cabinet members, such as how to go about allowing the states who seceded back into the Union.

When it comes down to it, the 13th Amendment is a congressional measure stating that slavery is now and forever illegal in the United States. While some people argued this was unconstitutional, many people believe it was the right move and Lincoln is still praised for the work he put into the 13th Amendment.

The main leadership lesson people can take away from the 13th Amendment is not to give up. Lincoln had a lot of odds stacked against him from the moment he was announced the 16th President of the United States of America. These odds were against him for four years as the country was at war. On top of these odds, more challenges were added that could have pushed someone further away from their goals. Lincoln, however, continued to do whatever he needed to do to keep his promises. While he couldn't keep every single one, he was able to keep the most important promises.

Lincoln's Leadership Lessons During the Civil War

The Civil War is full of leadership lessons from Lincoln. In order to give you the best description of most of his lessons, it is important to lay them out in an understanding way. Because so much happened during the Civil War, it is impossible to write about everything within the pages of this book. Therefore, it is important to take a look at the points below which discuss many of Lincoln's leadership lessons.

Don't Act Out of Spite

One leadership lesson people can take from Lincoln when they learn of the relationship between McClellan and Lincoln is that you should never react out of spite. Lincoln was a strong believer in this. It was one of the many principles he focused on throughout his life. Lincoln believed in this quality for many reasons. First, he knew it was necessary to keep a cool head if he wanted people to be comfortable talking to him about anything, especially when the Union was in the middle of a war. Many people, however, felt that this was also one of Lincoln's weaknesses as a leader.

Always Forgive

When it comes to pardons, Lincoln allowed more than any president before him. Lincoln became so popular with his pardons that his two youngest sons caught on and often started playing in ways where they would pardon their toys or even the Thanksgiving turkey. Many people felt this was a weakness because it allowed people to try to take advantage of Lincoln. But, the reality of pardons for Lincoln was that they couldn't further damage the Union. Lincoln did everything in his power to ensure that as little damage as possible was put on the Union, especially after the start of the Civil War.

Furthermore, pardoning is way to forgive people for what happened. While people lived with the events of the Civil War until they passed away, especially people who lived through the event, it is still important to forgive. Lincoln believed that a great leader would not only forgive others but also themselves. Lincoln struggled with the Civil War for many reasons, one was that he felt he was one of the many causes of the war. In reality, Lincoln was merely a step toward the Civil War as the steps began with the founding of the United States.

The more Lincoln took time to forgive, the more he was able to work through the events that unfolded within the Civil War. He was also able to put certain situations behind him and focus more on the good that was happening. For example, the Union was working toward two main goals. The first goal was to bring the Union back together. The second goal was to emancipate the slaves.

Keep Your Personal Life and Work Life Separate

For Lincoln, keeping his two main worlds, his personal life and work life, separate was a challenge. Part of the reason for this was because his family lived with him in the White House, which is also where he worked. Another part of this was because everyone who spent time with him on a daily basis knew what he was going through on a personal level. They knew when he was suffering due to the loss of a child. They knew the struggles he was having with his wife. They knew the struggles he had with mental illness.

Although Lincoln took the time he could to grieve for his son while focusing on the Civil War, he also made sure that this was not in front of his mind when he was speaking with soldiers. He made sure that when he was working, his focus was on how the government could help the Union soldier and the Civil War.

Possess Charisma and Use It

You have probably heard about Abraham Lincoln and John F. Kennedy. Both became among the most popular presidents in the history of the United States. Both men worked toward establishing more equality within the United States and had a certain amount of charisma. The comparisons between Lincoln and John F. Kennedy are almost endless. One reason for this is because both men, especially Lincoln, possessed charisma that made him like a magnet when it came to people.

If you have done any other type of reading on Abraham Lincoln, you might have come across information that talks about how Union soldiers would cheer for Lincoln once he made his way onto the battlefield. Many people have speculated why this is and came up with several reasons. One reason is people saw Lincoln as a hero. He was fighting for the rights of humans who weren't even thought of as humans. While this mindset had started to change by the 1800s, historically, most Caucasians saw African Americas as second-class citizens who shouldn't possess any rights. Another reason is because of Lincoln's charisma or even magical presence. When it comes down to it, some people often give off a certain light and presence that makes people pay more attention to them. Whatever this feature is, Lincoln had and he used it to get people to pay attention to what he was saying and doing. It helped him gain attention when it came to getting Union troops for the Civil War and when he made speeches in front of thousands of people to gain votes.

Lincoln Redefined the Presidency

By the time Lincoln was nominated as the Republican presidential candidate, he was hopeful for a win. The bottom line for Lincoln was he wanted the win so he could keep Stephen Douglas out of the White House. The other reason was throughout his early political career, he had grown to love what the world of politics gave him and what he could give politics. This only continues as he entered the White House as the 16th President of the United States.

While Lincoln never thought of doing this at the time, he brought more power into the presidency than ever before. The main reason for this was because Lincoln was in a special situation–one no president had ever before been in. He was fighting to keep the United States of America in one piece. He was fighting the Civil War. While other presidents had gone through wars, none of them had fought a war that was so deadly and bloody. Other than the Revolutionary War, the citizens of the United States had been pretty protected by war coming onto American soil. That was until the Civil War.

Because of the special circumstances the Civil War often brought to Lincoln, he had to improvise with many policies. Lincoln, however, would do this more with action that words. For instance, Lincoln placed a call for troops in ways that no other president had done before. He gave speeches, such as the Gettysburg Address, which brought different views of what the president could do to honor certain people or situations.

Lincoln spent more time out of the office than in the office. He made sure he spent time with the Union troops, generals, and citizens of the United States. He could often be seen walking around the streets of Washington, which would make some people worried due to all the death threats that surrounded Lincoln. But in the best way he could, he didn't allow people to worry about the threats or him.

Furthermore, Lincoln responded to harsh criticism or demands from people by giving them a quote or part of a saying to think about. For example, when people would come into Lincoln's office to discuss what they believed he was doing wrong in the war effort and how he should change it, Lincoln would simply give them a passage from a book he read or a quote. It was his way of telling the person what he thought without having to be rude or getting angry over what the person said. This is an action that was known to be rare from previous presidents. Most presidents demanded that people listen to them and didn't go into their office telling them what to do. Lincoln is considered to be the first modern day president for many reasons–and this is one reason.

Be Results Oriented with the Goals You Set

While many people don't think about this–Abraham Lincoln had goals he wanted to accomplish as the president. Of course, the most obvious goal is that he wanted to preserve the Union. Another goal is that he wanted to do what he could to end slavery. Lincoln didn't just come up with these goals because they were in the situations he was given as president, though that is part of the reason. Lincoln came up with these goals because it is what he believed he needed to do to be a great leader.

When it comes to Lincoln, however, the need to set goals and achieve them were more than a focus on developing leadership skills—it was an obsession. Lincoln had always dived head-first into his work and gave it his all. This could often become a problem, as it can for everyone. But Lincoln was able to work out situations in a way that he could achieve his goals. For Lincoln, it was one of the ways he received motivation to succeed. It was also a way that he was able to connect to other people.

The key for Lincoln was he had to see results to believe he achieved the goals. As Lincoln's law partner, Herndon, knew this better than most other people, even his Cabinet members. Herndon often compared Lincoln to a train that never stopped to rest. He just kept going and continued to work toward reaching his goals.

Don't Let Anything Hold You Back

When you take a moment to think about everything Lincoln went through as a politician, you will realize nothing could hold him back. Abraham Lincoln won the presidency and immediately started working. He didn't do this purely out of excitement for the win, he did this because he had to. He needed to get ahead of what the slaveholding states were about to do. He had to ensure that he took a step before they did as they were going to try to hold him back and keep him from keeping the Union together.

Of course, no one could have predicted then that the Confederacy would lose the war and have to rejoin the United States of America. What Lincoln did know is that if he allowed this situation to bring him down, he wasn't going to be able to run a successful presidency. Instead, he would start to have or fall into a great depression, which could create more problems within the Union. Therefore, Lincoln did what he did best–he kept going. He didn't allow anything or anyone to hold him back, no matter what happened.

Lincoln: A Final Farewell

John Wilkes Booth was an actor who always had an agenda against Lincoln. He was never supportive of Lincoln's ambitions to end slavery and he was even less supportive of the Civil War. Booth had been watching Lincoln for years and, as many historians believed, tried to assassinate him before that fateful night at Ford's Theatre.

John Wilkes Booth didn't act alone, though many people thought he did. While his friends had other roles that night, Booth was the one who shot and killed Lincoln during the play of "Our American Cousin."

The whole day before Mary and Abraham Lincoln decided to part the White House and head to Ford's Theatre, it seemed like the universe was telling them not to go. First, the couple had trouble finding friends to go with them. Second, Mary started to complain of a headache and told her husband she wasn't up to going. Lincoln, however, informed her that they had to because people knew he would be there as the newspapers made an announcement. Right before they were about to leave, Lincoln's bodyguard started to ask him not to go. He told him that he needed to because he had promised people he would. As he was about to walk out the door, Lincoln reportedly stated that he would rather stay home than go, but felt he had to.

About halfway into the play, Booth entered the balcony where Mary, Lincoln, and their guests were seated. No one directly knows when or how Booth officially got into Ford's Theatre or, more importantly, up the steps that were supposed to be guarded for Lincoln's safety. But, it was at this moment, Booth took his small pistol and shot Lincoln in the back of the head. He then jumped off the balcony and onto the stage, hurting his ankle in the process.

Lincoln was quickly brought across the street to the Peterson's home where doctors came only to find that they could not save Lincoln. He laid on the bed diagonally as he was too tall to lay any other way, and passed away the next morning.

While many people in the Southern states were joyous and considered Booth a hero, more people were in a state of shock and mourning. Many places around America declared April 15 as a period of mourning. The Northern states and many border states had grown to adore Abraham Lincoln over the years. They were celebrating with him a few days before as it was announced the 13th Amendment was approved in Congress. Now, they were devastated by the loss of their Great Emancipator.

Conclusion

Now, you have the story of one of the greatest leaders in American history. Abraham Lincoln was more than America's 16th president, he was a family man, politician, lawyer, and Commander in Chief. No matter what role he held, Lincoln put all his effort into it and continued to strengthen his leadership skills.

Today, people still look at Lincoln as a way to strengthen their leadership skills. Not only do politicians often quote Lincoln or discuss his leadership role in their speeches, but people look at Lincoln to help them become successful in their daily jobs. This is because Lincoln possessed many qualities of a great leader. For example, he was willing to learn on the job, controlled his emotions, aware of his weaknesses, willing to take and share success, he knew how to communicate, and would listen to varying viewpoints.

When Lincoln spoke, he did so with authority and humor. He was a naturally sarcastic person who enjoyed giving people a good laugh. While some people found his humor to be dark, he was a man who wasn't afraid to be himself. This doesn't mean that Lincoln couldn't be a serious leader, however. He knew when he needed to put the jokes aside and focus on the situation. Still, he would spend some of his time joking with the troops to keep their spirits up.

There are many great traits of a great leader, but one that many don't hold is the balance of comfort and business. Fortunately for the Union army and his followers, Lincoln found his balance. He helped bring The United States through one of its darkest times. Even though he never truly lived long enough to see the complete end of the Civil War, he was able to see the end of slavery; an institution he despised throughout his life.

As a bonus, here are some of Lincoln's notable leadership skills that he carried with him from his days as a young man working odd jobs in Illinois all the way to the end of his presidency and life. These skills are life lessons that we can add to our own lives.

1. No matter what Abraham Lincoln felt or was going through himself, he always made sure to relay positive messages to people. When he was an attorney, he kept his client's hopes up. When he was the President of the United States, his speeches and forms of communication related positive messages toward winning the Civil War and bringing the Union back together. Lincoln knew that people looked up to him and he used this power in order to inspire them and send them positive messages.

2. Lincoln had strong communication skills. No matter what case he took on or what event was happening in

the world, Lincoln made sure he communicated with the people who deserved to know what was going on. Lincoln could easily and clearly convey messages to his audience and was known to do so in a way that told a story.

3. Abraham Lincoln had great social skills. Although he was typically a quiet man, he was also known to be personable, honest, funny, and compassionate. Lincoln had a lot of empathy for other people, which helped him make strong connections to his supporters and audience. Lincoln knew who he could place his trust in and depend on when he needed it. He was also a great persuader and could negotiate rather well.

4. Lincoln had a lot of motivation, even when times were tough. He would always do what he could to put his principles into practice and make certain they were clear so other people could understand them. He also had the ability to work together with others, who would hold the same motivation as Lincoln to get the task accomplished.

5. Lincoln could accept advice and criticism no matter how difficult it was to digest. Lincoln would listen to other people, whether they were offering him advice or criticism. He also took their words to heart. Lincoln was also known to follow his own instincts above

anything else.

References

Abraham Lincoln. Retrieved 8 August 2019, from https://www.whitehouse.gov/about-the-white-house/presidents/abraham-lincoln/

Abraham Lincoln and the Election of 1860. Retrieved 8 August 2019, from http://www.abrahamlincolnsclassroom.org/abraham-lincoln-in-depth/abraham-lincoln-and-the-election-of-1860/

Abraham Lincoln Presidential Career Timeline. Retrieved 8 August 2019, from http://www.abrahamlincolnonline.org/lincoln/education/presidentialtimeline.htm

Abraham Lincoln, Banking and the Panic of 1837 in Illinois. Retrieved 6 August 2019, from http://www.abrahamlincolnsclassroom.org/abraham-lincoln-in-depth/abraham-lincoln-banking-and-the-panic-of-1837-in-illinois/

Abraham Lincoln's Childhood: Growing Up to Be President. (2013). Retrieved 5 August 2019, from https://americacomesalive.com/2013/02/12/abraham-lincoln-1809-1865-president-from-1861-1865/

Abraham Lincoln's First Inauguration. (2019). Retrieved 9 August 2019, from http://www.abrahamlincolnonline.org/lincoln/education/inaugural1.htm

Abraham Lincoln's Law Office in Springfield, Illinois. Retrieved 8 August 2019, from http://www.abrahamlincolnonline.org/lincoln/tours/lawoffice.htm

Coutu, D. (2009). Leadership Lessons from Abraham Lincoln. Retrieved 8 August 2019, from https://hbr.org/2009/04/leadership-lessons-from-abraham-lincoln

Experiences with Slavery. Retrieved 5 August 2019, from http://www.mrlincolnandfreedom.org/pre-civil-war/experiences-with-slavery-2/

Gantt, M. (2019). Abe Lincoln, rail splitter to well-paid railroad lawyer. Retrieved 8 August 2019, from https://qconline.com/editorials/abe-lincoln-rail-splitter-to-well-paid-railroad-lawyer/article_86e67981-2112-54dd-a4db-bb15ee1aa8a9.html

Glass, A. (2016). Lincoln is born in a Kentucky log cabin: Feb. 12, 1809. Retrieved 6 August 2019, from https://www.politico.com/story/2016/02/lincoln-is-born-in-a-kentucky-log-cabin-feb-12-1809-219025

Hale, J. (2019). Abraham Lincoln, the Almanac, and a Murder Trial. Retrieved 7 August 2019, from https://www.almanac.com/lincoln-almanac-murder

Johnson, G. (2016). The Irony of the Matson Trial in Abraham Lincoln's Life. Retrieved 8 August 2019, from https://tbilaw.com/blog/irony-matson-trial/

Lincoln, A. (1953). Collected Works of Abraham Lincoln. Volume 1. Retrieved 7 August 2019, from https://quod.lib.umich.edu/l/lincoln/lincoln1/1:92?rgn=div 1;view=fulltext

Lincoln-Douglas debates. Retrieved 8 August 2019, from https://www.britannica.com/event/Lincoln-Douglas-debates

Norton, R. A Very Brief Summary of the legal career of Abraham Lincoln. Retrieved 7 August 2019, from https://rogerjnorton.com/Lincoln91.html

Political Career 1830-1860 - Lincoln Home National Historic Site. Retrieved 8 August 2019, from https://www.nps.gov/liho/learn/historyculture/political.ht m

Presidency of Abraham Lincoln. Retrieved 8 August 2019, from https://en.wikipedia.org/wiki/Presidency_of_Abraham_Li

ncoln

United States presidential election of 1860 \. Retrieved 8
August 2019, from
https://www.britannica.com/event/United-States-
presidential-election-of-1860

Winston Churchill

Table of Contents

Introduction

Winston Churchill (1874-1965), is one of the most famous politicians in the history of the world. The Oxfordshire native reached the climax of his stardom as the valiant prime minister of the United Kingdom during the Second World War (1939-1945). Churchill gave to his people "toil, sweat, tears, and blood," conducting them to the victory against antagonists. Churchill was also an author, a gifted speaker, soldier, war reporter, and painter.

At the beginning of World War II, the United Kingdom was attacked by Nazi Germany. Churchill and his fellow citizens refused to abdicate despite the fierceness and impressive armament of their opponents. Winston Churchill's boldness and his keen sense of positivity inspired the people of Great Britain to victory.

The sleek style of this intrepid, devoted man, skilled on the battlefield and facing the public with two fingers in the air forming a "V" symbolizing victory, conquered people. British saw in Churchill the charisma of John Bull, a mythical figure of England.

Not only did Churchill make history, but he wrote it as well. As a war reporter, historian, and biographer, the "British Bulldog" showed a foolproof mastery of English language, a competence rewarded in 1953 with his triumph of the Nobel Prize for literature. As a schoolboy, Churchill had enormous difficulties, most notably an impediment of speech, but became a refined gentleman as he grew.

Churchill rallied in 1895 in the armed forces with the status of an army lieutenant and finished his career 69 years later, in 1964 in the House of Commons. His achievements and sacrifices would be etched in their minds forever. In world history, few men served their homeland with so much consecration and zeal.

Chapter 1: Winston Churchill's Early Life

Winston Churchill was born one year after his parents' wedding. As a child, he had some difficulties but ultimately became a fine gentleman. This first chapter sheds light on the birth of Winston Churchill, his academic background, and his entry into the military academy in 1895.

Birth

Churchill was born on November 30, 1874, in Oxfordshire during a time when Britain was the absolute dominant world power. His parents were direct descendants of Marlborough's Dukes and were among the British aristocracy's highest levels. Winston Churchill was then born into the United Kingdom's governing elite. John Spencer-Churchill, his paternal grandfather, had been the 7th Duke of Marlborough and a Member of Parliament for ten years. He had belonged to the Conservative Party and served in Prime Minister Benjamin Disraeli's government.

Lord Randolph Churchill, Winston Churchill's father, had been elected in 1873 as Conservative Member of Parliament for Woodstock. Jennie Churchill, Randolph's wife, was from an American family.

Randolph Churchill and Jennie Churchill were engaged in August 1873 after meeting each other the same month. In April 1874, they married in Paris, at the British Embassy. Appointed Viceroy of Ireland in 1876, John Spencer-Churchill chose his son as private secretary. Randolph moved to Dublin with his family, at a time when Ireland was part of Great Britain. It was there that Jack, Jennie's second son, was born in 1880. There was nevertheless a doubt about the boy's paternity, and many rumors claimed he was not the son of Lord Randolph Churchill. Jennie was pregnant with Jack while having limited contact with Randolph Churchill, who very unsteady because of his administrative duties.

In Dublin, the children were cared for by their nanny, Elizabeth Everest. Randolph was busy at work most of the time and had almost no relationship with either of his sons, especially Winston, whom he found bothersome. It was the same with Jennie, who was never very present in home life.

Academic Background

As a little boy, Churchill's education was almost a disaster. He had a very strict and stern governess who used to inspire fear. Winston's fear was so intense that Mrs. Everest, his favorite nanny, made him read a book with the title "Reading Without Tears." The aim was to help him read without crying, but the book, unfortunately, was not helpful.

Despite his governess's efforts to teach him, the young Winston was stubborn and too rebellious to be a brilliant student. In his childhood, he studied in three different schools and had considerable difficulty, for he was a chubby boy with a speech impediment. Therefore, Winston couldn't receive very appreciable grades in school. Winston's father, an accomplished scholar and a brilliant man, spent nearly no time with his son because he found him annoying. The boy's mother was a beautiful woman with a fondness for social events, where she could appear as a charming and impressive guest. Then, she too, did not have time for her son.

Winston Churchill's education began at the age of 12, as he entered Harrow School, a boarding school not far from London. Despite his previous academic failures, his time at the boarding school significantly helped him grow. In Harrow, he started a lifelong love of literature and writing, which accompanied him until his dying day. Curious about the world's wonders and especially fascinated with the written word, Winston imagined himself as a gifted student praised by England's top universities. Nevertheless, his dreams would go unfulfilled because his grades were poor.

Even from the boy's childhood, Winston's father was displeased with his son's inability to excel academically and decided his future would be in the army. Leaning on his formal education, Winston kept teaching himself by reading and learning on his own. He had a particular fondness for works by Edward Gibbons and Thomas Macaulay.

Entry Into The Military Academy

At the time Winston Churchill came in the Royal Military College of Sandhurst, very few knew he would become one of England's most celebrated war leaders. The young man passed the entrance exam after trying three times. He was not interested in the infantry and only applied to cavalry training because it accepted a lower grade and he would not have to learn mathematics.

Winston had a new start at Sandhurst. He found his work exciting and made a drawing of maps of the area. For the rear guards and advanced guards, he designed paper plans and even invented simple tactical schemes. Winston learned how to make bridges out of wood and jump over masonry bridges.

In December 1894, he graduated from Sandhurst, eighth out of a squad of 150. Although he could now be transferred, as his father had wanted, to an infantry regiment, he chose to continue with the cavalry. On February 20, 1895, Churchill was commissioned in the Fourth Queen's Own Hussars as the second lieutenant.

He had an annual income of $300 but did not find it enough. Indeed, he thought he needed at least $500 to have the same lifestyle as the other officers in the regiment. Winston's mother helped her son with an annual allowance of $400, but he often overspent that amount.

Intending to boost his wage, Churchill started war correspondence and wrote for two newspapers as a paid reporter.

Chapter 2: Winston Churchill's Early Days In Politics

When he entered the military academy, Churchill quickly showed fervor and proved to have a tremendous ability to take the initiative. This was an omen of a brilliant and long political career he started in 1899. This chapter goes into detail about Churchill's intervention during the South African War, as well as his entry into Parliament and appointment to the post of Under-Secretary of State for the Colonies.

The South African War

In 1899, after completing his tour of duty, Churchill left India, resigned from his commission and returned home. By the time the South African War increased in intensity, Churchill had negotiated a contract with a newspaper and was paid a monthly wage of $250 and all expenses paid.

Moving to the battlefront, Winston Churchill was escorting an armored train during a reconnaissance mission on November 15, 1899, when the train happened to be ambushed. Without panic, he took the lead of the situation and successfully freed the engine. Churchill, however, was captured with other British captives in Pretoria. It was alleged that he promised his captors that if they released him, he would not fight them.

Unable to obtain any promise of release, Churchill convinced Sergeant Major Brockie and Captain Aylmer Haldane to include him in an escape plan. As the plan was seemingly secure, Churchill was the first one to climb out. He soon discovered the other two were unable to come with him, so he mustered courage and set off alone. Following a series of adventures, Churchill triumphantly arrived in Durban after escaping via Portuguese East Africa.

Lord Randolph Churchill's son became a hero as he stood out in sharp relief after South Africans' disasters. Thanks to his new found fame, he was able to override the War Office's objections. He assumed the role of officer-lieutenant in the South African Light Horse regiment while remaining a war correspondent. In April 1900, Churchill joined the column headed by Sir Ian Hamilton, a friend of his.

Walking with his boon companion and cousin Charles Richard John Spencer Churchill who was Marlborough's ninth duke from 1871 to 1934. Churchill was often solicited as far as fighting was concerned and each time proved to be a very gifted war correspondent. The man turned his dispatches into two books, with little adaptation this time. The books were entitled "London to Ladysmith via Pretoria" and "Ian Hamilton's March." The first was about escape story while the second described his experience in the Second Boer War while escorting the British army. The South African war left an enduring imprint on Churchill's mind. He understood that war was very dangerous and should be assigned to more ranks than generals.

Churchill Enters Parliament

In Parliament, Winston became aligned with an association of Conservative dissidents. That group, known as "The Hughligans," was headed by Lord Hugh Cecil. Churchill's first speech in Parliament happened to be an attack on St. John Broderick's proposal. The Secretary of State for War's suggestion was to expand the army so that there would be six corps. Among them, three would have the freedom to get organized into an expeditionary force overseas.

For his first speech, Winston spoke without notes for an hour after training for more than six weeks. The speech spread his rhetorical skills and was highly appreciated.

In 1902, the young parliamentarian impressed at Michigan's University in an interview published only six decades later. His speech in the interview focused on "the ultimate partition of China" and Churchill expressed a lack of concern about Russian expansion towards India and China.

In 1903, he moved away from the group led by Lord Hugh but remained a friend of his. Churchill had been supported by Lord Hugh, as he opposed Joseph Chamberlain, the Liberal

Unionist Leader. Chamberlain suggested extensive tariffs for the protection of England's economic dominance, whereas Churchill was advocating free trade. Lord Hugh was not the only person supporting Winston. Other Conservatives, such as C. T. Ritchie, who was Chancellor of the Exchequer, also supported him. As Chamberlain's movement gained strength and split the Conservative-Union alliance, Winston Churchill continued his attacks on the Conservatives on several topics. Many causes could explain the growing dissatisfaction that led him to make personal attacks on certain leaders, including Chamberlain. As a reply, Conservative backbenchers once led a walkout while Churchill was speaking, and a lot of those people were hostile to him. At a certain level, his constituency happened to express disagreement and deselected him.

In 1904, his dissatisfaction grew so strong that, as he was coming back from the Whitsun recess, Winston crossed the House of Commons' floor to join the Liberal Party. He was followed by Ivor Guest, a cousin of his. The reasons that drove Churchill to change sides have included the search for a ministerial post likely to provide a significant wage, a desire to eradicate poverty and difficulties of the working class. In 1962, he became a liberal and kept campaigning for free trade.

Between 1903 and 1905, Churchill engaged in writing a biography of his father, Lord Randolph Churchill. Published in 1906, the biography received much acclaim. Nevertheless, filial devotion led him to mitigate certain of his father's ugly aspects. The book was been reviewed by Theodore Roosevelt, a man who had known Randolph. Historians thought Churchill could flaunt the book to partially vindicate the reason he had chosen his career and to justify the fact he crossed the floor. Winston himself later confessed that his father's life happened to be a major source of his conflict with the Conservatives.

Churchill, Under-Secretary Of State For The Colonies

In December 1905, Balfour resigned from his post of Prime Minister. King Edward VII then called Henry Campbell-Bannerman, the Liberal leader, to take Balfour's place. With the hope to have a working majority at the level of the House of Commons, the Liberal leader organized a general election in January 1906, won by Liberals.

A new government then was set up, and Churchill was appointed Under-Secretary of State to serve the Colonial Office. He worked under Victor Bruce, Secretary of State for the Colonies. In this position, Churchill first had the mission to help to elaborate a constitution intended to be applied to the Transvaal. In 1906 he was assigned for oversight when a government was to be granted to the Orange Free State. Churchill strove to establish equality between the Boer and

British while dealing with South Africa. He also announced an end of contract of Chinese working in South Africa.

Churchill expressed issues concerning the relations between the black African population and European settlers. After the launching of the Bambatha Rebellion by Zulu, he denounced the autochthons' disgusting butchery Europeans were confronted with.

In August 1906, he spent a holiday in Deauville, France, and gambled or played polo most of his time. From Deauville, he flew to Paris and then to Switzerland. There, he climbed to the top of the Eggishorn before reaching Berlin and Silesia to take up an invitation from Kaiser Wilhelm II. Churchill then moved to Venice and rallied from there with Lionel Rothschild, a friend of his.

He holidayed in May 1907 in Biarritz before embarking in the autumn on a tour of Africa and Europe. He flew through Italy, France, Cyprus, and Malta and afterward reached Aden and Berbera via the Suez Canal. Churchill sailed to Mombasa and went through the Kenya Colony on a rail journey. On his way, he stopped in Simba for big game hunting before heading to the Uganda Protectorate. To finish his adventure, Churchill sailed up the River Nile. The young Under-Secretary of State wrote for Strand Magazine about his experiences and subsequently published them in a book entitled "My African Journey."

Chapter 3: Churchill's Political Career Explosion

After a successful debut in politics, it was time for Churchill to move on to the next stage. His hierarchical superiors noticed it and assigned responsibilities to him. This chapter will explore Churchill's achievements as President of the Board of Trade, Home Secretary, and First Lord of Admiralty.

Churchill, President of the Board of Trade

In 1908, when Asquith replaced Campbell-Bannerman, Churchill was commissioned as President of the Board of Trade. In the Cabinet, Churchill worked along with David Lloyd George, a Liberal politician, to support social reform. He stated in a speech that even though the British people enjoy all the passions throughout the ages, their rearguard fights into conditions harsher than barbarism. Churchill was promoted to deal with this, what he referred to as a network of "state intervention and regulation," similar to that of Germany.

The young president of the Board of Trade negotiated on the River Tyne a dispute between some employers and their ship-workers. He then instituted, to settle future industrial disputes, a Standing Court of Arbitration. Churchill argued that workers' hours should be reduced, and initiated the Mines Eight Hours Bill, which supported laborers not working for more than eight hours a day. He introduced in 1908 the Trade Boards Bill, intended to institute a Board of Trade assigned to prosecute exploitative employers and establish a minimum wage. That Board of Trade also instituted the right laborers to benefit from meal breaks. The bill was largely approved. In May of that year, he initiated the Labor Exchanges Bill intending to implement more than 200 Labor Exchanges, by which people without employment would be offered work. Churchill also advocated an unemployment insurance scheme, partially financed by the government.

To make sure these social reforms would be funded, he denounced, with Lloyd George, the growth of warship production of Reginald McKennas. Churchill openly thwarted people who considered conflict with Germany was compulsory. He attempted, in autumn 1909, to improve Britain's relationship with Germany, visiting the country and meeting with the Kaiser. The Liberal government, headed by Asquith, presented social reforms as the People's Budget in order to pass them into law. Conservative antagonists of the reform established the Budget Protest League, and people who supported it set up the Budget League, which was headed by Churchill. The budget, accepted in the House of Commons, did not have the approval of the Conservative peers. Given that they had domination over the House of Lords, Churchill's social reforms failed.

Churchill anticipated that an upper class obstruction of that type would repel working class and could drive to class war. The government, to break the deadlock, called a general election in January 1910. The Liberals won, and Churchill maintained his Dundee's seat. He proposed in a cabinet memorandum, after the election, the eradication of the House of Lords. He suggested it should be replaced by a unicameral system or a reduced second chamber without prerogative for the Conservatives. The Lords relented in April, allowing the budget to pass.

Churchill, Home Secretary

Churchill was appointed Home Secretary in February 1910. He gained control over the police as well as prison services and then launched a prison reform program. Afterward, he introduced a nuance between political prisoners and criminals, with relaxed prison rules for political prisoners. Churchill attempted to set up libraries for prisoners. He then introduced a measure according to which every prison has to initiate either a concert or a lecture four times per year for the distraction of prisoners.

He lowered first offenders' solitary confinement to one month while the one of the recidivists was reduced to three months.

Churchill expressed disagreement about what he considered as the extremely extended sentences applied to culprits of some crimes. He proposed afterward the eradication of automatic incarceration for people unable to pay fines. He then abolished the incarceration of young people between 16 and 21, unless in cases of very serious offenses. Churchill succeeded in commuting 21 of the 43 sentences he passed during his Home Secretary's term.

At that time, one of the significant domestic issues in the United Kingdom was women's suffrage. Dealing with the point, Churchill suggested that women should vote, even though he would only initiate a bill thereupon in case of majority support from men. His suggested way out was a referendum that should take place on the issue. Unfortunately, this was not approved by Asquith. Therefore, women couldn't have access to vote until 1918.

In 1910, Churchill moved to the Mediterranean. After spending two months there, he came back to Britain and was assigned to find a way out for the Tonypandy Riot. It was a strike in which Rhondda Valley's coal miners strongly objected to their conditions of work. Glamorgan's Chief Constable asked the police to suppress the riot with the help of troops. When Churchill heard that the troops started flying, he allowed them to move far up to Cardiff and Swindon, but made their deployment difficult because he thought the use of troops was likely to drive to bloodshed. Churchill sent 270 police officers without firearms, assigning them to assist their counterparts.

Nevertheless, the riots lived on, and he arranged an interview for protesters allowing them to meet the chief industrial arbitrator of the government. Personally, Churchill thought the miners and owners on strike had the wrong attitude. "The Times," a national newspaper, and other media blamed him of being too kind with the rioters. By contrast, many members of the Labor Party considered him to be too clumsy.

In December 1910, a general election took place, by Asquith's call. The Liberals had a new victory, and Churchill succeeded in securing his seat at Dundee. In January 2011, Churchill was assigned to care about the Siege of Sidney Street. Three Latvian burglars killed several police officers. The murderers were hidden in a London apartment surrounded by police. With the scale of the situation, Churchill rallied the police. After the house was burned, he asked the fire brigade to stay far from the house, due to the danger posed to them by the armed Latvians. When the fire had consumed the apartment, the policemen found two burglars inside, dead. Although he was criticized for this decision, Churchill said he considered watching the house burn was better than putting valued British lives at risk rescuing criminals.

In March 1911, Churchill introduced to parliament the second reading of the Coal Mines Bill. When adopted into law, that bill had the goal to offer more safety to coal mines. Likewise, he proposed the Shops Bill, aiming to give better working conditions to shop workers. The bill was rejected by shop owners and passed into law with a fragile acceptance. In order to have a proper oversight on this issue, Churchill headed the Early Closing Association. He remained president of that association until the beginning of 1940. In April 1911, Lloyd George introduced the National Insurance Act, which Churchill has helped to draft. In 1911, Churchill was asked to find a solution to the escalating civil strife. He sent troops into Liverpool for the repression of protesting dockers. When the Agadir Crisis rose, Churchill indicated that Britain, Russia, and France should form an alliance in order to save the independence of the Netherlands, Denmark, and Belgium from potential German expansionism.

Winston Churchill, First Lord Of The Admiralty

In July-August 1911, the Agadir crisis occurred and revealed the strategist's skill in Churchill. For the cabinet, he composed an important paper titled "Military Aspects of The Continental Problem." Invited by Herbert Henry Asquith, the then Prime Minister of Great Britain, Churchill attended a meeting organized by the committee of imperial defense. The meeting revealed there was a huge lack of coordination between the War Office and the plans of the Admiralty. Highly impressed by Winston Churchill's apparent desire to seize command of the Royal Navy, Asquith appointed him in October 1911 to first Lord of the Admiralty.

Churchill's had at the Admiralty the mission to modernize. A significant number of his reforms were inspired by Jackie Fisher, the retired first sea Lord, with whom Winston was in nearly daily contact. The new First Lord of the Admiralty, however, was ready to act boldly, as he was confident in his judgment.

To begin, Churchill replaced three among the four sea lords. That way, Sir Francis Bridgeman gained the position of Sir Arthur Wilson, the first sea lord, while Prince Louis of Battenberg was designated second. David Beatty, a dashing officer, became Winston Churchill's naval secretary. A little after, in December 1912, Bridgeman was coerced into retirement by Churchill, the latter appointing Prince Louis of Battenberg in his place. Churchill had little respect for most of the Royal Navy's senior officers, as he found they were without imagination and set in their ways.

Following Fisher's advice, he established a naval war staff composed of three divisions that had the task to elaborate and coordinate war plans. Relying on Herbert Richmond's assistance, Churchill gave more interest to naval officers in strategy and story. He also launched a new periodical entitled "The Naval Review." With his desire to explore all aspects of naval affairs, Winston strove to entertain his political friends every so often. With a vigilant eye, he inspected dockyards, ships, and naval installations. He sometimes, in defiance of protocol, sought information from ordinary seamen or junior officers, avoiding senior naval officers.

Most of the admirals were frustrated. One of them was Sir John Jellicoe, who thought Churchill was not humble and unable to realize he was a civilian with limitations.

With Fisher's support, Churchill developed a division of battleships named "the Queen Elizabeth class." The latter was equipped with the 15-inch gun. With the First Lord of the Admiralty's devotion, the fleet from coal-fired became oil-fired engines.

He announced in June 1914 that he had negotiated with the British government for the purchase of 51 percent of the Anglo-Iranian oil company's shares. Thus making sure the fleet would have a significant supply of oil. He strove to promote the development of air power and submarines. In 1913, with Clementine's alarm, Churchill took up flying lessons. He then took the air several times before Clementine convinced him to stop for a while.

Winston Churchill was devoted to England, retaining a significant margin of naval supremacy over Germany. On February 8, 1912, in a speech he made in Glasgow, he argued that Britain's large navy was a necessity ,whereas it was a luxury for Germany, a comment that provoked much anger in Germany. When a new naval law was drafted in Germany and proposed an increase of the German fleet's size, Churchill wanted the cabinet's approval for the British naval program's expansion. Simultaneously, he renovated his Liberal credentials with an idea of "naval holiday," which means both countries should suspend naval construction. After Germans rejected this idea, the tenacious Churchill found a naval arrangement with the French people. Under that arrangement, the British Mediterranean Fleet would withdraw and concentrate on home waters so France would have the ability to patrol the Mediterranean.

After complex arguments that took considerable time, the cabinet finally agreed in July 1912. Nevertheless, the Anglo-French was strengthened and Winston's expansionist naval policy troubled the Liberal Party's radical wing. And speculation grew over the thought that he was preparing to rally the Conservative Party.

During the winter of 1913-1914, the first Lord of Admiralty's insisted on the construction of four other dreadnoughts and an increase of the naval estimates. That brought a crisis in which he was in opposition with Lloyd George, the majority of the Liberal Party, and most of the cabinet. Only Asquith's delaying tactics and a last-minute decision of Lloyd George to satisfy the majority of Churchill's complaints prevented his resignation.

Chapter 4: Warlord And Accomplished Politician

Churchill had henceforth demonstrated that Britain could rely on him. He couldn't stop when doing so well. Discover in this chapter, Churchill's actions during the Ulster crisis and Britain's federal devolution, his achievements during the First World War and when he was appointed to the post of Secretary of War and Air.

Ulster Crisis And Great Britain's Federal Devolution

With his status of first lord, Winston Churchill was highly concentrated on naval matters. Nevertheless, he was significantly involved in the biggest political issue of the moment: "Irish Home Rule." Churchill accused the Conservatives and Bonar Law of inciting rebellion. In February 1912, in Belfast he attempted to confront a Unionist audience in the same hall where Randolph Churchill, his father, had spoken 26 years earlier. At the last minute, the meeting moved because there was a great threat to his safety.

In March 1911, he secretly proposed one possibility in the cabinet room: Associate Ireland with an all-round scheme debating federal devolution. That all-round scheme was supposed to welcome seven regional parliaments in Britain and other parliaments from Ireland, Wales, and Scotland. The cabinet, however, decided Ireland should have a single parliament for the whole country. Churchill caused a sensation in September 1912 when in Dundee he aired the federal devolution's concept across a speech. Two times in 1912 Churchill prompted, without success, the cabinet to move temporarily to predominantly protestant counties instead of home rule. During the 1913-1914's winter, he was the primary intermediary in many secret moves for the promotion of a bipartisan settlement. His principal contact on the Conservative side was F.E. Smith, a personal friend of his.

At the moment the Home Full Bill was to become law, there was a disagreement of the Ulster Unionists who rejected Asquith's offer to opt-out of the protestant counties for six years. Churchill then changed course. He argued that the Ulster Unionists should accept the opt out, as they had obtained a compromise. He was also determined to reestablish his status in the Liberal Party. On March 14, 1914, in a speech he gave at Bradford, Churchill issued a severe warning that there was one option for Ulster Unionists. According to his words, they have to agree to the government's plan, or they would suffer the consequences.

Meanwhile, many police reports alarmed the cabinet, informing that the Ulster Volunteers were planning a military coup. A cabinet committee controlled by Churchill ordered precautionary troop movements while Churchill himself ordered, as the first lord of the Admiralty, the 5th battle squadron to move to Lamlash, which was extremely close to Belfast. Churchill's actions happened in convincing the Conservatives that the government was planning an "Ulster pogrom," and the "Curragh mutiny" quickly confirmed that. When most of the 3rd cavalry brigade's officers, fifty-seven out of seventy, declared that it was better to be dismissed than help to coerce Ulster. Across the public platform, Churchill often spoke with provocative language while pursuing conciliatory policies behind the scenes.

Churchill And The First World War

At the beginning of the war, the Germans racked up many naval successes, and Churchill was heavily criticized. Two German battleships, the Breslau and the Goeben, escaped in August 1914 from the Adriatic via the Dardanelles to Constantinople. Churchill boasted on September 21 that the German fleet should come out and fight. Otherwise, they would be miserably dug out from their hole.

Angry, the Germans sank three British cruisers on the following day three, killing 1459 men and officers off the Dogger Bank. With Germans' zeal in their fight, two other British cruisers were sunk on the coast of Chile during the battle of Coronel on November 1. Some days later, on

December 16, 1914, German battle cruisers killed 500 civilians, as they bombed Scarborough and some other east coast ports.

Voices against the Admiralty multiplied and were only in part offset thanks to the successful actions of the Dogger Bank and the Falkland Islands. Fascinated by every aspect of the fighting, Winston Churchill felt eager to participate in the war and was ingenious in assuming the responsibilities of the Admiralty. He quickly took action and the naval reserve was converted into Royal Naval division. It was an infantry force composed of 15,000 men.

Although Churchill promised to transfer the division to the War Office's control, he now had a kind of private army on which he could rely. He also established a trident of squadron aircraft. Those squadrons shelled from airfields German defenses in northern France.

In October 1914, during nearly four days, Churchill led virtually a land battle while rushing along the channel coast. The Germans were threatening to invade Antwerp, a Belgian city. Churchill was dispatched by the cabinet to set up reinforcements and strengthen the Belgian government's resistance. Churchill did a great job. He succeeded in counteracting the German advance by setting up Antwerp's defenses. As soon as he was on the spot, Churchill's zeal for the lead of military operations rose up. He solicited the trident of three battalions and burnt a telegram with a message asking him to resign from his cabinet post in exchange for a high-ranking command at the level of the field.

At the time Asquith shared the telegram's message with his colleagues, they roared with laughter before Winston was ordered home. That laughter was the illustration of the gulf there was between Churchill and his politician colleagues. The politicians ultimately had command of the war, but they were obliged to rely on the admirals' and generals' judgment, since almost none of them had knowledge of military matters.

There was, however, a generalissimo inside Churchill fighting to get out. As Churchill's detractors could see it, his military ambitions were excessive, and his defense of Antwerp was a worthy prowess. When the city failed, he was heavily criticized in the press. This was perhaps the moment at which Churchill's critics in the political sphere settled into their belief that he was a man who lacked judgment.

Churchill, Secretary For War And Air

At the end of the First World War, when the Liberal Party was split, Lloyd George headed a Coalition Liberals and coalition of Conservatives. The most prominent personalities of the Coalition Liberals were himself and Churchill. In December 1918's general election, the coalition obtained an impressive majority and once again, Churchill won his Dundee seat. He expected to come back to the Admiralty. Lloyd George, however, put him in charge the posts of secretary for air and war. As soon as he had been commissioned, Churchill had to settle a crisis over demobilization. Many opposed existing arrangement because they didn't take into account the duration for which a man served. The resentment was so great that at Calais, a mutiny broke and generated riots. To find a way out, Churchill proceeded with the establishment of a new scheme. The latter was instituted with a "first in, first out" principle.

Some other consequences emerging from the war kept on showing up, and the stormy Bolshevik revolution invaded Churchill. He concluded that Soviet communism was the most harmful thing on earth and Trotsky and Lenin more dreadful antagonists than Germany and its Kaiser. Churchill was afraid of the fact that Bolshevism could conquer both Germany and Russia, thus generating a fierce and hostile bloc spreading in Europe and the rest of the world. Therefore, he prompted the winners to set up a policy of friendship and indulgence towards Germany. Churchill claimed to carry out a policy established by the war cabinet and arguing that the 14,000 British troops remaining in Russia after the war should be withdrawn from the country. But when the supreme war council held a meeting in Paris in February 1919, he supported a concerted attempt of sending money, supplies as well as extra troops to the Russian forces. He strove to convince others of his view, but no one listened to him.

Lloyd George was greatly dismayed by Churchill's memorandum on the subject. He complained he was engulfed in an obsession with Russia, but Churchill maintained his view. Lloyd George was strongly against trade negotiations with the Russian leaders and narrowly missed resigning in November 1920, when the cabinet approved a treaty instituting Anglo-Soviet trade. Churchill's conception of tyranny related to the Bolshevik regime has been vindicated later. Nevertheless, following the bloodbath that came from the First World War, the United Kingdom, and its allies could no longer mobilize a workforce, money, or popular opinion to engage in military intervention.

Developments at home were also a major concern for Churchill. The intelligence services read messages from Moscow giving the Soviet agents in Britain authorization to link to the British Communist Party, the Daily Herald, and other left-wing organizations. The Herald had already identified Churchill as the most harmful enemy of the Labor movement. For his part, Churchill implied that the Labor Party was not fit to govern and denounced the latter as a prey likely to be manipulated by extremists.

Churchill, absorbed by the "red peril" until early 1920, didn't realize that Ireland was diving into chaos. Sir Henry Wilson, the Imperial General Staff's chief urged for the establishment of martial law. All the cabinet, including Churchill, opposed this, but Sir Henry Wilson strongly supported Lloyd George in his policy of engaging the Black and Tans, two paramilitary forces as well as the auxiliary police force, "Auxis." The Auxis, through fierce reprisals inflicted on the IRA, killed many of them and also some innocent civilians. In June 1920, at the time Lloyd George urged him to preside over a cabinet committee on Ireland, Churchill had plenty of bold ideas that should serve to intensify the conflict. He even thought of setting up a force composed of 30,000 Ulstermen who would ensure Britain's authority on Ireland. But, as he also made the cabinet understand, his goal was to set up a position of strength that would allow constitutional concessions to be granted.

Chapter 5: Political Career Highlights

Churchill assumes responsibility and reaches his reputation's climax by leading Britain to victory during the Second World War after switching to Home affairs. But before all this, he had been appointed Secretary of States for the Colonies.

Churchill, Secretary Of State For The Colonies

In February 1921, Churchill was appointed Secretary of State for the Colonies. One of the major issues of that year was the Irish War of Independence. Churchill and six other British negotiators met Sinn Fein leaders at the level of Downing Street. Churchill argued that Ireland should be given home rule within the Empire, and the Protestant-majority Ulster's counties would have autonomy from the government of Dublin. The Ulster Unionists objected to this, therefore, it was concluded that Ireland would be divided. A major part of the country was to be called the Irish Free State, where the Protestant-majority spheres would be Northern Ireland and part of Britain. This division was included in the Anglo-Irish Treaty drafted by Churchill.

Following the treaty, Churchill succeeded in deleting the death penalties of Sinn Fein members who had committed murder. As a civil war emerged in Ireland between republican opponents and supporters of the treaty, weapons were supplied by Churchill to the forces of the pro-treaty government of Michael Collins. Churchill prompted to install an Arab government and remove most of Britain's troops from Iraq. In March British officials who had the mission to govern Iraq in Cairo. The British officials agreed to make Faisal King of Iraq while his brother, Abdullah, would be installed as King of Transjordan.

From there, Churchill flew to Mandatory Palestine. There, Arab Palestinians asked him to stop admitting Jewish migration. As he was an advocate of Zionism, he rejected this. He thought that he could support Jewish immigration to Palestine and appease the concerns of Arab people who were afraid they would become the minority. At that time, Turkey was eager to expand into the lost areas of the country during World War I. Churchill encouraged Lloyd George to hold Constantinople under British Control. Turkish troops moved towards Britain, leading to what is subsequently referred to as the "Chanak Crisis." Churchill considered the matter at hand and asked British people not to panic.

In the last part of 1921, Lloyd George gave Churchill a post in the Cabinet Committee on Defense Estimates. The committee's members met in early 1922 to decide how much military expenditure they would need without putting national security at risk. Churchill suffered from appendicitis and underwent an operation in October 1922. While this was happening, the Conservatives stood against the coalition government of Lloyd George and made haste for a general election in November 1922. This was a bad deal for Churchill whose Dundee seat was gained by the prohibitionist Edwin Scrymgeour after the latter had ranked fourth at the vote.

Churchill And The Second World War

In September 1939, the war broke out and Chamberlain put Churchill in the war cabinet. He once again became the first lord of Admiralty and returned to the same post he had been appointed to in August 1914. The whole direction of the war could now be found under Chamberlain and his war cabinet's control, acting following the military coordination committee's advice. Lord Chatfield was the chairman of that committee. Chamberlain, who was afraid at the beginning of Churchill's intrigues, discovered with surprise that the man was an impressively loyal colleague. This led to an unusual event, as Chamberlain and his wife dined with the couple. The two men were politician antagonists, however. While Chamberlain seemed not to be at ease in his post as war minister, the first lord of Admiralty's flamboyant face and sparkling look threatened to erase him.

Winston Churchill's dynamism was quickly noticed at the Admiralty. The man ordered that all merchant ships should be armed and all naval vessels fitted with radar. With the belief that Britain would easily overcome the U-boat threat, he announced figures that, according to him, characterize German losses. His advisers, however, thought those figures were greatly exaggerated.

In April 1940, under the first lord of Admiralty's instructions, Talbot was dismissed. Churchill was searching for a bold move by the navy, as ignoring bombers could endanger ships without fighter cover. Winston repeatedly prompted the naval staff for the adoption of a dangerous plan that would send a naval force at the level of the Baltic. That idea was eventually counteracted by Admiral Cork, the first sea lord. Another idea rose to Churchill's mind. He thought Norwegian coastal waters could be mined to prevent the Swedish iron ore from being transported to Germany. On November 30, 1939, the Russians invaded Finland, and Churchill sent an expeditionary force to take hold of the Swedish ore fields in Narvik, believing they were rushing to rescue Finland. It was only in the last days of March 1940 that the supreme allied war council gave the authorization of mining the leads. German forces marched on April 9 into Norway and Denmark.

As Chatfield resigned a couple of days before, Chamberlain asked Churchill to assume the function related to the military coordination committee. The first lord of Admiralty obeyed and started dominating operations. He dispatched, under Admiral Cork's command, an expeditionary force to Narvik. Churchill, however, decided a few days later to open up a second front around Trondheim. After that, the convoy's rear half was directed to central Norway. At the time Churchill proposed to shell Narvik, General Mackesy, the land commander retorted it would be a shame to bombard thousands of people in Norway. Churchill told Cork that Mackesy should be relieved or placed under arrest without hesitation if he happens to spread an evil spirit via the land forces. After Churchill made a quick change of plan, the troops dispatched to Trondheim were overwhelmed and evacuated.

Home Affairs And The Failed Election Of 1945

Because of his frequent absences from England and great concentration on the lead of the war, Churchill's didn't have permanent contact with home affairs. Most of the time, he had to delegate. The war economy's management was largely controlled by the committee of the lord president, whose successive chairmen were Chamberlain, Anderson, and Clement Richard Attlee. At that time, Bevin was appointed minister of labor and was in charge of industrial relations as well as the reconstruction committee. Woolton had to deal with post-war problems. It was a big mistake for a prime minister to ignore domestic political currents for a long time. Churchill indeed bore the brunt of his careless attitude, as he miserably failed in 1945's general election.

In December 1942, the Beveridge report was published and opened up a bank of peacetime questions. This has an immediate consequence of becoming a crisis that overwhelmed the coalition. A misunderstanding arose between the Conservative and Labor parties. In this situation, the war cabinet strove to find the adequate solutions and Churchill, in a broadcast in March 1943, sought a middle way between approval and refusal of the report. Nevertheless, he was devoted to postpone all legislation to the post-war period.

In March 1944, Churchill was surprised when the government happened to lose a vote in the House of Commons over equal remuneration for women teachers. Eager to teach his detractors a lesson, he converted the topic into a vote of confidence and won by a crippling majority. This experience confirmed the widespread impression that Winston Churchill was not able to be an efficient, peacetime leader.

In Europe, the end of the war approached, and Churchill hesitated between maintaining the coalition for an extended period and fighting a general election. In May 1945 he invited the Liberal and Labor parties to continue in office until Japan's defeat, which was not likely to occur for another eighteen months. Both parties refused, and Churchill after resignation headed a caretaker administration. During the election campaign's opening broadcast, he surprised a lot of admirers of his by informing that a Labor government was about to introduce Gestapo into Britain. Churchill had been significantly worried in wartime by state bureaucracy's inroads into civil liberty. He was also influenced by the anti-totalitarian tract of F. A. Hayek, materialized by "The Road to Serfdom," written in 1944.

In 1945, the new generation that went to the poll for the first time was predominantly Labor party, young people shaped by the left-wing propaganda and the egalitarianism of the war years.

Unusually, there happened to be an interlude between the July 5 polling day and the results twenty-one days later, during which Winston took part to the Potsdam Conference. There, he saw Stalin, who convinced him that he had benign intentions. After a short holiday, Churchill came back to Britain feeling eager to know the general election's result, but the winner was the Labor party. While Churchill was shocked by that defeat, Clementine found it could be a blessing in disguise. But he had a majority of more than 17,000 in his

Woodford's constituency. At 7 pm on July 26, 1945, Churchill rallied Buckingham Palace and announced his resignation.

Chapter 6: Churchill Heads The Opposition And Stays In Business

After failing in the general election in 1945, Churchill headed over the opposition and wrote about the Second World War. He took action against Union Soviet threat and fought for the establishment of European Unity before being appointed Prime Minister once again.

Leader Of The Opposition And Second World War's Historian

A lot of time remained before the next general election, and during this time Churchill often ignored his role as Conservative leader. He absented himself and couldn't be seen in the House of Commons for long periods. In foreign and defense policy, there was limited scope for the opposition, since Churchill fully agreed with the government policies.

On the other side, he was actively hostile toward the fact the economy was undergoing socialist mismanagement. He deplored the proliferation of controls, as he found them like totalitarian tendencies. Churchill also disapproved when the government prepared for the transfer of India's power. According to him, it was hurried and irresponsible. In March 1947, he warned that in handing over India's government to the so-called political classes, they were handing it over to doubtful men who would disappear a few years later. He added that it was with deep pain he watched the British Empire's clattering down after all the glories and the services it had rendered to humanity.

Nevertheless, Churchill had to recognize that it would be complicated to back up, and finally supported India Bill's independence. As he had lavish spending habits, Winston had never had consistent wealth. In 1938, Churchill and his wife made heavy losses at Wall Street, the New York Stock Exchange, and were compelled to sell the Chartwell, their apartment. Fortunately, Churchill was helped by some wealthy friends, one of them being Henry Strakosch.

Finally, a consortium of rich benefactors was led in 1946 by Lord Camrose and presented Chartwell to the National Trust after purchasing it, claiming that Churchill and Clementine would stay there until the end of their lives. To avoid penal rates related to income tax, Churchill handed his papers over to the Chartwell Trust, after selling the literary rights, granted the tax-free income for his children and grandchildren, paying him an annual wage of $20,000.

In order to write content about the Second World War, Churchill gathered a group of researchers, controlled by Sir William Deakin, his pre-war assistant. Churchill and his team took profit from the full cooperation of Norman Brook, the cabinet secretary. Brook gave them nearly unlimited access to wartime files. Churchill asked Whitehall to vet the drafts of the book, thus making it a semi-official history. He used that method to have access to all the relevant documents that are in a galley proof. He would then have to insert narratives of events or linking passages. The structure and tone of the final text would reveal the Churchillian style, as it was already the case with his personal recollections. Thus, readers at that time were surprised to learn that key passages, such as "The Evacuation from Dunkirk" or "The Account of the Rise of Hitler," were ghostwritten. Some other passages were even the work of Norman Brook himself.

The Second World War, appearing between 1948 and 1954 in six volumes, was translated into eleven languages and published in fifteen countries. Churchill insisted it was not history, but rather a contribution to history. But he engraved on a whole generation's mind his version of events. He attacked the policies of appeasement before arguing that timely action could have helped prevent the Second World War.

Union Soviet Threat And European Unity

The interpretation Churchill made of World War II was the first of many themes he strove to develop between 1945 and 1951; the Soviet danger was the second; and the third was

European unity. In late 1945, Churchill received a call for a series of lectures at Westminster school in Missouri. On March 5, 1946, he gave the first warning of an impending fight between the Soviet Union and the West. From Stettin to Trieste, he declared that an "iron curtain" had dropped over the continent. At the time the speech was delivered there was still a strong connection with wartime ally Russia. This friendship generated much criticism in Western Europe as well as the United States.

Nevertheless, the "iron curtain" speech matched the opinion of many insiders in Whitehall and Washington. Even Truman, despite pretending to ignore the contents of Churchill's speech, read and approved it in advance. Later, when relations between the Soviet Union and the West shattered, it granted acceptance of Churchill's views, and his speech at Fulton was applauded as widely prophetic.

By this time Churchill, was privately asking the United States and Britain to take advantage of their fleeting nuclear power to offer the Soviet forces an ultimatum. If this warning was ignored, it would deploy the atom bomb on Russia. In August 1949, it was widespread knowledge that the Soviet atomic test was successful, and this put an end to any fabrications.

In a speech pronounced in September 1946 at Zurich's University, Churchill provided the post-war world with his second contribution. As he did at Fulton, the British warlord was trying to make his audience break with the emotions of wartime and get ready to integrate the post-war reality. Churchill asked for the reconciliation of Germany and France as well as the birth of a united European continent in which states' sovereignty would be set for the common good.

Churchill had such great stature that, thanks to his speeches, a fiery impetus was given to the scheme for a united Europe. This made people regard him as one of united Europe's founding fathers. In addition, Churchill accepted to head the British European movement. He castigated the Labor Government that had failed to assume a more important task in the creation of European unity. In June 1950 Churchill attacked in the government after it refused to take part in the conference held for the implementation of the Schuman plan, which was intended to set up a European steel and iron community. When the session of the Council of Europe's consultative assembly opened up at Strasbourg in August, Churchill succeeded in moving a resolution for the establishment of a European army. Thereafter, he implied that the United Kingdom would participate in it. When some observers saw all this, they concluded that he was a full-committed European.

On October 9, 1948, however, Chwhile addressing the Conservative Party Conference, Churchill explained that he thought the United Kingdom had a single role to play, the one of being the connection between the great circles within the democracies and free nations.

Churchill's Second Term

Just shy of his 77th birthday, Winston Churchill was re-elected Prime Minister in 1951. During this time, it was his attempt to maintain what was known as a "special relationship" the link between Great Britain and the United States that was the most notable during this time.

The term "special relationship" was coined in "The Sinews of Peace" speech and refers to the narrowness of the connection between the two great countries in times of peace, and war, as well as politics. The Anglo-American relationship had notably changed with time and their different stances towards Communism, involvement in the Middle East, as well as the occupation of Germany acted as a strain between the link. He believed the "European Defense Community" that was proposed in West Germany would not be successful. Churchill made many visits to the States in an attempt to maintain and secure the "special relationship" in which he played a major role. He lobbied unsuccessfully for military support for Britain in its efforts to secure what was left of the colonies. While at the same time, he agreed to play a minor part in supporting the US during the Korean war.

Many would say he was consumed by international relations and this disproportionate focus lead to a decline in foreign policy. In 1941 during the Second World War, he stated he didn't hold the title as Prime Minister to allow the dismemberment of Britain's Empire. So his efforts turned to retaining as much of it as he could. On top of dealing with the decline of morale, and Britain's failing global influence, the Prime Minister had two rebellions on his hands. Sending troops to Kenya to deal with the Mau Mau rebellion that lasted from 1952-1960, as well as the "Malayan Emergency." Churchill halted these rebellions by assisting the people who swore allegiance to Britain and using military force on those who rebelled. These attempts to hold on to imperialistic power were fleeting as the British were still losing ground.

In January 1955, he introduced "Keep England White" as a slogan to support his belief in restricting West Indian immigration from the cabinet. He believed it was an important subject facing Britain at that time. His proposal to restrict colored workers and a chance to return to flogging as corporal punishment was reported only a year prior. It was not well received by colored citizens, many immigrants who fought against Hitler, and remains a spot on Britain's history.

One of Churchill's greatest speeches, The Fulton speech, coined a popular phrase used often during the remaining of the Cold War. Churchill referred to the "iron curtain" and warned of the rising influence of the Soviet Union in Eastern Europe. This speech received mixed reviews as it was met with applause on the home front of Britain and widely criticized as "imperialist entanglement" by American news outlets and politicians. History notes that many people on both sides of the pond generally disagreed with Churchill's message. It was only after some years later that his speech revealed itself to be a great prophecy as it was a spark the West needed to get involved.

In 1952, President Eisenhower was elected. Churchill was eager to meet the new leader of the free world to ensure a strong connection remained with the United States. Some considered this to be impossible because of Churchill's age and declining health. The former warlord of Britain had started showing losses of faculty and poor health. In meetings, he proved to be hostile towards any type of hearing aid, meaning most of the conversations they had were at a screaming volume. This only added to their tumultuous and difficult relationship. In his diary, Eisenhower remarked that Churchill was manipulative, stubborn, and set in his ways, but the close cooperation of the US and Britain was critical to solving the world's problems. In spite of not having a traditional and respectful relationship with Dwight D. Eisenhower, Churchill was always headstrong in his efforts to maintain clear contact between the two countries. They had an unbounded admiration for each other and the friendship spanned decades until Churchill's death.

Realizing the necessity, Churchill tried to establish a connection with the Soviet Union, unyielding even after Stalin's death in 1953. The Yalta conference left postwar peace in Europe something to be desired. Churchill thought it was time for a new leader to make a stand and positively influence the country. He saw Stalin's death as an opportunity to seize power in order to re-establish British-Soviet relations.

Chapter 7: Churchill's Key Allies

During his political career, Churchill forged strong relationships with some particular countries. He could share his views with the leaders of those countries and set up real ties among states. This chapter documents Churchill's relationships with the Soviet Union, USA and France.

Relations With The Soviet Union

When Hitler invaded the Soviet Union, Churchill quickly sent tanks and supplies as an aid to the Soviet Union. In January 1943, the Casablanca Conference was held in the capital of Morocco and lasted ten days. That meeting gathered allied powers and gave birth to what was known as the "Casablanca Declaration." Franklin D. Roosevelt, Charles de Gaulle, and Churchill were in attendance. Joseph Stalin had left the conference because he needed to be present for the Stalingrad crisis happening in the Soviet Union. In Casablanca, the Allies signed a commitment for the war's continuation through to the Axis powers. Nevertheless, Churchill was never fully convinced of the idea of "unconditional surrender," and was surprised when Roosevelt announced it to the world.

At the time, there was a settlement between the borders of Poland, with one boundary between the Soviet Union and Poland and the other between Poland and Germany. The agreement was seen as a betrayal in the post-war years in England and established against the exiled Polish government's opinions. Keeping a vigilant eye on this, Churchill strove to motivate Sir Mikolajczyk, the Polish government's prime minister, to accept Stalin's desires, but he refused.

Churchill considered a unique way to soften tensions between the countries, and that was to transfer citizens and balance the borders. Churchill also supported the idea of expelling the ethnic Germans from Czechoslovakia. On December 15, 1944, in the House of Commons, he declared that expulsion was the only method that would provide a satisfactory solution. He ensured there wouldn't be a mixture of populations provoking trouble and a clean sweep had to be made.

Nevertheless, the expulsions of Germans from Czechoslovakia, Poland, Romania, and Hungary were made in a way that provoked hardship and the death or disappearance of more than 2.1 million Germans. Churchill went against the domination of Poland over the Soviet Union and mentions that topic in his books, despite his inability to prevent it.

In October 1944, Churchill was in Moscow with Anthony Eden for a meeting with the Soviet lead. The Soviet Union's forces were starting their intrusion in many eastern European countries. Churchill understood that as long as everything was not be properly worked out during the Yalta Conference it was necessary to set an agreement defining who had to run what. On October 9, 1944, the most important of these meetings was held in the Kremlin between Stalin and Churchill.

Churchill decided he and Stalin should discuss problems between the Balkans and Poland in the Balkans because his armies, missions, and both interests were there. Churchill suggested to Russia 90 percent power in Romania and 90 percent for Britain in Greece before putting forward a 50-50 percentage in Yugoslavia.

Stalin agreed to the percentages. But in 1958, five years after the publication of this meeting's account, Soviet authorities denied Stalin's acceptance of Churchill's proposal. At the Yalta Conference, one of the decisions was that Allies would return all Soviet citizens in the Allied zone to the Soviet Union. That rapidly affected prisoners of war of the Soviet Union set free by the Allies. The Yalta Conference's decision also affected the refugees in Eastern Europe.

Relations With The USA

Churchill had good ties with Franklin D. Roosevelt, president of the United States. The two men exchanged much and met 11 times between 1939 and 1945. That's the reason Churchill was happy for Roosevelt's re-election in 1940. Upon reelection, Roosevelt immediately found a new method of supplying and shipping military hardware to Britain without payment.

President Roosevelt convinced Congress that the United Kingdom would ensure repayment for that service by defending the US. That is how lend-lease was born between the countries. Churchill had 12 strategic conferences with Roosevelt that covered Europe strategy, the Atlantic charter, the Declaration by United Nations as well as other war policies.

As soon as the attack on Pearl Harbor occurred, Churchill thought that they should win the war. He engaged the US Congress through a joint meeting on December 26, 1941, asking himself and people around if Germans and Japanese knew what the US Congress stood for. Under the Ministry of Economic Warfare headed by Hugh Dalton, Churchill launched the Special Operations Executive. Once established, that program helped occupied territories as it drove and fostered covert, partisan and subversive operations with great success. This made the Russians refer to Churchill as the "British Bulldog."

Churchill signed treaties that were likely to redraw Asian and European boundaries of post-Second World War. Those treaties were discussed early in 1943. He drafted in 1944 the Second Quebec Conference and signed, together with

Roosevelt, a less-rough version of the Morgenthau Plan. In their version, they promised to convert Germany following its surrender into a pastoral and agricultural country.

Roosevelt died in April 1945, and Churchill mourned the death of his friend, before continuing the path with Harry S. Truman, the new president of the United States. Joseph Stalin, Harry S. Truman, and Churchill agreed at Potsdam on proposals of Europe boundaries and settlements. Churchill developed a strong relationship with Truman not unlike the one with FDR, and that was very profitable for both countries.

Relation With France

On June 16, 1940, Germans were about to descend on France. Churchill and Charles de Gaulle met for lunch in London and agreed that France and Britain would merge into a single "super country" that would be referred to as the "Franco-British Union." This occurred some weeks after French and British troops were saved from Dunkirk's beaches, where German troops had surrounded them. On May 10, 1940, France had undergone a relentless assault from Germany. After fighting for a month, the French army was devastated.

As the assaults continued and on June 14, Paris was invaded by German troops. During the following days, French and British civil servants developed a proposal asking to declare the Franco-British Union. Far from being a mere wartime alliance, the goal of this Franco-British Union was to create a country. As read in the prepared document, the two countries had come to a moment in modern history where two governments, one of Britain and the other of France could unite.

The two countries were ready to sweep, at a stroke, centuries of constitutional history under the rug and have a common foreign finance policy, defense control, and economic policy. On June 16, even though Churchill was personally doubtful, he introduced the idea to the British cabinet. Contrary to what he thought, there had been a wave of enthusiasm about the idea.

That same day, Charles de Gaulle flew to London, with great enthusiasm for the scheme's achievement. After that, Churchill got on a train with leaders of several major parties, moving towards an appointment with destiny. It was planned that the train would rally the coast and once there, the party would get on a ship and deal with the Act of Union's signing.

But when Reynaud moved towards the French Council of Ministers with the proposal, it was rejected. The plot had been regarded as a deceitful way for the British to take hold of the French empire. Even though the scheme collapsed, the connection between the two countries has never been broken, notably due to Churchill who, several times, traveled to France to meet French leaders.

Chapter 8: Winston Churchill's Married Life

Like most traditional men, Churchill had a marital life, despite dedicating most of his life to his first love, his homeland. This chapter talks about Churchill's wedding, his progeny as well as his relationship with his wife and children.

Wedding

It was in Crewe house, at a ball, that Winston and Clementine met each other for the first time. Four years later, they met again in March 1908 at a dinner party. Lady St. Helier, a relative of Clementine's, was the one hosting the party. On their first brief encounter, Churchill had appreciated Clementine, since he found her beautiful and unique. On this second encounter, after spending an evening in her company, Churchill realized Clementine was a girl with a great character and impressive intelligence. They kept meeting each other for five months and had frequent correspondence as well. On August 11, 1908, at Blenheim Palace, during a house party, Churchill asked Clementine to become his wife. Churchill and Clementine got married on September 12, 1908 in St Margaret's. Their honeymoon was at first in Baveno and afterward in Venice and Moravia. They lived at 33 Eccleston Square in a London home.

Churchill and his wife had five children. Diana, the elder, was born in 1909. Three years later, Randolph was conceived, succeeded by Sarah in 1914, Marigold in 1918, and Mary in 1922. Marigold died when she was only two years old but the other children all lived relatively long lives. Sarah, Diana, and Randolph died around their 50s, and 60s and Mary lived as long as her parents -- dying in 2014 at the age of 92.

Churchill's Progeny

Although the marriage reflected a happy shared life at the beginning, there were regular arguments. Clementine was strong-willed and high principled while Winston was an ambitious and stubborn man.

In 1909, Clementine and Winston's first child was born. As a little girl, Diana proved to be naughty and pestered her parents long into adulthood. She married John Bailey in 1932, divorcing three years later after an unsuccessful marriage. In 1935, she married Duncan Sandys, a Conservative politician with whom Sarah has had three children. But once again, the marriage fell apart. After a string of hospitalizations for nervous breakdowns, Sarah committed suicide in 1963.

The Churchills' second child and only son was born in 1911. Winston decided to name him Randolph, after his own father Lord Randolph Churchill. He was a very handsome boy, and his father had enormous ambitions for him. Randolph tried to join parliament several times during the 1930s but failed each time as many regarded him as a political maverick. He became a very successful journalist and started writing his father's official biography during the 1960s. Randolph married twice, first in 1939, when he took Pamela Digby as a wife. They had a son, and he was named Winston, like his grandfather. Randolph Churchill married June Osborne in 1948, and they had a girl, Arabella. But once again, the marriage did not last.

Sarah, the third child of Churchills was born in 1914. She began in their home as an amateur actor and later had a successful career in the dramatics. Sarah had two marriages, but neither of them was successful. She became a widow after her third child. Her first husband was Vic Oliver, a musician. Their marriage didn't last because Sarah's parents didn't agree with the relationship from its beginning. Sarah then became the wife of Anthony Beauchamp. Unfortunately, their relationship didn't last; Anthony Beauchamp committed suicide shortly after they divorced.

In 1918, a fourth child was born in Churchill's house. The third girl of the family, she was named Marigold. In 1921, before her third birthday, Marigold contracted septicemia during a seaside holiday while in the company of the children's governess. Marigold died some days later, leaving Winston grief-stricken. Clementine was shocked and lamented during the long days following the death of her beloved little girl.

In September 1921, the Churchills had another girl, their fifth child, and she proved to be the last of the family. Her name was Mary. Unlike her siblings, Mary didn't cause sorrow to her parents. She was instead a great support for Clementine and Winston. She married a man named Christopher Soames in 1947. At the time of their wedding, Christopher was an Assistant Military Attaché serving in Paris. Mary's husband had a brilliant diplomatic and parliamentary career. Throughout the years, Christopher became a great friend to Winston, always listening and supporting him in any way he could. Their marriage was a long and prosperous one. They raised five children.

The Relationship With His Wife And Children

Even though they would go long periods without seeing each other, Churchill and Clementine managed to preserve a successful marriage. As it happens with all couples, there were some failings and fights. Churchill's worst offense, according to his wife, was buying Chartwell, their country estate in Kent, without consulting her first. Clementine couldn't bear the fact that her husband was able to make a purchase of that magnitude without involving her in the decision.

Churchill stayed away from his household for a good portion of his marital life. He was busy with work most of the time; and when he was not dealing with business, Churchill was on holiday, far from family. Even though work ranked first in Churchill's life, he had affection for his children. Throughout their conjugal years, Clementine had most of the time found her husband's company tedious and had never appreciated to go out with him.

On rare occasions, the family would go on holiday together but Churchill preferred to spend holidays with friends and acquaintances. In all the time they spent together, the family took eight cruises.

Chapter 9: Winston Churchill, A Gifted Speaker And Writer

Although his life was dedicated to politics, Churchill had a taste for literature and proved to be a very skillful writer as well. Discover throughout the following chapter Churchill as a speaker and writer.

Writing Career

In 1895, Churchill was appointed second lieutenant. He had an annual wage of $300, which he found insufficient. Churchill wanted to live the same way with other officers who had more consistent salaries. To earn the required amount, he gained from his colonel an agreement for observation of the Cuban War of Independence. Churchill was helped by his mother who secured for him a contract as a war reporter. He was posted to his regiment located in British India. From that place, he could send war reports that were published in The Daily Telegraph and The Pioneer. Those reports were the basis of Churchill's first book, "The Story of the Malakand Field Force," which was published in 1898. Subsequently, Churchill wrote "Savrola," a novel published in 1898. He was transferred that same year to Sudan with the mission to participate in the Mahdist War which lasted from 1891 to 1899. There, Churchill took part in September 1898 in the

Battle of Omdurman. His recollections were published in 1899 in "The River War."

That same year, Churchill flew to South Africa after resigning his commission. He became a correspondent of The Morning Post during the Second Boer War's time and had a monthly salary of $250 plus all expenses. The Boers captured Churchill, but he managed to escape and continued sending reports to the newspaper, as he remained in South Africa. His dispatches were subsequently published in 1900 through two works, "Ian Hamilton's March" and "London to Ladysmith via Pretoria." Churchill returned to Britain the same year and became a Member of Parliament. As a parliamentarian, he started writing his answers and speeches in pamphlets for publication. Many of those writings were later compiled into collections, some of them edited by Randolph, his son, and others by Charles Eade of the "Sunday Dispatch." Churchill wrote, apart from his parliamentary duties, a two-volume biography of Lord Randolph Churchill, his father.

After the general election of 1923, Churchill couldn't maintain his parliamentary seat. He moved to the Southern part of France. There, he wrote a six-volume history narrating the First World War. The work was entitled "The World Crisis" and its publication was done between 1923 and 1931. The book was appreciated, despite Arthur Balfour, the former Prime Minister dismissed the work. Sir Balfour considered that in "The World Crisis," Churchill just narrated his brilliant achievements in World War I instead of writing on the events that occurred.

At the general election of 1924, Churchill came back to the Commons. He wrote in 1930 "My Early Life," his first autobiography. After that, he began his research for the book, "Marlborough: His Life and Times" written published 1933 and 1938. It was a four-volume biography of John Churchill, his ancestor who was the 1st Duke of Marlborough. The final volume of that book was not yet published when Churchill wrote for newspapers a bank of biographical profiles, which were subsequently gathered and published in 1937 under the title "Great Contemporaries."

In May 1940, Churchill was appointed Prime Minister, eight months after the Second World War broke out. He didn't write any history during his tenure, but many of his speeches were still collected and published. After the war ended, the 1945's general election occurred, and Churchill was ejected from office. He continued writing and produced "The Second World War," a six-volume history with a research team lead by historian William Deakin. The books were published between 1948 and 1953 and became a bestseller in the UK as well as the US.

Churchill's final great work was "A History of the English-Speaking Peoples," a four-volume work published between

1956 and 1958. In 1953, Churchill won the Nobel Prize for Literature. This triumph was a reward for his mastery of biographical and historical description and also for his sparkling oratory in defending human values. As an author, Churchill had nearly always good wages and writing, during most of his life, was his primary source of income.

Wartime Speeches

In 1940, Churchill read some speeches that were the most scintillating ones of his political life. In a statement made on May 13, Churchill promised tears, sweat, blood, and toil for to his fellow countrymen. Some days later, on June 4, while talking to the House of Commons, he vowed that British army officers would struggle on the beaches. On August 20 of the same year, while paying tribute to Britain's fighter pilots, Churchill stated: "Never in the field of human conflict was so much owed by so many to so few."

Following the fall of the French empire on June 18, Churchill was invited to repeat in a radio studio a speech he had made earlier the same day in the House of Commons. When thousands of people gathered around their wireless, they could hear Churchill suggesting to his fellow citizens that they would have to brace themselves for duty if Britain's empire and the Commonwealth should last for a thousand years.

Churchill had patriotic rhetoric, which helped to generate emotion. Likewise, his speeches captivated attention for another reason. They pierced the fog of speculation and rumor with authoritative and vivid commentaries on the army and its strategic situation. Despite the fact that there was a consistent element of propaganda in his description of the facts as well as hidden secrets, Churchill did well to convey instructive information in his speeches. While listening to him, it was easy to see Churchill was a brilliant parliamentary democrat and a great leader.

In July 1940, opinion polls were taken that revealed 88 percent of people interviewed accepted Churchill as prime minister. That same high level of support continued throughout the years of his political career.

Churchill's Oratory

Churchill unmistakably ranks among the most celebrated political orators of all time. His words during wartime are regularly included in collections featuring the best speeches of history. His rhetorical techniques and style are often used to advise business executives and speech-makers to this day. Churchill had a taste for words and colossal accuracy in their use. The British statesman had a great mastery of the English language.

Churchill was known to work on his speech making diligently. He was not a natural public speaker because of an impediment he developed early in life. That was one of the reasons he never excelled in school. But as the years passed, he became a skillful orator, studying the best works in the world and picking eloquent techniques from them.

For his speeches, Churchill used to rely on detailed preparation. He liked to be dependent upon carefully written scripts and sometimes took breaks when speaking. In spite of the fact he developed rhetorical skills, he had weak powers of improvisation. His oratory could then be unyielding and, when debating, Churchill could give the impression he was speaking at an audience.

One of the qualities that made him a great speaker was his ability to speak in a casual everyday style as well as in a heroic, opaque manner. Thus, he was able to use an ornate and flat vocabulary with simple words and at the same time, an active lexicon with colorful images when making his points. Another critical aspect of the British warlord's oratory proved to be his performance element. Indeed, Churchill had an impressive physical presence, a perfect gesture, and a good sense of timing. Likewise, his voice and his way of delivering messages were absolutely astounding.

Chapter 10: Churchill, Man Of Deeds

Committed politician, Churchill was a man of deeds who didn't hesitate to take action. In respect of the choice of his political parties, Churchill was a man guided by personal interests. This chapter describes in detail Churchill's conduct during wartime, the performance of his duties as a Chancellor of the Exchequer, and relations with political parties.

Churchill's Conduct Of The War

Churchill had high authority, but never the attitude of a dictator. Most of the time, he used to be careful in relying on the war cabinet when it came to significant decisions in foreign or domestic policy. More than once, his wishes have been overridden by his colleagues. When he was appointed prime minister, Churchill was given the responsibility of the minister of defense. Likewise, the war cabinet's military secretariat and the whole staff committee proved to be incorporated into a department under Churchill's direction. Major General Hastings Ismay was heading Churchill's defense office with the support of his two deputies, Ian Jacob, and Leslie Hollis. Those men were then assigned to propose operations and to inform about the feasibility of schemes coming from Churchill and the staff. Ismay also assumed the functions of Churchill's representative to the leaders of the staff committee. Churchill had, however, as minister of defense, the right to summon the staff's leaders and command them concerning the management of the war.

The new machinery applied to the management of the war was significantly the result of Churchill's thinking. Machinery that successfully prevented the rifts between brass hats and frocks had emerged during World War I. Churchill called frequent meetings of the war cabinet's defense committee. The defense committee was composed of Beaverbrook, Attlee, as well as the three service ministers. When Churchill's power grew, the committee wasn't needed as often and the service ministers found themselves assigned to only administrative roles. Afterward, Churchill himself ran the war's military side in conjunction with the staff committee's leaders.

With his fertile imagination and bulky energy, he sometimes conducted his professional advisers to distraction. Churchill's favorite colleague was Admiral Pound, the first sea lord. The latter had a dogged loyalty that was nevertheless lessened by indirect methods of resistance.

With his functions as prime minister, Churchill acquired an excellent source of power. He gained knowledge enough to defeat the enemy and also an incredible skill for his negotiations with his allies and Chiefs of Staff. On May 22, 1915, the code-breakers cracked the primary functional key of the Enigma enciphering machine of Germans' Luftwaffe. This led to Ultra, the flow radio messages' transcripts sent by the German army.

Even though Ultra was constantly monitored and the fact there was continuous reporting on it, Churchill insisted on having an independent and direct connection to the raw materials. Sir Stewart Menzies, the Secret Intelligence Service's head, was instructed in September 1940 to send the completeness of the original transcripts to the prime minister via a daily box. As the transcripts were of a considerable volume, Churchill allowed him to select and send some of them. But as he was eager to know everything about Ultra, he kept receiving a box of transcripts during nearly all the wartime. The wartime expansion been noticed at the level of British intelligence services, as well as the valued repute they obtained in Whitewall, was due to Churchill's support.

When Italy declared a conflict with the United Kingdom in July 1940, a new series of operations began in the Middle East. A month later, Churchill sent, at enormous risk to home defense, 154 tanks for the reinforcement of the British commander-in-chief Wavell in Egypt. He had then to deal with a new war against a weaker enemy. But was still unable at that time to say how the United Kingdom was about to defeat Germany. In the hope of having communication with Stalin, Churchill sent Sir Stafford, an influential left-wing politician, as ambassador to Russia. After drawing inspiration from a vision of Europe's occupied people rebelling against their German oppressors, he created the Special Operations Executive (SOE). This was intended to set the continent ablaze.

To harass the opposition, Churchill surrounded occupied Europe's coasts with commando raids. Likewise, he was aware of the usefulness of strategic bombing, even though his main hopes were attached to the perspective of American intervention.

Churchill, Chancellor Of The Exchequer

In November 1924, Churchill became Chancellor of the Exchequer and walked through 11 Downing Street. He entered the Conservative Party and with his new position, tried to continue with what he called "the same type of measures." Churchill had previously advocated that ideology at the time of Liberal Social Reforms. In January, he negotiated a set of war repayments, from other nations to Britain, and from Britain to the US. The Bank of England, as well as others, asked Britain to get back to the Gold Standard, but Churchill disagreed with that idea. He consulted different economists, most of those who approved the change. Churchill, at last, repented and accepted the measure.

In April 1925, Churchill announced in his first budget the return of the gold standard. That first budget contained measures to help widows start earning their pension just after the death of their husband and lowering the age from 70 to 65. Churchill's budget also announced that, for people with lower salaries, there would be a ten percent reduction in income tax. The British statesman thought this would encourage small business. To deal with such expenditure, he asked to lower the naval spending, stating it was useless in peacetime.

Churchill also persuaded the government that year to offer a subsidy to the mining industry, which would allow mining bosses to keep paying the same wage to their employees. In April 1926, Churchill announced his second budget. The latter contained a tax on heavy lorries, on petrol, and luxury car purchases. In 1926, during the General Strike, Churchill oversaw the British Gazette's publication and the anti-strike publication of the government. At the end of the General Strike, he was requested to serve as a go-between for the striking miners.

Churchill suggested that any reduction of wages should be the owners' earnings. He went further, becoming an advocate for the calls of miners reclaiming a legally binding minimum salary. At the beginning of 1927, Churchill flew through the European continent, visiting Athens, Malta, Paris, and Rome.

In Athens, he spoke highly of the parliamentary democracy's restoration. In Rome, he spoke to Prime Minister Benito Mussolini. There, Churchill told the Italian press that if he were Italian, he would have been with them from the beginning of their glorious fight against Leninism. He ensured he and his fellow countrymen had not yet had to deal with that threat in the same intensity. He finished the talk with the Italian press by saying that they, British, had their own way to proceed.

In April, Churchill came back to London and presented his third budget. The budget announced new concerning taxes on imported wines and car tires. Likewise, it announced increased taxation on tobacco and matches. Later that year, he started elaborating the idea of stamping out local rates to reduce taxation on Britain's agriculture and industry. After some criticism from the cabinet, he suggested lowering only local rates by two-thirds. His fourth budget contained this berating scheme when it was presented in April 1928. A year later, he dealt with the presentation of his fifth budget, including the eradication of the tax on tea.

Relations With Political Parties

Rhodes James remarked that Churchill was a politician without permanent faithfulness to any party. Likewise the author highlighted that Churchill's shifts of allegiance were all the time linked to his interests. In 1899, when he was campaigning for his seat of Oldham, Churchill made people considered him as a Tory Democrat and a Conservative. And to make haste to post as someone belonging to Liberals the following year. In a letter he sent to a fellow Conservative in 1902, Churchill asserted that he had tolerant, extensive, and moderate views. He ensured he had a taste for agreement and compromise, a disregard for the cant of all types, contempt for extremists and confess his ambition of a central party with loyalty and patriotism.

In 1924, when Labor supplanted the Liberals as the main antagonist of the Conservatives, Churchill had the desire to form a new party that would have as name the "Liberal-Conservatives." Churchill was disappointed by the Conservatives earlier in the century, partly because they promoted economic protectionism. His attitude then had earned him the hatred of a lot of party members. He knew that this situation might be an obstacle on his way, leading to a cabinet position at the level of the Conservative government.

Then, the Liberal Party was gaining increasing support, and therefore, Churchill's defection may likewise have been motivated by personal ambition. He wrote a letter in 1903 stating he was an English Liberal. He confessed in this letter his disdain for the Tory party, their methods, words, as well as their men. Jenkins remarked that Churchill formed with

Lloyd George a partnership of positive radicalism. The author praised a pair of reforming social New Liberals with the merit of foregoing the ancient Gladstonian tradition that strictly dealt with libertarian political issues, leaving social conditions in bad shape.

Along with Churchill's political career, there had been a rocky relationship between him and the Conservative Party. This did not escape the attention of Addition, who stated that Churchill's loyalty to the Conservative Party was never complete.

Chapter 11: Churchill's Political Interventions In Specific Issues In Britain And India

Thanks to his influence and the political power, Churchill provided services in some sensitive situations in Britain and elsewhere. Discover in this chapter his role during Bengal famine in India, Germany's rearmament in 1936 as well as during the abdication crisis that involved King Edward VII.

Churchill's Role During The Bengal Famine

Churchill was considered responsible when millions of Indians died in 1943 during the Bengal famine. Some commentators thought the cause was maladministration of the province and the marketing system's disruption. Churchill said that the starvation in Bengal was less alarming than the one of sturdy Greeks.

He made Indians understand that the famine was their fault because they used to breed like rabbits. This led Adam Jones of the "Journal of Genocide Research" to consider Churchill like a "genuine genocidaire," Adam Jones said the British statesman took Indian Hindus for a foul race and requested the air force chief of Britain to send some bombers to devastate them. In a letter, Churchill told India's Commander-in-Chief that he had to rely on the martial races.

Arthur L. Herman, the author who wrote "Churchill and Gandhi" stated that the true cause of the Bengal famine was the hegemony of Japanese over Burma, which prevented India from importing rice when the country's sources fell into drought. Even if Churchill was hostile to the importation of food supplies in India, he was not to be blamed because it was wartime.

When Leo Amery, India's Secretary of State and Wavell, India's ruler urgently prompted Churchill to liberate food stocks for their country, he answered in a telegram to Wavell that Gandhi would have already died if food was so scarce. Newly in office in July 1940, he heard reports about the emerging conflict opposing the Indian Congress to the Muslim League and hoped it would be bloody and fierce.

Madhusree Mukerjee wrote the famine was amplified by Churchill's decisions as well as the ones of the War Cabinet, in part because of food's export and also indifference at the time Britain's raw materials and storing of food mounted to 18.5 million tons. There were warehouses brimming with oil seeds and sugar, which had to be stored under tarpaulins outside.

In the book "Drought and Famine in India" written between 1870 and 2016, some American and Indian researchers, after studying soil moisture, confirmed that the famine in Bengal was not caused by drought, but rather British policies. The same study revealed that the fact Japanese captured Burma, which had been India's food supplier so far, caused the hecatomb of the Bengal famine in 1943.

Churchill And Germany's Rearmament In 1936

In 1936, Churchill was on holiday in the Spanish territory when the Germans came back to the Rhineland in February. The Labor opposition showed antagonism and was ready to implement sanctions while there was a difference of opinion within the National Government. Some people felt eager to advocate economic sanctions, and others said they would drive a discreditable back down by Britain because the French government would not support the interventions.

On March 9, 1936, Churchill made a measured speech, which Neville Chamberlain praised as positive. But after some weeks, Churchill was appointed Minister for Coordination of Defense and had to work alongside with Attorney General Thomas Inskip. This was strongly criticized by A. J. P Taylor.

On May 22, 1936, Churchill attended a meeting gathering Old Guard Conservatives at Shillinglee Park and was hosted by

Lord Winterton's house. Churchill's presence at that meeting had as aim to take action for greater rearmament. In June 1936, he organized a delegation composed of senior Conservatives who went to meet Halifax, Inskip, and Baldwin. After it had been demanded to hold a Secret Session, the senior ministers accepted to attend the committee. This was, according to them, better than listening to a speech by Churchill, which would last for hours. Churchill had made sure he had delegates coming from the two parties. He subsequently wrote that it would have been possible to impose remedial action if the Liberal opposition and Labour's leaders were present at the meeting.

When Churchill measured the Luftwaffe that Ralph Wigram had leaked to him at the Foreign Office, he had got figures less accurate than the ones revealed by the Air Ministry. Churchill then believed that Germany was preparing to hit London with thermite bombs. Ministers underlined that Hitler's intentions were not clear and so it was urgent to maximize England's long-term economic power via exports. Nevertheless, Churchill thought that British industry's 25 to 30 percent should be placed under state control for rearmament's purposes. Baldwin suggested they needed a victory in the election to have useful approaches for rearmament. He then agreed at the meeting's end to Churchill's view, according to which rearmament was necessary to counteract Germans.

On November 12, 1936, Churchill came back on the topic. In a speech, he gave some specific instances as far as the preparedness of Germany's war was concerned. He asserted that Britain would strive to prepare more months and years vital for the country's greatness.

Abdication Crisis

In June 1936, Churchill was told by Walter Monckton the rumors that King Edward VII was eager to marry Wallis Simpson were true. She was an American lady, previously divorced. Churchill advised the King not to do so. As Edward was the nominal head of the Monarch Church of England, which didn't allow two divorced persons to get married if their ex-partner is still alive. Thus, most British people argued Edward couldn't marry Wallis Simpson and remain on the throne. In November, Churchill refused Lord Salisbury's call to belong to a delegation composed of senior Conservative backbenchers planning to meet with Baldwin for the matter's discussion. On November 25, Churchill, Attlee, and Archibald Sinclair, the Liberal Party Leader, held a meeting with Baldwin and received the confirmation of the King's plot. The King then asked if they would set up a governing administration in case Baldwin resigns.

Both Sinclair and Atlee asserted they would not feel eager to take office if they were called to do that. Churchill replied that he would be on the government's side. In the following days, the abdication crisis mushroomed and reached its climax in December 1936. Churchill, at that time, supported the King. On December 3, the first public meeting of the Covenant Movement and the Arms was held. Churchill saw, later that night, the draft of the wireless broadcast proposed by the king. He spoke about it with the king's solicitor and Beaverbrook.

He met with Edward VII on December 4 and encouraged him not to abdicate. The following day, Churchill issued a lengthy statement suggesting that the Ministry was putting pressure on Edward VII to push him towards a decision. He then attempted to convince the Commons to allow a delay. Churchill was booed and left, as the disagreement was unanimous among members.

This significantly damaged Churchill's reputation in Parliament and all of Britain. Some people said he was striving to set up a King's Party, and Alistair Cooke was one of them. Others such, as Harold Macmillan, were saddened by the harm Churchill had done to the Covenant Movement and the Arms by backing Edward VII. Churchill later wrote he was slaughtered in public opinion, and there was a nearly universal view that his political life had finally ended. There is no unanimity about Churchill's reasons in his support for the King. Some people, like A. J. P. Taylor, saw it as an attempt to overturn the government of weak men. R. R. James and others saw Churchill's reasons honorable and selfless.

Chapter 12: Churchill, Implausible Character

Churchill was an incredible character. He made great achievements and behaved like an exceptional person. This chapter discovers Churchill's sense of sacrifice, his lifting of the United Kingdom to a great power status and the legacy he left behind.

Churchill's Sense Of Sacrifice

It may seem like an exaggeration, but between 1940 and 1941, Churchill seemed to carry the world on his shoulders. He bore huge burdens and anxiety that would have crushed a weaker man. As Major-General Ismay, who worked along with him would say, Winston Churchill was not ordinary and proved to be different from anyone he would ever meet. As a warlord, he was considered above anyone Britain or any other country could produce. Ismay goes on to boast that Churchill was an indispensable figurehead who was irreplaceable. He was a man who revered tradition and ridiculed convention.

When the occasion required it, he could behave like a man with great dignity, and when the spirit grasped him, he was able to act like a kid. Indeed, Churchill's industry and enthusiasm were unfettered, and his loyalty absolute.

Churchill could be without compassion while leading his commanders. Sometimes he would warm to the charm with a dash of Alexander and later employ Wingate's radical qualities. In his relationships with the admirals, Churchill used to wield the executioner's ax with absolute blindness and without attempting to verify if his victims were unable.

The war cabinet's secretary who worked with Churchill divulged the extent of the British warlords' incredible devotion to work. According to Bridges, under Chamberlain's dominion there were formal meetings to deal with government business at hours determined in advance. But when Churchill came into office, things were never the same.

The man implied there were no borders between the office and home and work hours could not be differentiated from the hours of rest. Churchill could work everywhere, in the bedroom or dining room, and often relied on an associate at any moment. Bridges kept saying one could be summoned at nearly any hour of day and night to achieve some task. With Churchill, one might be sharing a male with one's family and take orders.

Churchill Lifting Britain To Great Power Status

Eventually, Churchill was eager to have a quiet life at home to help him focus on his main goal, Britain's restoration as a prominent power. When the time came for the British government to get involved in the Schuman plan and show interest in the establishment of a European army, Churchill didn't feel enthusiastic. Instead, he dealt with a last-ditch defense concerning the United Kingdom's military base at the Suez Canal, opposing Egyptian leaders asking the British army to withdraw.

Author Roger Louis noted that Churchill never hesitated to express his view that the British were superior to the nation of Egypt and regarded them as cowardly. This was a concern on which Churchill used to deploy along with Anthony Eden, his foreign secretary. By 1954, however, Churchill felt compelled to realize that his opinions had little value.

When he came back to power, Churchill's first goal was to reestablish the Anglo-American's relationship. He crossed the Atlantic in January 1952 to meet with President Harry Truman. Although the connection looked great between the two countries, Churchill's request of an Anglo-American alliance was not accepted by the American president and his advisers. They rejected his request of American military support at the level of the Suez Canal Zone. Likewise, the Americans didn't show interest in Churchill's concern of reestablishing the Quebec agreement and adoption of nuclear weapons. In November 1952, when Eisenhower succeeded

Truman for the American's presidency, Churchill hurried to Washington to meet with the new leader.

Despite Eisenhower's admiration for Churchill, he considered his conception of Anglo-American relations irrelevant and thought the British statesman was still living in the ancient wartime. Churchill's request of diplomatic support upon Egypt was rejected. John Foster Dulles, the new US Secretary of State notably displayed disregard towards Churchill's proposals.

Even if Churchill negotiated regular meetings with the Kremlin in Moscow, he had been unable to define the terms of a specific arrangement, and his ideas seemed to blend. Churchill was invaded by voices whispering that he was no longer fit for office. He was then under heavy pressure to let Eden assume his functions. Whatever his motives could look like, his ultimate great wish was to set himself in peacemaker. When Stalin died on March 5, 1953, Churchill's hopes of relaxation emerged, but his illness thwarted him before he had time to seize any initiative.

In December 1953, at Churchill's invitation, Eisenhower rallied Bermuda to attend a conference, but once again rejected his proposals about a common approach towards Russia. In June 1954, when he traveled to Washington, Churchill noticed with surprise that Eisenhower proceeded with the withdrawal of his proposals before asking him to return alone to Moscow. On his path of return from the meeting with Queen Elizabeth, Churchill, without consultation of the cabinet, sent a telegram to Molotov. This leads to a cabinet crisis, and he gained the fierce disdain of Eden as well as other senior ministers.

Churchill was not a unilateral disarmer. In June 1954, under his chairmanship, the cabinet's defense committee recommended that the United Kingdom should build its hydrogen bomb to deter a Soviet attack. But Churchill also understood that if both the Soviet Union and the United States get nuclear weapons, it would seriously put the word's safety at risk. On March 1, 1955, he spoke in the House of Commons about the dangers related to nuclear holocaust.

Churchill's Legacy

Robert Rhodes James, a historian, stated that Churchill's life has been tremendously long, controversial, and complex while Addison noted that Winston Churchill had become a famous historical figure. Throughout the years, Churchill offered himself a reputation of high rank among the great British Statesmen. In 2002, when the BBC made a poll about the 100 Greatest British men of all time, Churchill people voted Churchill number one.

Churchill had, throughout his career, an outspokenness that made many become enemies of his. Addison wrote that

Churchill considered as a politician with an obsession for personal interest. His detractors found he was a self-absorbed and egotistical man who had poor judgment. His decisions in politics, up until 1939, produced widespread hatred and mistrust. Addison meant that according to the Conservative Party's High Tories, Churchill appeared like a traitor when he became a member of the Liberal Party. As the First Lord of the Admiralty, a lot of detractors had negative things to say. They called him ignorant, reckless, as well as a statesman who did not understand the prestigious methods and traditions of work related to the Royal Navy.

How he responded to the Rhonda Valley bustle and anti-socialist rhetoric earned him disregard from the left. According to Addison, they accused Churchill of being an authentic reactionary. The opposition he manifested against the General Strike made many strikers hate him, and the number of his enemies in the labor movement increased. Although, when Churchill switched to Britain's left for the resistance against Germany, a lot of leftists thought he did it to protect the British Empire from Nazis and without personal interest.

Edward Moritz Jr., a historian, noted that when the left accused Churchill of being a vicious reactionary as well as an enemy of the working class, they did not take into account his domestic reforms. Jenkins noted that Churchill, as a social reformer, had a glorious record for the work he did during his early parliamentary career. Rhodes James shared Jenkins' opinion, meaning that Churchill, as a social reformer, had brilliant achievements.

For Rhode James, those achievements have been possible because when he was a minister, Churchill had three wonderful qualities. At first, he had been a hard worker. Secondly, he had always found a good way to put his proposals through the Parliament and Cabinet. And thirdly, he had strongly been linked to his department. Rhode James granted these ministerial merits to Churchill, even though everybody did not share his opinion.

Churchill's racial views have been often underlined and heavily criticized, and his imperialist views have earned him significant controversy. Likewise, his attitudes towards policies concerning Indians have been hugely deplored and have overwhelmed his personality by a contentious mark. Churchill had had an awful relationship with India, a country in which he had very bad conduct.

Churchill's legacy has been exploited by Randolph Churchill, who published an eight-volume biography of his father between 1966 and 1968. Randolph started that work, and Martin Gilbert completed it. By 1980, fifteen years after Churchill's death, there was already in Britain, as well as in the rest of the world, a very broad range of published work on Churchill.

Up until today, Churchill's legacy keeps on producing intense debate in the universe of historians and writers. In 1980, Addison asserted that many people in the world are so prejudiced against or for Churchill that it would not be realistic to consider him a historical figure. Afua Hirsch described, in 2018, meetings with two historians who were told by their colleagues that researching the less known parts of Churchill's life could end their careers, or turn them into outcasts in academia.

For Allen Packwood, who presided over the Churchill Archives Center, Churchill was, in his lifetime, a hugely contradictory, complex, and larger-than-life human being, with the custom to combat those contradictions.

Chapter 13: Specific Things About Winston Churchill

Churchill was a multi-faceted man. One must have read about him without knowing some of his hidden faces. Indeed, Churchill happened to be a seer. He was also an imperialist and had a fondness for painting.

Churchill, The Seer

At the beginning of 1930, Churchill was without a government position. The British warlord seemed to be exhausted of opposing individual political decisions such as the one giving broader independence to India. Churchill kept writing newspaper articles and books from Chartwell, and many believed his political career had come to an end. He only appeared to manifest his opposition to the Nazi dictatorship of Hitler in Germany and to go against the perspective of British rearmament.

Churchill, during the 1930s, regularly strove to urge the British government to policy measures able to deter the German weaponry. He insisted that Britain should get ready to prevent a probable assault from Germany, but no one paid attention to his warnings. Later, he explained in his WWII memoirs that his warnings during the previous six years occurred in such great number and had then been so broadly vindicated, to such an extent that no one could deny him.

Churchill's attitude during those years has been compared to the one of Jeremiah, the Biblical prophet who stood in the desert, shouting to Israelites to repent. Churchill's warnings concerning Hitler were not just related to the numbers of planes and tanks. He grasped that war was not only a matter of armaments but could be reflected in the conception and the character of a country's leaders. He understood at an early stage that the passion for conquest generated by the First World War would emerge the probability of another European conflict. Churchill's years of consecration came to an end when the war was over in September 1939.

Churchill, The Imperialist

Churchill was an absolute imperialist. He exhibited a good image of Britain's empire and saw British imperialism as a form of selflessness that was profitable to its people. At the beginning of his parliamentary career, Churchill suggested bias towards the well-being of different African groups. For the author Addison, Churchill thought that conquering and having hegemony on other peoples would allow Britain to make them believe that civilization is more valued than barbarism, no matter the way the conquest's process might affect the conquered. Churchill's writings, according to

Adams, show a militarist ideology and a cavalier pace in favor of imperial war.

In the cabinet meeting of November 1921, where a suggestion to return Weihaiwei to China came up, Churchill was alone with another imperialist, George Curzon, to oppose the proposal. During the time Churchill lived, there was a strong belief concerning racial superiority in Britain, even among socialists and liberals, and Churchill also shared that conception. Nevertheless, Addison found it to be unfair to consider that Churchill was a racist, given that he have any opinion of race by way of a biological entity. The author believed that Churchill was unable to make immigrants experience racial hatred or persecution.

Although he upset both George V and Edward VII during his political career, Churchill was a great monarchist, exhibiting a bright image of Britain's monarchy. Jenkins asserted Churchill's antagonism towards protectionism was based on a deep conviction, even though many people questioned the authenticity of his anti-protectionist beliefs during his political career. In spite of the fact he proved to employ sanctioning executions when he was a Home Secretary, Churchill did not approve the death penalty abolition. He had, around 1912, the eugenicist idea to sterilize the disabled people.

Churchill's Love Of Painting

When he was 40 years old, Winston Churchill happened to be at a political career low. As a matter of fact, after the First World War, he was dismissed in May 1915 from his post of First Lord of The Admiralty and became an army officer. Overwhelmed by anxiety after being deflated of power, Churchill found a new hobby, which was painting. For the giant British politician, that hobby became a source of bliss that helped him relieve the stress related to his political career.

In June 1915, Churchill started his adventure with painting in his country house's garden. Lady Gwendoline Bertie, his sister-in-law, was painting watercolors when she noticed Churchill's interest in her activity. She then gave him a paint box and prompted him to try. The trigger came instantaneously, and although he was unfamiliar with the technique, it didn't lessen his devotion. As he would explain later, bravery was the first quality needed.

Churchill started then with his new hobby, which he had a real fondness. Painting became the perfect solution against his clinical depression. He found in that art a passion that gave him a new delight in life. With advice from prominent teachers and artists, he was able by 1921 to make an exhibition in Paris. Nevertheless, he was humble concerning his ability and exhibited under the pseudonym of Charles Morin. When the Royal Academy acquired his services as a painter in 1947, Winston Churchill used David Winter as a pseudonym.

Chapter 14: Churchill's Evening Of Life

After a hectic life, Churchill had some health problems and was obliged to retire. His health went from bad to worse, and he finally died in Chartwell, his country home. Churchill has been honored with valued funerals.

Health Problems And Resignation

During the war, Churchill's health decayed. He suffered a heart attack at the White House in December 1941, and two years later, in December 1943, he was a victim of pneumonia. In spite of this, Churchill flew over 100,000 miles to meet other countries' leaders throughout the war. As he was getting old and due to his poor physical health, Churchill again experienced clinical depression. Many authors have asserted that during he suffered from or was a risk of depression his whole life.

During the 1949's summer, while he was on holiday, Churchill suffered a stroke in the southern part of France. The strain he had, carrying the Premiership as well as Foreign Office, was certainly one of the reasons that provoked his second stroke on June 23, 1953, at 10 Downing Street. Despite that, he was partially impotent, he directed the following morning a cabinet meeting without any sign of incapacity. His condition deteriorated afterward, so badly that some people believed he would die the same week. The news spread, and it was told that Churchill was a victim of exhaustion.

In spite of his fragile health, Churchill was still eager to pursue his political life and appeared publicly to make a speech in October 1953 at Margate, during the Conservative Party Conference. Two months later, in December 1953, he met Eisenhower, the US President, in Bermuda.

Churchill was unhappy about the friction that occurred between Dulles and Eden in June 1954. As he was coming back from an Anglo-American conference, Pierson Dixon, the diplomat, made an analogy between the United States' actions in Guatemala and Soviet policy in Greece and Korea, obliging Churchill to reply that he had never known a more "bloody place" than Guatemala. Churchill was still wishing to travel to Moscow, threatening to resign. That provoked a huge crisis in the Cabinet when Lord Salisbury asserted he would resign too if Churchill bowed out. Finally, Soviets suggested a five-power conference, but the latter was not held before Churchill's retirement. After postponing his resignation many times, Churchill, aware of the fact he was getting weak physically as well as mentally, retired in 1955 as prime minister and Anthony Eden succeeded him.

Retirement And Death

After Churchill left the premiership, he spent little time in parliament before he bowed out at the general election of 1964. Most of his retirement time, Churchill stayed in Chartwell and Hyde Park Gate, his residence in Central London. Although he was publicly supportive of Eden's Suez Invasion, he was privately scathing it. In the following years, Churchill some visits to the US in an attempt to contribute to the repair of Anglo-American relations.

At the time of the general election of 1959, Churchill could sometimes be found in the House of Commons, a place he had rarely frequented since 1955. It was then without surprise that his majority fell by over a thousand. Many were those who believed that his physical and mental faculties' decaying had made him overwhelmed by depression, a pain he has fought since his young age. But the incidence and nature of that depression were uncertain, and some people even rejected the existence of such a pain in Churchill's life. One of those people was Anthony Montague Browne, his personal secretary during the last ten years of life. The man wrote that Churchill never referred to depression in his speeches and strongly disputed that Britain's former warlord was victim of depression.

Some people speculated that Winston Churchill may have suffered from Alzheimer's disease during his last years.

Nevertheless, other people thought that his dwindled mental capacity was just the consequence of the strokes and the deafness he had undergone between 1949 and 1963. When US President John F. Kennedy, acting following authorization conceded by an Act of Congress, proclaimed Churchill an Honorary Citizen of USA, he was unable to attend the ceremony in the White House.

In spite of his health problems, Churchill kept trying to be engaged in public life. On St. George's day in 1964, he sent a message to congratulate the surviving veterans after the Zeebrugge Raid of 1918. Churchill's message was appreciated by people who gathered in Deal, Kent to attend a service of commemoration related to the event. In fact, two casualties of the tragedy had been buried in that place. On January 15, 1965, Winston Churchill suffered a major stroke. He passed away nine days later at his London home, January 24, 1965. Churchill was 90 years old.

Funeral

Churchill's funeral was the largest one in history up until that point, as it gathered representatives from 112 countries. If they were in Great Britain, 25 million people stayed in front of their televisions to watch Churchill's funeral, there were 350 million people on the entire European continent watching. Churchill's corpse was laid in Westminster Hall for three days and the British government held a state funeral service on January 30, 1965, at St. Paul's Cathedral. One of the widest reunification's of statesmen in world history was observed for the service. The Queen came to the funeral, an unusual occurrence due to the fact that Churchill was, since William Gladstone, the first commoner to lie-in-state. When Churchill's coffin was taken from the River Thames through Tower Pier and MV Havengore's Festival Pier, dockers lowered crane jibs to salute the late giant.

The 19-gun salute was fired by the Royal Artillery and a flyby of 16 fighters from English Electric Lightning. Churchill's coffin was taken to Waterloo Station. There, the coffin was loaded into a painted and prepared carriage for its rail journey leading to Hanborough, a railway station in Oxfordshire. Churchill's birthplace is situated in the northwest at seven miles of Oxford.

Churchill's family was carried in a funeral train driven by Pullman coaches in Battle of Britain class locomotive. In the fields across the way, and at the level of the stations the train went through, thousands of people paid their last respects standing in silence. As Churchill had requested, he was buried at St. Martin's Church, Bladon, in the family plot, near Woodstock and the place he was born at Blenheim Palace.

Conclusion

Winston Churchill's school days seem to be the only unhappy days of his fulfilled life. After having numerous difficulties as a schoolboy, Lord Randolph Churchill's son grew to refine himself, moving upscale before becoming a gentleman and national hero. The major bright spot of Churchill's young days occurred when he discovered the wonder of books. He developed at the military school a skill of self-learning that has proved to be useful in his brilliant and lengthy political career which came later.

When Churchill entered Sandhurst military school in 1895, very few could have seen him as a future great army officer, but he proved himself on the job and gained the trust of all as the years went by.

Churchill had a penchant for action and incredible love for his homeland, two major keys of his impressive political career sprinkled with resounding exploits. Churchill's patriotic feats reached their climax when the Second World War occurred in September 1939. Heading the British troops, he bravely faced Nazi Germany, Hitler and conducted Britain to victory.

And even if Winston Churchill is more known for his political feats, the native of Oxfordshire also made significant achievements in the world of literature and painting as well.

He then built a huge reputation throughout the years, leaving a wealthy and emotional legacy to Britain and the rest of the world.

Resources

Winston Churchill in politics, 1900-1939 (n.d.). Retrieved from
https://en.wikipedia.org/wiki/Winston_Churchill_in_politi
cs,_1900%E2%80%931939

Winston Churchill. (n.d). Retrieved from
https://en.wikipedia.org/wiki/Winston_Churchill

An introduction to the Life of Winston Churchill. (n.d).
Retrieved from https://www.kibin.com/essay-examples/an-
introduction-to-the-life-of-winston-churchill-M2ucQ3yB

Churchill, Sir Winston Leonard Spencer. (2014, September
25). Retrieved from
https://www.oxforddnb.com/view/10.1093/ref:odnb/97801
98614128.001.0001/odnb-9780198614128-e-32413

Later Life of Winston Churchill. (n.d). Retrieved from
https://en.wikipedia.org/wiki/Later_life_of_Winston_Chur
chill

1945 United Kingdom general election. (n.d). Retrieved from
https://en.wikipedia.org/wiki/1945_United_Kingdom_gen
eral_election

Winston Churchill as a writer. (n.d). Retrieved from https://en.wikipedia.org/wiki/Winston_Churchill_as_writer

When Britain and France Almost Merged Into One Country. (2017, August 8). Retrieved from https://www.theatlantic.com/international/archive/2017/08/dunkirk-brexit/536106/

Winston Churchill: His Childhood, Life, and Memorable Speeches. (n.d). Retrieved from https://www.historyonthenet.com/winston-churchill-childhood-life-memorable-speeches

The Oratory of Winston Churchill. (2015). Retrieved from http://eprints.whiterose.ac.uk/85035/1/Conservative%20Orators%20Churchill-4.pdf

Winston Churchill's Personal Life. (n.d). Retrieved from https://www.captivatinghistory.com/winston-churchills-personal-life/

The Churchill School of Adulthood Conclusion: Thought + Action = An Awesome Adulthood. (2015, February 11). Retrieved from https://www.artofmanliness.com/articles/churchill-conclusion/

George Washington

Table of Contents

Introduction

Politics and politicians have their way of both winning and losing hearts, lighting some on fire and turning others into stone.

It is truly uncommon that a politician is as unanimously beloved and highly appreciated as George Washington was and still is.

More than a politician, Washington is the father of his country in all the ways you can think of and more. A paternal figure dominating American history and setting in stone its very first independent steps, George Washington is the kind of character that still instills admiration and inspiration.

There are a thousand reasons to love George Washington. You may love him because he helped create the country you call home or, for that matter, the country you wish you called home. You may love him for his military abilities or for the way he treated those around him. You may love him because he was right, because he was able to see past his own interests, because he laid the foundations of the place that has been, for quite some time now, the leader of the world in so many different ways.

No matter what you think of George Washington, you probably hold at least some grudging admiration towards him and the life he managed to lead -- a life that did not necessarily promise to change the world when George came into the world. He was his father's third son and his mother's first, so it was a life that probably did not promise *that* much success and glory, even after he was inspired by his older brother and chose to join the military.

George Washington's life was simple yet fascinating at the same time. At his very core, he was always, and will always, embody the essence of America: an entrepreneur, a military genius, a visionary.

Born into a family that was not necessarily poor, but also not extremely well-off, George Washington's early years have mainly faded into the mist of times. There was nobody who thought to document little Georgie as he made his first steps, but there were plenty who wanted to document his most important ones.

We don't know his first words, but we know his last.

We don't know what George Washington imagined his future to be like when he was a kid. Most probably, he wanted to be a farmer and landowner, just like his father. But we do know what he dreamed for the future of his country.

Many parts of George's life still remain unknown, such as whether or not he knew his future wife, Martha, and her first husband prior to the latter's death, or how he truly felt about the fact that they were never able to have children of their own.

We don't know what George thought when, in the trenches, he fought side by side with his soldiers and won the war that gave America its freedom. But we do know what he thought when he left his office after two mandates.

We don't know what George and Martha talked about the first time they met. We do know, however, that they built a relationship forged from mutual respect and support and that they ended up being partners above everything else.

There was nothing glamorous about George Washington's life. He was a promising young fellow, of course, but unlike the future leaders of European countries, there was nothing special about his birth or his station. He wasn't particularly rich before he met Martha. He wasn't particularly educated. He wasn't particularly keen on creating a country out of nothing.

But he made himself into that figure. He became special, he became wealthy, he became educated by surrounding himself with educated people, and he ended up keen to do his very best to create a country out of nothing.

The book you are holding in your hands right now is not meant to be a historical introspection into each and every step George Washington ever made. It is, however, meant to help you understand how you can come from simplicity and grow to be one of the most influential people in the world. You can come from a modest education and still grow to be the one who sets the first stone into the pavement of a new world. And more importantly, you should stay honest and modest no matter how high up the mountain of influence and power you climb.

George Washington cut an imposing figure -- one that many did, and still do, find attractive. What drove Washington to change had nothing to do with his physique, however, and it had everything with his psychology. He confronted every challenge that came along at face value and overcame every single one like the true leader he was.

Don't pick up this book if you want a step-by-step timeline of his actions and his life. He did this and he did that, and then the other thing - and yes, pretty much everything he did in the years prior to after the war was more than notable. This book doesn't aim to give a complete historical view on George Washington's evolution. Instead, we will give you a bird's eye view of his life and the moments that marked his personality and the path of his development. Therefore, the first part of the book, made up of the first three chapters, describe the three pivotal stages George went through: childhood, ascension, and presidency.

The second part of the book, which is the fourth chapter, is all about showing you the most important lessons that George Washington left behind, beyond his political actions and affinities. We aim to give you ten lessons in leadership, to show not only what an amazing human being George was, but also how you can take his influence and use it in your own life.

We do hope, in all honesty, that this book will give you wings and hope so you can fly and dream on your own, all while staying true to your one true self.

Chapter 1: George Washington's Formative Years

Not many people can say that they have laid the foundation of a country that has grown to rule the world, economically, politically and culturally.

There's an even smaller number of people who can say that they did this after coming from nothing. In fact, you can count them on your hands and have fingers left over.

George Washington is one of the few people who fall into this category. He was not only the president of a country, he was the *first* president of a country. And it was not just any country -- it was a country that, less than 200 years later, would grow to what many would view as the *first* in the world.

The same could be said about Napoleon, or Peter the First, or other rulers who made history. What sets Washington apart from them, however, is the very essence of who he was and who he became.

George Washington had a relatively modest upbringing. It is frequently claimed that many leaders in the Western world of the 20th and 21st century came from very homogenous backgrounds. But George Washington actually *did* come from a very modest family, perhaps not in terms of fortune but definitely in terms of education. In the 18th century, only a very select few could afford an education, so it wouldn't be fair to George Washington or to any of his contemporaries to compare his academic achievements with the standards we look up to today, in 2019.

The boy who was destined to become the first president of the United States of America was born in 1732. To be more specific, it was the 22nd of February, 1732, when George Washington came into the world and into a family of prosperous farmers. His father, Augustine, owned several plantations in Virginia and he had already been married once before marrying George's mother. When George was born, he had two step-brothers, Lawrence and Augustine.

As was the norm in an 18th Century household, George, Lawrence, and Augustine were not the only children in the Washington family. Five more were born after George, so by the time he was eleven, the family had grown to be quite large.

Throughout his childhood, George Washington moved with his parents from one farm to another. At the age of six, George and his family settled at Ferry Farm, located on the Rappahannock River, in Virginia. This is where the future first president of the USA would spend the rest of his childhood.

His childhood was no different than that of any other boy his age, but even from a young age George proved himself to be a winner. He was allowed to plant his own garden when he was little and, once he grew old enough, he even received his own pony. He grew to become very good at riding horses, something that would be a huge benefit to him in the future.

George spent his evenings at home with his mother and brothers, reading from the Holy Bible. As you will discover later on in this book, his mother's religious education would end up playing a monumental role in the life of George Washington even once he had left her sphere of influence.

Aside from the evenings in which their mother read the Holy Bible to them, George did not receive any type of formal education. Like most of the boys his age, he was home-educated, so he learned the very basics of arithmetic, astronomy, geography and handwriting. Most of this was done by copying from a book that was very popular back then, called the *Rules of Civility and Decent Behavior*. This was one of the main ways that children were educated at the time, and George was no exception.

You wouldn't think that the man of words like the politician George Washington became (because, well, politicians *are* men of words) once hated reading and writing, but little Georgie did. In fact, of all the subjects he learned as a child, arithmetic was his favorite. Perhaps with a nature as diligent as his, he would have grown to be a mathematics professor or a physician. But then events overtook him, and he ended up on the path of politics.

It can be said that Washington's childhood was generally happy. His family was well-off and nothing out of the ordinary happened while he was still a young child. When he turned eleven, though, tragedy struck the family. His father, Augustine, died and left most of his fortune to his first-born son, Augustine, and his widowed wife, who still had young children to look after.

Soon after their father's death, George moved in with his older brother, Lawrence. The second-born son of the family became a substitute paternal figure in little George's life, taking care of him until he was old enough to work.

There was nothing too special about the Washington family. Although they were rich, they were not too influential, and they definitely weren't among those who were meant to rule the world. They were just a normal family. So, as you would expect, there was nobody documenting little George's childhood. There was nobody to recount his misdemeanors, his personality as a child, or the little things that eventually pushed him to become *George Washington, the first president of the United States*. Why would there have been? He was not a royal, nor did he belong to any kind of aristocracy. He was part of a family who was fortunate enough to have a good financial situation, but that's all.

Because of this, little has been told or found out about the childhood of this utterly important man in history. Some stories traveled across time and distances to us, which have become associated with George's personality and the micro-events that grew to shape him as an adult. Somewhere between make-believe and quasi-verifiable truth, these stories keep the flame of his legend alive. Because of a lack of a better-documented alternative, history has created stories and made sure that George Washington did not just rise from *absolutely nothing*, and that he did not just *pop* into life out of the blue.

Whether or not these stories are 100% accurate doesn't matter. In the end, all that matters is that they say something about George's personality -- as a kid, if you deem these stories to be true, and as an adult, even if you don't believe in them.

Of all the stories that surround the narrative of the childhood of George Washington, two stand out as especially revealing for what he grew up to become.

The first one tells the story of a colt, a horse that George's mother held very dear to her heart. Augustine had raised horses all his life and he took a lot of pride in the purity of their blood lines so, after his death, Mary Washington continued the tradition and raised horses as well. One colt was her absolute favorite. Despite being unbroken and extremely difficult to control, this horse was close to Mary's heart precisely because he was high-spirited and unique.

One day, George and his brothers went to the pastures. As the determined child he was, George asked his brothers to hold the horse in place so that he could ride him. It was difficult, but they finally managed to hold it still, and George got himself on the horse. As you would expect from a wild horse, he fought to get George off his back, but the boy did not give in. He held onto the horse so hard that it died in the effort to rid itself of the boy on its back.

When George and his brothers got home, Mary asked them about her favorite colt. Without hesitation, George told her that the animal was dead and that he was the culprit. It is said that although she was sad about the death of her favorite horse, Mary took pride in her son telling the truth without shame.

Truth would go on to become one of the most quintessential values within George Washington's life. As the father of the Founding Fathers themselves, he always took pride in being honest. He may not be as well-known for his honesty and righteousness as Abraham Lincoln was, but Washington is right there, on a high pedestal of genuine values, and this story is meant to reveal that he has been this way since childhood.

The other, and perhaps more popular, story about George Washington's childhood also has, in fact, controversial origins. Some say this story is real and that it was passed down to writer Mason Locke Weems, who wrote about Washington right after his death. Others, however, maintain that this story was invented.

As mentioned before, though, whether or not this story (or any of the others we will recount here) is true is not even that important. In the end, the actions of George Washington the man, the adult, are those that speak loudest about who he really was.

This story is about a cherry tree that George's father loved very much[1]. As a six-year-old child, George received a small hatchet from his father and started to play around with it on anything he could find. The story says that one day he tested his hatched with his father's cherry-tree and maimed it. The next day, his father noticed the problem and gathered the family to ask who had done it, although he already had a very strong suspicion as to who it could have been. When he asked

---

[1] Jay Richardson, George Mason University. Sourced: https://www.mountvernon.org/library/digitalhistory/digital-encyclopedia/article/cherry-tree-myth/

little George, the boy wanted to deny it at first, but then very quickly changed his mind and told his father that it was he, and that he simply could not lie about it. Hearing this, his father was very happy and told George that his honesty had repaid him far more than the cherry tree could have ever done it.

At the age of sixteen, George Washington got his first job as a land surveyor. This job involved being in the outdoors a lot, riding horses and even sleeping outside, but young George did not mind at all. He loved what he did, and he took pride in his job.

Three years later, his brother and replacement father figure, Lawrence, got extremely sick, which prompted him and George to go spend some time in Barbados in an attempt to help Lawrence to recover. Unfortunately, this did not happen, and Lawrence died on the tropical island.

Following his beloved brother's death, George decided to become a soldier just like he had been. Perhaps unsurprisingly, he turned out to be very good at it. At the young age of twenty, he had already reached the rank of major in the colonial English army, whose main purpose was that of defending the English colonies on American soil. The story goes that George's first big job was actually very dangerous, as he had to persuade French colonists to move their forts from a colony that belonged to England. What is most revealing about George's personality is the fact that he wasn't *forced* to do this job, he volunteered.

It is equally unsurprising that the French did not listen to George's words. So, as the creative young man that he was, he had the idea of building a British fort right next to the French one. History states that an ambush between Washington's troops and a French colonial battalion was the beginning of the war between the English and the French colonies. Depending on which society you live in, this is called the Seven Years' War, the French and Indian War, or the Fourth Colonial War.

George Washington played an important part in this war, and this war played an equally important role in his life. Although he was already quite skilled in the art of war, the French and Indian War taught him different tactics, precisely because, although the English were very straightforward in their strategies, the Indians (American Natives who fought alongside the French) had many other tactics.

After the war, George went back home to Virginia, but the lessons he learned in that military endeavor were priceless and it is not an exaggeration to assume that they shaped his personality, his character, and even his entire future.

At the age of twenty-seven, George met and married Martha, the woman who was to become the first First Lady of the

United States and who became such a major influence in George's entire life. For the first years, the two lived in Martha's house, as her parents were quite well-off, and George was still quite poor.

This marks the end of the first chapter in George's life. These were the years that shaped him as a man and as a politician. The moment he met Martha was a defining one not only in his personal history, but also in what would become the history of the United States itself.

As we said earlier, there was nothing notable about George's childhood. He lived just like most boys his age. He lost financial and social status after his father died, but he did not allow this to keep him down. Instead, he took a job and excelled at it. When his true vocation called, he took another job. Needless to say, he excelled at that too.

As a child, George was nothing remarkable. He did not have the spark of genius, or at least, there is no record that he did. Even if there had been anything like that in his life, there would have been nobody there to actually tell the story. With the simple background of the Washington family, who didn't even know how to trace their precise ancestry, there was nobody to jot down every move of all eight children and their parents.

Such is the history of America itself, and this is perhaps why, of all the people who could have taken the empty place of leader, George Washington was *the one*. The one to shape America. The one to lay the foundations of what is today one of the greatest powers in the world. The one to inspire millions upon millions of future Americans.

Just like George Washington, America itself was not in any way different to the other colonies of Europe elsewhere in the world. But just like George Washington, America excelled at what it did and became a legend in the fullest sense of the word.

Chapter 2: The Beginning Of A New Era

There are two major storylines that intertwine to lead to George Washington becoming the First President of the United States of America. The first is the story of George and Martha Washington. The second is George's rapid ascension to leadership within the revolutionary army, up to the point where he became the general of the American Revolution and, later on, the First President.

In our opinion, neither of these storylines is more important than the other and they cannot be separated. They both equally contributed to the "creation" of Washington, the President. They both carved his path, and gave birth to his future and, together with this, the future of America itself.

Martha And George -- A Common Love Story, An Extraordinary Love Story

We all like to think our own love stories are Earth-shattering, unique, futureproof. And, of course, they are, because in each of us lies a micro-universe that is completely torn apart and re-built when we fall in love.

Only a handful of these incredible partnerships, however, change the world in the fullest sense of the word. Beyond novels and movies, there are not very many true stories of love that changed the face of the Earth.

Antony and Cleopatra.

Napoleon and Josephine.

George and Martha Washington.

Arguably, there was nothing passionate about George and Martha when they first met. There were no fireworks and they were not particularly influential people. There was nothing to predict that they would eventually end up as the Father and Mother of a nation, of its dreams, and of every single action that nation took from there onwards.

Martha and George met the way many couples used to meet back then: at a cotillion. She was the child of a planter from Virginia, just like George had been. Clearly, she was not from a very modest background, as her father had been much more successful than that of Washington. What not too many people know is that George was not Martha's first husband. Before him, she had been married to another man, Daniel Parke Custis, with whom she had four children. Only two of them survived past childhood, the other two did not survive past young adulthood. Daniel Parke Custis himself passed away when Martha was only 25, leaving her a very rich widow with a 25,000-acre plantation.

Martha and George got married two years later. Although she had also been courted by another wealthier man, Martha chose George. We don't know exactly why she made this decision, however. We can only imagine that she was conquered by George's honesty and ambition.

Martha and George lived in Martha's house for a few years, but when the Revolution started, she followed him into encampment. Some go as far as to say that she lived with the common soldiers but, in the spirit of honesty with which Washington lived his life, it is quite important to mention that this is only partially true.

Martha *did* follow George throughout his travels as the general of the Revolution. But she probably did not travel with the common soldiers. She was, after all, a woman and a woman of means. She dressed well, and she was very independent in herself.

Everyone around the couple noticed how much Martha loved her husband. It takes courage and a whole lot of love to follow your man through the type of revolution that changed and re-shaped the country and the world. It also takes a special kind of character to be as beloved as Martha was by the common soldiers. In the encampments, she was a motherly figure, the same figure that would later on grow to be beloved as the Mother of the United States of America.

We don't have exact sources to attest to how much of an influence Martha Washington had on her husband. Given the fact that she was an assertive woman herself and that she followed her husband throughout the entire Revolution, it is fair to assume that she did play at least a small part. She may not have been out in the trenches, like an equivalent Joan D'Arc for the Americas, but she was the support George needed.

Martha is frequently characterized as being attractive and feminine, socially adept, intelligent and very strong-willed. She was also known to be honest and charming. Unlike most women of the time, she knew how to read and write, although her family had given her this education so that she would know how to run a household.

It is easy to understand how the petite Martha, who stood at 5 feet tall, was charmed by the rapidly ascending military man George Washington. He had an imposing stature of 6 feet 2 inches and had already been recognized for his apt military leadership.

The couple continued to love and respect each other throughout the rest of their lives. Before George Washington became the President of the United States, Martha was not exactly supportive of him taking the role, but when it actually happened, she quickly realized how she would support him. She dictated the rules by which First Ladies from thereon would rule in an unofficial office that is just as well respected and beloved as that of the presidency itself.

Martha and George never had any children of their own. This bothered Washington until late in his life, but he learned to live with it eventually. Without children, both Martha and George directed all their parental instincts towards the shaping of the new nation that was only just learning how to walk on its own two feet. Together, they built the foundations upon which the new country was meant to be built.

Martha and George met like many others did. She was a rich widow; he was a preeminent and ambitious figure of the military. She was eight months his senior, and he was far less well-off than she was. They got married. They stood by each other. And, eventually, they passed away, leaving behind a legacy that continues to live on more than *two hundred years* later.

George Washington passed away in 1799. In 1801, two and a half years later, Martha followed him on his last travels, but not before following his last will and testament and releasing all his slaves.

George: The Right Man, The Right Time

There is no doubt that George Washington had an innate inclination towards military strategy. It may not have been his first job, but it was the job he chose as he associated it with his brother, whom he loved very much. He had no formal military education as a child, but he learned to be strong and quick-witted, and this military mind shaped his entire adulthood, from the moment he joined the military to the moment he passed away.

To understand George Washington's ascension to what is now one of the most coveted presidential offices in the world, you must first understand the social, economic and political background upon which the events played out. Of course, George Washington may have become a great man of his era, even without all the events preceding the American Revolution. It was these events, however, that paved the way to his success.

When George was born, North America was a promising land that was constantly being fought over by the Spanish, the French, and the English, along with the Dutch and other smaller nations that laid claim to the land. Native American numbers were rapidly decreasing because of the smallpox the Europeans had brought from the Old Continent and continued conflict with the colonizers, which led to the three major powers on the continent being the warring European states. The great battle was set to be fought between three main nations that dreamed of being the rulers of a land they had not yet even finished mapping.

It took more than 150 years for conflict to settle down on North American soil and the English prevailed as the principal nation of the new land. By the time George Washington came into the world, New York City was 65 years old and the English ruled over most of the North American coastline, expanding into the South.

Seven years after George's birth, Great Britain and Spain declared war on each other over territory in North America. The spark was a dispute over the territory of Florida, but the war also moved across to Georgia, one of the more recent colonies of the New World.

When George was 13, the English tried to take over Louisville, in what is now Kentucky. Three years later, in 1748, as George was starting his career as a surveyor, the English were obliged to give Louisville back to the French. This event marked Washington, who believed that the interests of the people within the colonies had been made redundant by the interests of the government in the Old World. This was perhaps the beginning of the aversion he developed towards the ruling Crowns of Europe and how they handled everything from afar, without knowledge of what truly happened in the life of the colonies. Despite this aversion, however, he joined the English Colonial Force and dedicated his life to fighting for his country.

In the area west of Virginia, the French continued to be a threat, despite all the efforts of the English to secure their location and their regency in the area. George, who was a true representative of his generation and a man who held his beliefs above everything else, stood up for his nation and eagerly volunteered to ask the French to move away after they occupied an English-held fort. This dedication to his beliefs also explains why he was so eager to find a solution against their refusal.

With English being the official language of the United States of America today, it is quite clear who ended up ruling the New World. But back then, the French were vying with the English to take over land in North America. The English possessed larger territories, but in many respects, the French had a strategic advantage. Unlike the English, they had actually managed to create alliances with Indian confederations and settlements. They went as far as dressing up as Indians and encouraging intercultural marriages, all for the purpose of gaining their trust and their loyalty. For the English, actions like these were inconceivable. For the French, it was the foundation and framework of their entire strategy. In contrast, the only way the English were able to win over the Native American population was to provide them with cheap manufactured goods.

Fate also seemed to be on the side of the English. While back in England the birthrate had been low, in the New World, the English birth rate rose almost exponentially. Within the first years of colonization, it reached a level twenty-four times higher than that of their co-nationals on the Old Continent.

In fact, aside from the smallpox that the Europeans had brought with them, the density of the English settlements was a major contribution in the extermination of the native population. With the increasing numbers of British subjects in America, it is quite understandable why the English wanted to expand into the West, where the French had already gained a foothold in the country. George Washington was part of these expansion plans as a surveyor, and then as a military professional. As a surveyor, George's main ambition was that of earning enough money to buy a larger piece of land that he and Lawrence could work on. Lawrence had inherited some of his father's land, a plantation called Mount Vernon, but the brothers were ambitious. To reach his goal, George endured unfortunate conditions, working in locations that were frequently lying at the very borders between civilization and wilderness.

George Washington succeeded in his endeavor. After his brother's death, he continued to acquire land and continued to increase his wealth in his mid-twenties. Because the land had to be defended *and* worked, George also became an officer with the local militia. At the age of 21, George was appointed as major by the governor of Virginia. Although young for such a role, his imposing appearance helped him ensure that people obeyed his commands.

This is when George's military career began: when he was given the task to tell the French to move their fort off English land. It was also a moment when, for the first time but not the last, George's actions and ideas would define the course of history in the New World. Because the French did not respond positively to Washington's request, a plan was devised in response that would throw the English and the French into war with each other for the next seven years.

In the words of historian Francis Parkman, "The volley fired by a young Virginian in the backwoods of America set the world on fire"[2].

This "young Virginian" was none other than the hero of our book here. And the backwoods of America were truly set on fire by his actions. Who knows what the world would have

---

[2] Francis Parkman, Historical Handbook Number 19, 1954. Sourced:

https://www.nps.gov/parkhistory/online_books/hh/19/hh1 9a.htm looked like if, on that fated day, George hadn't set a trap in the "backwoods of America" and lit the colonies on fire?

Obviously, we are not here to debate the ethical, moral, legal or political actions of current-day America, or even that of the America of George Washington's youth. But although the English eventually prevailed in this war in the New World, the sparks of freedom and revolution were formed as colonists started to believe that they could, perhaps, be masters of their own fate.

America eventually managed to bring a whole new ideal into the world: that of democracy and freedom.

Following his first military actions, George gained a reputation as a man of his word, a courageous man and a man who knew how to stand up for what he believed in. As a result of his actions and his reputation, he was made a Colonel and Commander-in-Chief in Virginia, at the young age of 23.

If, before this promotion, George had been determined and eager to succeed at whatever he attempted, his military ascension gave him even more self-confidence. But, more importantly, these experiences also taught him invaluable lessons, not just about military actions, but about other arenas of life.

George Washington played a big part in the events that led to the American Revolution, as well as the Revolution itself. The internal wars within the territory of what is now the United States of America defined the new country. But, undoubtedly, the moment that marked and re-routed the course of history forever was the victory of the colonists over the British Crown in the American Revolution.

Like most Revolutions, the American one did not simply spring up out of the blue. It simmered and simmered with the frustrations of the colonies and of all those who were trying to truly build something *new* in the world they had grown to inhabit. This revolutionary simmer is precisely what George Washington was brought up in, and the atmosphere in which he became an adult, a man of the military, a civilian with influence and reputation, a husband, and, later on, a father to an entire nation.

Of course, it might seem a little bit hypocritical for George Washington to be growing in resentment towards the British, while still fighting wars and winning battles for them. Nevertheless, how the Crown handled international wars was one matter, and it was entirely separate from the control they levied over their own subjects. There was increasing discontent over taxes and amounts of money colonies had to pay to the crown, which came to a head in 1767, when Great Britain passed the Townshend Acts. These enabled the government to collect even more money in taxes for products that had not previously been liable for customs taxes, such as tea.

George Washington had, by this time, left the military after being passed over for promotion by his British superiors. His own dissatisfaction with the colonial regime was growing, as his own business and livelihood was threatened by increasing taxes. From 1759 to 1975, he concentrated on his plantation but also emerged as an influential political figure in Virginia, holding local office and acting within the provincial Virginia legislature.

By 1770, the American people had had enough. When a large group of them gathered around a group of British soldiers in Boston and threw different objects at them to show their displeasure, one of the soldiers was hurt. Although they were not ordered to shoot, the soldiers started to use their weapons against the population. No less than five people died in the incident, and the moment remains known in history as the Boston Massacre.

Amid frustrations, tax increases, and the violent reactions of the British soldiers against civilians, it is easy to see why American sentiments towards the Crown deteriorated very rapidly over the course of the next few years. Washington helped to lead protests and demonstrations against the Townshend Acts and the Coercive acts.

The American Revolutionary War was declared in April 1775, with Washington leaving Mount Vernon to join Congress at the beginning of May. George Washington was nominated to be the Commander-in-Chief of the American revolutionary army, and the war began in earnest. America declared its independence from the Crown on July 4th, 1776, but Britain would not surrender and acknowledge this until September 1783 when the Treaty of Paris was signed.

Chapter 3: The First Presidency

The American colonies had won the war against Great Britain. They had been, perhaps, the unlikely winner, given the resources of the Crown, but the colonies quickly proceeded to organizing their newfound freedom.

George Washington had been the very core of the American Revolution, the Commander-in-Chief for more than eight years. Because of this, a lot of people expected him to try to keep hold of his power once independence was won. But Washington returned to Virginia and relinquished his power. He wanted to show that the new republic would be ruled democratically, not just by people who had influence and tried to keep hold of it. In fact, legend says that, when King George was told Washington would most likely return to Virginia, he said that this action would make him the greatest man in the world.

We all know, however, that Washington didn't stay in Virginia as he had planned, at least, not for very long.

It took some time for the Colonial Congress to write a Constitution and set the legal and procedural foundation of what was to become The United States of America. But in 1789, the states unanimously voted George Washington the First President of the thirteen colonies that made up the USA.

To travel from Virginia to New York for his inauguration, George borrowed 600 pounds. We don't know the range of thoughts that may have crossed his mind as he was traveling from his beloved Mount Vernon in Virginia to New York to take the reins of a country.

We do know, however, that he arrived safely in New York. He was the only president who never set foot in the White House, because at this time New York was still the capital of the nation. After it was changed to Philadelphia in 1790, the White House started to be constructed but it was not finished until Washington had left office.

George Washington was sworn into office on April 30th. Although he had borrowed money to arrive there, he refused to be paid for his job. He believed that he was in the service of the people and that he should not make money out of this. Thomas Jefferson, the man appointed to be Secretary of State and future President himself, stood by him in this decision. The other members of the Congress, however, didn't, and neither did members of the administration. They believed they should all be paid for their services, which meant that the President had to set the precedence, even though they were all from wealthy backgrounds.

Washington eventually gave in and accepted a salary of $25,000 a year. Nevertheless, the government was bankrupt, so he did not get paid until after it got back onto its feet.

One of the first actions Washington took once in office was to appoint Alexander Hamilton as the Secretary of the Treasury to take charge of the national finances. The two men had been discussing this matter since before the end of the war, as inflation had been a major issue even before the declaration of independence. Later on, in the 19th and 20th centuries, other newly founded countries suffered from the same type of problems, dealing with a valueless currency that simply couldn't work. Some of these countries recovered from the financial disaster but some are still carrying the problem into the 21st century.

Under the leadership of George Washington and with the financial savviness of Hamilton, America prevailed. They started by paying off their debts collectively, which was met with skepticism and some anger by states that had already paid off their own debt. Nevertheless, Hamilton managed to persuade the senators of the South and all the states ended up participating in this collective effort.

Eventually, America repaired its finances and its credit. Because of this, they were capable of raising $11.25 million and purchasing Louisiana from the French in 1803. Although they were not necessarily popular, the financial measures adamantly imposed by Hamilton brought the newly formed nation back to its feet. What's more, they allowed George Washington to continue to run the government without constantly worrying about the crippling debt the country was in.

Without those financial measures, America would not be what it is today. Of course, Washington had his major role to play in the shaping of the new country, but as the musical bearing his name makes clear, Hamilton also played his part.

Since there were no political parties at this point in the American story, George Washington ran the country on a non-party basis. This is not to say, however, that everyone involved in the leadership of the newly-free America was on the same side. On the contrary: ever since the beginning, the politics of the US were based on duality. On the one hand, there were federalists like Hamilton, who believed that America should be run using the English model, with a very centralized government. On the other hand, there were those who supported Jefferson, who believed that the new country should be more decentralized with states having a lot more power for themselves.

In between the two, George Washington himself had no strong opinion either way. On the one hand, the situation and the circumstances had pushed him into making a lot of choices that leaned towards the federalist approach. On the other, he was still a farmer and landowner from Virginia and knew for a fact just how important it would be for people like him if regions were better represented in front of the central authorities.

The power struggle between federalists and decentralists was, at its very core, a war between an old world, built on an English system, and a new one, where factories and manufacturers played a crucial role in the development of the country. Washington was a landowner, so he, like Jefferson, believed in letting the people and the states have more power. In practice, however, he was more inclined to apply the experience that leading an army had given him, as this was the moment when he observed, for the first time, the huge impact of the industrial revolution on the future.

In between the power struggle, Hamilton's career was flourishing, although this was much to the resentment of Jefferson, who saw everything he did as an act of tyrannical leadership. Aside from creating the plan that would eventually pull America out of debt, Hamilton also founded the first American Bank. Perhaps not very originally, its name was to be "the Bank of the United States."

Washington was not a keen aficionado of the banking system in general, but he knew very well that the country would not rise from its ashes unless a proper banking system was put into place. So, he gave Hamilton this project, trusting him and his knowledge in the art of finances.

Likewise, Washington may not have been a keen aficionado of the industrial revolution itself. But he understood very well that, in order to grow a country from an economic point of view, transportation was needed. In order to create fast and reliable transportation routes, factories and manufacturers were also needed.

One of the great qualities of George Washington's presidency was that he knew how to distinguish between what he would have chosen to do himself and what needed to be done. His view on ceremonies and official status was no different than that of any other farmer and landowner in the country, but he understood that that was what the people needed.

He had a very broad view of what was going on within the wider population, largely because he chose to surround himself by people with varying and often divergent opinions. It is said that he frequently played the part of an old man, acting like he didn't know what was going on, just to see what other people were truly thinking. Playing the fool enabled him to make those around him expect less of him, so that he could then deliver so much more.

As he had been as a surveyor and, according to the stories we have already relayed in this book, as a child, President Washington was an extremely diligent man. Although some critics of the era complained that he didn't do anything of substance while he was in office, the truth is that he was extremely attentive: ranging from the paperwork he carefully handled at the early hours of morning to the major decisions he took as a President.

George Washington preferred to be seen as someone who would much rather return to their farm in Virginia than rule a country. As President, he lived a good, decent life in New York, but he never dabbled into excess or grandiosity. It is said that his household was quite small for the time period, with just fourteen people taking care of the household including himself and Martha.

He also worked hard and woke up before dawn to get a large part of his daily administrative tasks finished before breakfast was even served. Even so, he frequently let people believe he worked much less than he did. In fact, at times, he might have seemed idle and aloof, rather than the focused, determined, and agile person and President that he truly was.

He was also warm and frequently met with the public. At the same time, however, he made sure that he established various types of protocols -- not because he distrusted people, like Jefferson did, but because procedures and protocols allowed him to see more people in a smaller amount of time. He especially didn't want to see people in his office; he wanted to see them at home, in their natural environment. This is the main reason he went on two tours and met hundreds of thousands of citizens who needed, more than anything, someone to believe in.

Not only did he travel around rural America and meet so many people, he did it with grace and dignity, maintaining his ceremonial spirit and his sense of humor. Instead of getting mad at the accidents that often held him up on the harsh roads of rural America, he laughed at them.

He may have seemed idle to many, but he was a man of action through and through. He is frequently credited as the person who managed to strike a careful balance between constitutional law and federal law, and many of the Presidents that succeeded him walked in his footsteps in this respect.

For instance, in 1791, a tax on whiskey was imposed by the central government. Some whiskey makers in the Frontier area believed this was a direct affront to their work, especially since they frequently found themselves using the alcoholic beverage as a currency. So, a few of them refused to pay the tax. When some of these tax evaders were caught in Pennsylvania, a riot burst out. The governor of Pennsylvania, however, refused to send in the militia to shut down the rioters. In response, as the man of action that he was, Washington pulled together a militia that was stronger and more numerous than any he recruited previously, with men from the three states of Virginia, New Jersey, and Maryland.

He believed that the actions of the tax evaders and rioters were treasonous, so it made all the sense in the world to him to gather the militia and put down the riots. He did not believe in hanging the insurgents, though. In his view, he had made his point by bringing in the army. That was enough for him.

His ability to take action when needed was passed to future generations of Presidents, and this shaped America more than many people imagine. From the way Washington reacted to riots to the way George W. Bush reacted to terrorism, all these actions seem to have roots to that single whiskey tax law passed in the 1790s.

The way that the American Constitution is created, with all of its amendments, can be traced back to Washington's views and those of the people who surrounded him. America had to be a free land and therefore, the first amendment protected the freedom of religion, speech, press and assembly. Those first men of America ensured that states had their own power as well. Whatever was not delegated to the United States as a federation fell into the jurisdiction of each state individually. The same general rule still applies today.

There are so many things that can be said about George Washington's presidency, and yet so little room to describe them all fully. He ruled for two mandates and retired after eight years in office, tired of the political scene, returning to his much beloved Mount Vernon. The four-year mandate and the two-term limit for any president still stands today.

Before he retired, however, Washington made sure he laid the foundation of what we now call America. Aside from being the President that helped to draft the Constitution itself, George Washington is also credited with being the man who created the six-member Justice system comprised of one Chief Justice and five Associated Justices. Furthermore, he is also credited with the creation of the cabinet system. And, being the first President, he was also the first President who gave an inaugural address.

He defeated the British and gave America its much-needed independence, but he also became the man who mended the rift between America and Great Britain in 1795 when he signed Jay's Treaty. Apart from this, he also made sure America and Europe stayed fully independent from one another when he declared his country to be neutral in the face of the Napoleonic wars of Europe.

Ultimately, he laid the foundations of the America we know and love today. His farewell address circled back to his beginnings as a President and to the beginnings of the United States of America as an independent country. This speech is widely considered to be one of the single most important speeches in the history of America and the world, precisely because it revised everything Washington stood for as a President of this new country and set the rules for the future.

When George Washington retired, rumors of his senility abounded, spread mostly by Jefferson. Yet, every single document from his last years suggests otherwise. He was lucid, very sensible, and he stood by the values he believed up to his last moment.

Unfortunately, George Washington did not enjoy a very long retirement. He survived for just three years after he stepped down from office, time that he spent with his family, guiding his step-grandson who was doing badly at Princeton. He remained the same honest man who, in childhood, did not have the heart to lie to his parents about his misdemeanors. His last portrait captures him wearing his army attire, a sign of respect for himself and for all the years he had proudly and courageously served his country.

George Washington passed away in 1802 on a dark December night. Feverish and fragile, at the age of 71, George's last words were *"Tis well"*.

And well it was. He passed away with the same simplicity and honesty with which he had lived his entire life. He and Martha, who followed him on his last journey two years later, are both buried at Mount Vernon, in the New Tomb, and they can be visited every day of the year by people wanting to pay their respects to the parents of the nation.

Chapter 4: Lessons In Leadership

As you would imagine, the men called the Founding Fathers were nicknamed this for a reason. They created what we now call The United States of America, and they set the foundation of the future country not only in a political and legal sense, but also in a philosophical one.

The teachings of the Founding Fathers live on more than two centuries later, and they are still considered to be perfectly applicable for the modern day. The Founding Fathers were, above all, *leaders*.

As the Major General of the Revolution and as the first President of the United States of America, George Washington is, without a doubt, the father of the Founding Fathers. His teachings are just as poignant and as important today as they were in the 18th century.

We will dedicate this entire chapter to teaching you the lessons in leadership that George Washington has passed on to us. Regardless of who you are, what you do for a living, and even where you come from, these lessons are important for you to learn and develop.

We hope the chapter ahead will help you grow as a leader and, most importantly, as a human being. Sure, Washington made his mistakes, but when he did something right, he performed miracles. And this is the belief that we should pass on to future generations: His ability to find balance in his life and still be a human being, with all the flaws and the qualities that this entails.

Seeing The Larger Picture

George Washington always managed to concentrate on the larger picture. He was a slave owner and landowner, but he left aside his own ambitions as a farmer to do something bigger. As we mentioned above, one of Washington's greatest merits was connected to the fact that he always, *always,* worked to reconcile the two diverging currents of thought of the era. He could have tried to develop an America that was decentralized, but instead, he saw the larger picture and admitted that this would not be possible or advantageous for the rest of the country.

He saw beyond the borders of the views he had been raised with since childhood. For instance, although he was not particularly educated and only received a home education like most boys of that time, he believed in education for all young boys:

"A primary object should be the education of our youth in the science of government. In a republic, what species of knowledge can be equally important? And what duty more pressing than communicating it to those who are to be the future guardians of the liberties of the country?" [3]

The very fact that he lay the foundations of the United States of America as it remains today is extremely relevant to this. George Washington was the father of a nation in the same way he would have been the father of a son. He donated his love, his passion, his determination and put them to the service of a country that was struggling to stand on its own two feet.

He believed, in every respect, that America could rise from the ashes, pay its debts, and start organizing itself like a proper country - and one that would be better than those of the Old World, that would be strong, faithful and determined.

Many would say that his dream did come true, for America is today exactly what Washington envisioned it to be.

"Nothing can illustrate these observations more forcibly, than a recollection of the happy conjuncture of times and circumstances, under which our Republic assumed its rank among the Nations; the foundation of our Empire was not laid in the gloomy age of Ignorance and Superstition, but at an Epoch when the rights of mankind were better understood

---

[3] George Washington, Eighth Annual Message of George Washington. 1796. Accessed:
https://avalon.law.yale.edu/18th_century/washs08.asp

and more clearly defined, than at any former period, the researches of the human mind, after social happiness, have been carried to a great extent, the Treasures of knowledge, acquired by the labours of Philosophers, Sages and Legislatures, through a long succession of years, are laid open for our use, and their collected wisdom may be happily applied in the Establishment of our forms of Government; the free cultivation of Letters, the unbounded extension of Commerce, the progressive refinement of Manners, the growing liberality of sentiment... have had a meliorating influence on mankind and increased the blessings of Society. At this auspicious period, the United States came into existence as a Nation, and if their Citizens should not be completely free and happy, the fault will be entirely their own." [4]

It would have been straightforward for Washington to fall back on his own education and see the future of America from an agricultural viewpoint. Instead, he used on his own learned experience as a military leader to show how important it was that the US modernized and adopted the science and technology that the rest of the world was welcoming.

---

[4] George Washington, Circular to the State. 1783. Accessed: http://press-pubs.uchicago.edu/founders/documents/v1ch7s5.html

George Washington was a pioneer. America did not delay the Industrial Revolution later than any country in Europe. Instead, it aligned itself with the modern thoughts of the era and built railway after railway, factory after factory, a country that would eventually become prosperous, powerful, and unique.

One of the biggest ideals that Washington held was to see America as a country independent of the British Crown. And he did accomplish that dream. As the highest military leader in the American War of Independence, he proved that he was not only a great strategist, but also the kind of man that people genuinely looked up to and appreciated.

His thinking was completely independent of the archaic rules by which Europe was governed. He had never visited Europe so, to him, European nobility was nothing but a vague concept. That is, perhaps, why he never considered the nobility to be entitled to rule over the land he loved so much or understand how it could create the laws and collect taxes from people living in a context so wildly different from that of Europe.

Washington's beliefs were based on a concept that might feel shockingly modern to many: privacy. The right to be left alone, to be independent, to be free was the main thing for which George Washington fought. It was the underlying motif of the Revolution he led and was the underlying leitmotif of all the actions he and the other Founding Fathers took in the wake of the newly acquired independence.

In America, where the Crown had only seen another source of income, Washington saw potential for growth. He may not have known the route of that growth, or how it would occur, but he believed that Americans were destined to grow past their colonial limitations and create a prosperous, independent, free country.

It may not seem like a big idea for someone looking at contemporary America and seeing what it has become. But as a colony, America was not supposed to move out of the political, social, and economic boundaries imposed by the Crown.

Washington believed that America could be much more than that. He believed the value of his land would grow over time, so he purchased parcels of land with the very purpose of collecting the profits once they appreciated.

George Washington was a politician but, more than anything, he was an entrepreneur. This can be seen in the way he led the country through its first two presidential mandates. From the compromises he made, to the fact that he saw land as one of the greatest values of the United States of America, George Washington acknowledged that the new country would eventually have great potential for businesses.

He also believed in the power of the people living on American soil. He saw the people as resourceful and creative, true pioneers who had not been afraid of living on a land that was still predominantly wild and untamed.

Washington was a man ahead of his time in so many ways, and we would do him a severe injustice if we were to judge him by one angle of his character. By no means was he without fault, but, as the honest man that he was, he knew when to admit his own mistakes and how to compromise.

The saying goes that the sky's the limit, and Washington proved this very well. A boy born into a good family without much of an education, who grew up in the colonial system, somehow managed to gain the independence of his country and then lead it through its first free steps.

Nothing could have predicted this when he was born, when he got his first job, or even when he joined the army, but he did it. This was largely because of his visionary approach to life.

"For if Men are to be precluded from offering their Sentiments on a matter, which may involve the most serious and alarming consequences, that can invite the consideration of Mankind, reason is of no use to us; the freedom of Speech may be taken away, and, dumb and silent we may be led, like sheep, to the Slaughter." [5]

Being Brave And Determined

It takes courage to become a public surveyor and explore lands that were far from friendly.

It takes courage to join the military.

It takes even more courage to stand up to the Crown and lead men into battle against your colonial mother, then to *win* that war.

It takes all the courage in the world to be the one to lead a whole new country through the first tumultuous years of chaos, debt, and sheer danger.

---

[5] George Washington, Address to the Officers of the Army. 1783. Accessed:

https://www.mountvernon.org/library/digitalhistory/quotes/article/for-if-men-are-to-be-precluded-from-offering-their-sentiments-on-a-matter-which-may-involve-the-most-serious-and-alarming-consequences-that-can-invite-the-consideration-of-mankind-reason-is-of-no-use-to-us-the-freedom-of-speech-may-be-taken-away-and-dumb-/

Say what you will about George Washington, but you have to admit that the man was full of courage. In fact, if it weren't for his courage, America would not be the country that it is today.

Washington's courage did not come with his ascension through the military, as, if we are to believe the childhood stories that have been relayed in this book, courage was always a part of George Washington's character.

In battle ever since he was a young colonel, George Washington had always proven his courage. In fact, after escaping a near-death experience on the battlefield, he said:

"I fortunately escaped without a wound, tho' the right Wing where I stood was exposed to & received all the Enemy's fire and was the part where the man was killed & the rest wounded. I can with truth assure you, I heard Bullets whistle and believe me there was something charming in the sound." [6]

Those may have been the words of a young man who had gained a little too much confidence, but it was precisely that confidence that pushed Washington onwards. Without it, he wouldn't have grown to become the general of the army that

---

[6] Letter from George Washington to John Augustine Washington, 1754. Accessed: https://founders.archives.gov/documents/Washington/02-01-02-0058

won the Revolution or, later on, the man who took what was presumably the hardest job in the country.

Some may think words like the above were spoken out of arrogance, and so they might. But George Washington was not just a man of *words*, he was a man of action. Like the country he was laying the foundations of, he believed in hard work and taking action without hesitation.

Even as a general, George Washington did not sit back, merely giving orders. He was out there, in the trenches, as much as he was needed. For instance, in 1778 during the battle of Monmouth, General Charles Lee ordered the troops to retreat. When he learned about this, Washington countermanded Lee's orders and went to the front to fight with his men.

Washington's bravery pushed the entire army to go further. It wasn't just that they were winning battles, it was also the fact that this man that so many looked up to was confident and steady and, most importantly, he was *present*. The same can be said about Martha Washington as well. She followed her husband throughout the entire war, seeding hope among the common soldiers and supporting her husband in what was the craziest and bravest endeavor of his life.

George Washington was courage by definition, and not just in battle, but also when it came to admitting his own mistakes and giving up his own wants for the better of the cause.

Many brave men have filled the pages of history. Few, however, are as well-regarded and respected as George Washington was and still is. The legends of his acts of courage live on, not just on American soil now, but across the world.

By building one of the most influential countries in history, George Washington became universal. From East to West and from North to South, people look at his life and gain hope. There is nothing more encouraging than seeing a person who *made it* despite all the odds, a person who stood up in the face of adversity with dignity, courage, and, perhaps, a slight dose of madness.

No matter where you go and what you do in life, remember that Washington believed. In himself. In his men. In the cause he was fighting for. You can have all the money and the education in the world but without this kind of belief, you won't get very far. It takes a leap of faith to make that one step that pushes you over the edge of the ordinary and become *extraordinary*.

Being Honest At All Times

George Washington is the kind of role model you want your children to really look up to. Bravery might be foolish at times, and visionary ideas rarely just *happen* overnight, but when it comes to Washington's honesty, we should all learn a lesson. His was more than just simple sincerity. His honesty should be deemed an act of bravery in its own right.

The stories we have already relayed about George Washington's childhood might have been invented, but the *deeds* of this man remain as true as they come. Throughout his entire life, George Washington did nothing but stay true to his ideals. One of them helped him win the war against the British. Another helped him shape America.

In a letter written in 1778, George Washington told Alexander Hamilton: I hope I shall always possess firmness and virtue enough to maintain (what I consider the most enviable of all titles) the character of an honest man. [7]

He viewed his honesty as the main trade he could offer the world. During the Revolution, many tried to question his military talents and his decisions, but. But there is no trace of anyone ever doubting his honesty.

It is precisely this honesty that brought people closer to him, making close friends and common soldiers alike rally around

---

[7] Letter to Alexander Hamilton from George Washington, 1788. Accessed:
https://founders.archives.gov/documents/Hamilton/01-05-02-0025

the ideals Washington held dear to his heart. In return, Washington expected nothing but loyalty from the people who followed him.

This is why he was absolutely devastated when Benedict Arnold betrayed the cause. Although they couldn't catch him, they did manage to catch John André, a Major who had been found guilty of being a spy and collaborating with Arnold.

In his typical manner, George Washington stayed true to his own self and his principles. Tradition dictated that officers found guilty of treason had to be executed by firing squad. But, Washington despised treason so much that he hung everyone convicted of it. So, when the time came to execute John André, he stood by his own principles, rather than tradition.

Aside from the stories shared by those who came into contact with Washington, there are more than 20,000 of his own letters that stand as evidence for his honesty. He might have flattered a friend with a "white lie" here and there but when it came to telling the unaltered truth about everything else, he was always true to his character. Not one lie can be found in all of these letters. Through good and bad, through thick and thin, Washington stood by what he believed in: pure, unaltered honesty, both in his relationships with others and in his relationship with himself.

This kind of honest leadership is extremely valuable no matter who you are. Whether you are a team leader, a project manager or a CEO, standing up and staying true to yourself and to the others around you is a crucial policy that you must adopt. People can smell a liar from a thousand miles away, especially when they are in a leadership position, and while they might forgive you once or twice, they will not forget.

What happens next?

They will lose their trust in you as their leader, and, consequently, they will lose their trust in your judgment and in the actions you take.

Can you imagine what would have happened if, in the trenches of the War of Independence, people had lost faith in George Washington? What kind of disaster would have ensued?

The same goes with modern leaders as well. The minute you lose the trust of your team is the minute you lose their respect and their willingness to follow you. That is the moment you lose the game because, without a team, you simply cannot develop, and you simply cannot become your best self.

Holding On To Your Goals

Most things that are worth achieving aren't easy. This is a belief you hear about so often that it has become a cliché.

But there is a reason most clichés echo on through time and space. It is related to the fact that, well, *they are true.*

You can achieve a lot of easy things in life. A new haircut. A new T-shirt. A new TV. Finishing a book, even. And these can give you a certain level of satisfaction.

But genuine growth happens beyond the trivial and the minimal achievements. Just think about how far mankind has come. From the first man to light a fire to the engineers working on terraforming Mars, nothing truly great has ever happened without a struggle.

Do you think it was easy for that first man to learn how to make a fire? It took the first human beings hundreds of thousands of years (at least!) to control fire. [8]

And it will most likely take engineers and scientists another several decades before they can even bring to life the dream of terraforming Mars.

No, nothing easy comes without struggle, and George Washington knew this very well. Like the good entrepreneur

---

[8] Anonymous, Accessed:
http://www.beyondveg.com/nicholson-w/hb/hb-interview2c.shtml

he was at heart, Washington knew that the single most important struggle in any grand endeavor is with *yourself*.

You can fight all the armies in the world and defeat all the laws of Physics. But when *you* feel defeated in your path to success, there's no point of returning. You *must* hold on to your goals, no matter how unrealistic, how impalpable and how downright crazy they might seem.

Washington is the first of a long line of Americans who *believed in their dream.* There was Ford. There was Bill Gates. There was Steve Jobs. There was Mark Zuckerberg. America is filled with role models who believed they could really change the world, one car, one computer, one Facebook account at a time.

George Washington is the father of his nation in more ways than one. He was the military leader of independence and freedom and, later, he was the political leader of reformation and reorganization.

Let's make this clear: Despite his occasional arrogance, Washington was a humble person who never boasted of his achievements. As a young man, he dreamed of serving his country and achieving fame. And when that happened, he set another goal.

It's not like George Washington dreamed of becoming an elected "King" in America, either when he was a kid or even much later on when he was already in the military. Instead, he set goals that were somewhat realistic for the time and for his own evolution as a human being.

He believed in his dream of a free America, up to his very last breath. That was his lifelong goal, the very engine behind all the other achievements that eventually paved his way to success.

George Washington was the kind of man who knew how to hold on to his goals. But, as a practical man, he also knew when the time had come to realize them.

Even more, he knew goals like his don't happen on their own and that he simply could not make them happen if he stayed sitting in a social bubble his whole life, feeding his thoughts and nothing else. Just like Martha, George was a socially adept man who knew the value of networking and friends, and who recognized he could inspire the country in a way that would eventually support his dream of building *America* as he had envisioned it.

Some may argue that Washington's near obsession with his goals led him to less ethical actions. For instance, many have pointed out that he married Martha for her fortune. But evidence from the era shows that the relationship was mutually profitable. He was successful and respected, and he owned a farm of his own. She was personable, loveable and very wealthy.

Their relationship evolved into one of mutual help and respect. She stood by him and helped him accomplish his last wishes. He valued her for who she was and for everything she did for him as a good wife, but maybe even more importantly, they learned how to love each other in their partnership. They learned to pursue, together, the same goals of freedom for the land they called home.

George Washington was not an upstart. He was a man with a big goal who found a woman who shared that goal with him. She may not have agreed with his choice to run for President at first, but as time passed, the love and respect they had for each other eventually won out. She played the part of the first First Lady of America the way nobody else could have.

Sticking to goals that seem impossible is the catalyst of all evolution in the history of mankind. You simply can't have one without the other, and history is written by those people who somehow managed to be foolish yet precise in their chase for glory.

You should follow their example. True leaders know their goals are crazy, that their companies have a high chance of failing, and that there are a thousand and one mistakes they could make along the way. This strength of your character and adherence not only to your goals, but also to the very principles that drive you forward.

Finding A Balanced Judgment

It is extremely hard to be the *person in charge* and leave your own interests aside for a greater cause. In the end, we are all human and that means we are programmed to be biased by our own education, interests, and the points of view of those that shape our lives.

The pressure of finding the best path for everyone is even harder when there is no precedent, and when your goal is to lay the foundation of something entirely new and entirely different.

Washington must have been terribly torn between what he wanted as a Virginia landowner and what he wanted as the leader of a new country. In between those who wanted to centralize the power and those who wanted to split power between those first 13 incipient states, he managed to find a balance and make the decisions that would benefit the country he was leading, rather than his own interests.

Now, that takes true strength of character and a special talent. Human beings are bombarded with thousands of pieces of information every day, so being able to filter through all of them to draw a conclusion and take the best course of action is more of a superpower, than an inherent ability.

George Washington had this power. He knew exactly how to take decisions that would benefit everyone, not just the few at the top of the social hierarchy. Although he was loved and respected by the people, he did not always take the most popular decision.

In fact, he is known to have taken the most unpopular path on many occasions, not because he wanted to "have it his own way" or because the opinions of others didn't matter to him. He did it because he knew the unpopular decision would eventually lead to greater success.

For instance, during the Revolution, he appointed the French Marquis de Lafayette as a general for the Continental Army. As you would imagine, this was a terribly unpopular decision amongst his peers. Lafayette was not English, nor was he of the same background as everyone else on that side of the fence. On top of everything, he was only 19 years old and people simply felt that he was too young to have been appointed general.

On the other hand, Washington knew that Lafayette would be a good choice. Not only did he like him for his enthusiasm and his true belief in the American cause, but he was also well-connected to strategic people in France. Because of how much the English and the French disliked each other and fought against each other in the New World, Washington knew that the revolutionary army needed the help of the French if they were to succeed in this crazy endeavor.

Lafayette joined their cause and grew to become extremely close to George Washington. They may have been of very different upbringings and backgrounds, but they had something that united them in spirit: the first American Dream.

This was not even by far George Washington's most debated decision. The man made a habit of making the difficult call and deciding to do things that were extremely unpopular at the time. For instance, when he gave Nathanael Greene the command to pull together a band of men to take over Boston, many around him were shocked.

You see, Greene had plenty of military expertise under his belt and he was truly *in* for the cause, but he had a very pronounced limp, which many people judged him for. The first impression he left everywhere was that of a disabled man. Congress itself refused to commission him as an officer, despite his extensive experience.

Washington saw past that. He saw a courageous, loyal and energetic man who wanted to help. By the time the future President of the US ordered Greene to take over Boston, people had already started to believe in his military expertise and look past the limp, but they wouldn't have ever got to that point if Washington hadn't given him a chance to begin with.

Something similar happened with a man called Henry Knox. Unlike Greene, he had little military experience, but as a bookseller he had read pretty much everything connected to the military. He had the theoretical knowledge that nobody else had. So, it made all the sense in the world to George Washington to appoint him as the very first secretary of war in the United States. Given Knox's limited experience on the battlefield, few would have agreed with this. Washington took a leap of faith, however, and gave him the chance.

He was right to do so. Henry Knox ended up playing an instrumental role in creating the US Navy.

George Washington always chose to see beyond the obvious, beyond the first impression of the people he met along the way and the situations he had to manage. If it weren't for his good judgment of character and of the complexity of any given situation, America wouldn't be what it is today -- or it wouldn't be here *at all*.

As a leader, it is of the utmost importance to be able to see beyond the surface. Sometimes, the people you lead may not look like your "ideal" team, and they might make mistakes and stumble and fall. But, if you manage to see past the blunders and all the things that don't "recommend" them for the job, you might be in for a pleasant surprise.

Don't let your own biases or those of wider society tell you how to feel or what you have to do. Use your own judgment and follow your instincts. Some people might not look the part, but they play it tremendously well. In the end, it doesn't matter what the "part" should look like compared to the team, but rather it is about the hidden or overlooked traits that truly recommend them for the job.

It does take a leap of faith to follow your judgment, but it can pay off so well!

"While we are contending for our own liberty, we should be very cautious not to violate the rights of conscience in others, ever considering that God alone is the judge of the hearts of men, and to him only in this case they are answerable."[9]

---

[9] Letter from George Washington to Benedict Arnold, 1775. Accessed:

https://www.mountvernon.org/library/digitalhistory/quotes/article/while-we-are-contending-for-our-own-liberty-we-should-be-very-cautious-not-to-violate-the-rights-of-conscience-in-others-ever-considering-that-god-alone-is-the-judge-of-the-hearts-of-men-and-to-him-only-in-this-case-they-are-answerable/

Knowing How To Learn From Your Mistakes

Courage is not always all about going out onto the battlefield and fighting the enemy. Sometimes, it is about leaving behind people and situations that were holding you back, or admitting that you made one or more mistakes.

If you are the person in charge, admitting to your own mistakes is brave. It's not just that you are moving past your pride, but also that some people tend to perceive mistakes as weakness. Traditionally, of course, leaders should never be perceived as weak in any way, shape, or form.

George Washington was an honest man. He believed in loyalty and truthfulness perhaps even more than he believed in his American Dream. From this honesty spawned an inherent desire to be fair when it came to recognizing his own mistakes.

"In politics as in philosophy, my tenets are few and simple. The leading one of which, and indeed that which embraces most others, is to be honest and just ourselves and to exact it from others, meddling as little as possible in their affairs where our own are not involved. If this maxim was generally adopted, wars would cease and our swords would soon be converted into reap hooks and our harvests be more peaceful, abundant, and happy." [10]

No one is perfect. We are human and we are flawed by nature. But when you make mistakes and are able to admit to them, you will become an entirely different kind of human being. You become stronger, not weaker, as the traditional view on leadership might lead you to believe.

Washington knew all of this. To him, how he perceived himself was far more important than how everyone else did. At the end of the day, he could lay his head on his pillow and know that he had done right by those who believed in him and, ultimately, by his own principles.

Many people imagine George Washington to be self-contained and cool in the face of danger, just how portraits make him look: a demi-God among men, looking down on America and what has become of his dream of freedom.

Perhaps he was, according to the records that history has left us. But in his youth, he was frequently perceived as arrogant and short-tempered. But he quickly learned from his mistakes

---

[10] *General George Washington: A Military Life* by Edward G. Lengel. 2005. Accessed:
https://www.ilibrarian.net/biography/georgewashington/quotes.html

and tempered himself down until he became quite the opposite: a humble leader with a very balanced point of view.

Furthermore, courage is frequently associated with mere foolishness. Washington himself may have been foolish when, as a young military man, he told the French to move along and when his strategies started the French and Indian War. But the young George very quickly learned that war is not about much more than survival. This was especially true when, during the Revolution, the British had one main goal: diminishing the American army by killing as many people as possible or taking them prisoners.

Young George might have been impetuous in the face of this kind of danger. At times, he ordered his people to march on into pure slaughter. He believed that lives are the cost of all wars.

But George Washington, the leader of the Revolution, knew better than this. He left his tumultuous youth behind and took a balanced stance. He knew when to order his people to retreat with honor and how to recognize that the battle was lost. He knew that the life of his people was more important than anything else, both from a human standpoint and from a military standpoint.

Washington truly knew how to learn from his mistakes, which was largely due to the fact that he knew how to be honest both with those around him and with himself.

Time and again, Washington proved his adherence to his own principles of honesty and self-awareness. Not only did he do this as a military leader, he also did this as a person. As we were saying in the beginning, George Washington didn't grow up receiving a particularly good education. As he grew up, however, he admitted that he had educational gaps he needed to fill. So he became an avid reader and a self-learner. He looked up to his mentors, particularly his older brother, Lawrence, and he read everything he could get his hands on.

As in many other areas of his life, George Washington proved to have a very balanced approach when it came to his education. He knew that real life can't be found in between the pages of a book, and he knew when to put it down and take a weapon to defend himself and his people. But he also knew that literature and books could enrich his decisions and make him a better leader.

He was a man of action as much as he was a self-learner in literature, philosophy, and sciences. That is, perhaps, why it came easily to him to draw the path America would walk on. Although he believed that land would eventually grow to be America's biggest vantage point and although, as a landowner and farmer, he believed that the future of the US lay in agriculture, he also knew when to admit he was wrong.

He knew how to draw the best conclusions from all that was happening to him and around him. When, during the Revolution, he saw just what a huge difference industry can make, he knew that the future of the country would not lie solely in working the land, but also in industrializing it as much as possible.

A man ahead of his times, Washington felt the wave of the Industrial Revolution on the horizon and he pushed the entire country towards it, even though his original beliefs did not agree with these goals.

George Washington was the kind of leader you simply love. He was not a *boss* who hardly ever admitted to his own mistakes and never learned from them. Instead, he took every lesson to heart.

It is a universally acknowledged fact that bad leaders always find someone to blame, and then try to correct the mistake. Washington was the exact opposite, even when it came to his relationship with himself. He knew that spotting and recognizing a mistake means that you can mend it and prevent it. And, as he said:

It is much easier at all times to prevent an evil than to rectify mistakes. [11]

Being Humble

As we also mentioned above, George Washington was not always the man everyone now knows. As a young man, he was obnoxious and arrogant, frequently taking decisions that were not very well thought out.

He knew how to learn from his mistakes, however -- George Washington also knew that humility is the key to living a balanced life. He was an extremely powerful man who had managed to lead America to victory and pull the country out of the fog and chaos of its first years, and yet, he put all of his faith in God and the people around him. Perhaps the most revealing words he left us with are the very last paragraphs of his official resignation:

"While I repeat my obligations to the Army in general, I should do injustice to my own feelings not to acknowledge in this place the peculiar Services and distinguished merits of the Gentlemen who have been attached to my person during the War. It was impossible the choice of confidential Officers

---

[11] The writings of George Washington from the original manuscript sources, 1745-1799 (ed. 1797). Accessed: https://libquotes.com/george-washington/quote/lbh3i6u

to compose my family should have been more fortunate. Permit me Sir, to recommend in particular those, who have continued in Service to the present moment, as worthy of the favorable notice and patronage of Congress.

I consider it an indispensable duty to close this last solemn act of my Official life, by commending the Interests of our dearest Country to the protection of Almighty God, and those who have the superintendence of them, to his holy keeping.

Having now finished the work assigned me, I retire from the great theatre of Action; and bidding an Affectionate farewell to this August body under whose orders I have so long acted, I here offer my Commission, and take my leave of all the employments of public life." [12]

Of course, the official context of these words does influence them and the way they were arranged with grace and humility, but they are also very revealing of who Washington was and the kind of legacy he wanted to leave behind.

Humility is a rare trait, especially among the powerful. It is quite hard not to allow power and success to take over who

---

[12] Washington's Address to Congress Resigning his Commission. Accessed:
https://founders.archives.gov/documents/Jefferson/01-06-02-0319-0004

you are and what you believe in, especially when your achievements are as grand as those of Washington. He believed in a dream that felt nearly impossible, yet he made it through.

Most importantly, he left behind the same belief. Americans today believe that they can make their dreams come true precisely because of this one humble leader that took them to battle and then bought them peace in a country that became prosperous and healthy.

People don't like those who, having reached a certain level of fame, success, and power, throw their story in everyone's faces like it happened through their merit and their merit only. Truthfully, nobody ever *makes it* on their own. For some, family is the catalyst for their success. For others, it is the teams they work with. And for most, it is a combination of both.

George Washington is the result of his times, of his own hard work and power to believe, and of all the men and women he met along the way and stood by him. His merit is that of acknowledging the fact that not even the most powerful leader can achieve his goals without the help of everyone else around him.

Indeed, Washington was a humble man, especially when you compare his achievements to the life he lived life. He never enjoyed the luxuries of being the leader of a country, and never slept in late or left tasks unattended. With his honesty and humility, there came a work ethic that should be the model for all the generations succeeding him.

True leaders do not bask in their own glory. They are grateful and humble, and they acknowledge that their power is not *theirs*, but of all the people supporting their cause. Regardless of whether you are the leader of a two-person team or if you lead a country into success, you should always be self-aware and humble.

Without humility, it is very easy to forget your true goals and become a different person, one that is thirsty for power and glory, not thirsty for grand ideals and for dreams that come true.

Setting The Expectations Low

It's one thing to have a big dream and aim high, and it is a completely different thing to set unrealistically high expectations for those around you.

Washington believed in his America and, together with the Founding Fathers, he made his dream come true.

At times, Washington's thoughts were clouded by doubt. He thought people were expecting too much of him and that he might not be up for the task. Humble and honest, he rarely promised more than he could deliver.

The fact that he led the Revolutionary War against the British is evidence of this. Through his powers of persuasion and this belief in his dreams, he managed to rally around him people from all walks of life who were ready to fight and die on the battlefield to make the dream of a free America come true.

The task was more than difficult. The American numbers were low, and they clearly did not have the military power of the British who, back then, were considered to be the strongest army in the world. The courage it took to stand up to such an undeniable force is staggering, both for Washington and for those who followed him.

The Americans were the underdogs, least likely to win the war and most likely to perish in the fire and ash the British army would leave behind. And yet, fortune was on their side. Battle by battle, the Americans managed to send the British back home having lost one of their most valuable colonies.

Washington was careful in the way he communicated his doubts, choosing to do it only with those who were close to him. In the spotlight, he was nothing but inspiring and motivating. But behind the curtains, even he had his doubts which is precisely why he always aimed for *more* than he promised, and *more* than his people wanted.

But George Washington made it. He not only made it through the war alive and helped America gain its much-desired independence, but he also made it through two whole mandates as the President of the United States of America.

He also left behind something far more valuable than he would have ever promised to anyone, even to himself: his legacy. The man built America not just politically and militarily, but also socially. The core of the modern American Dream is built on George Washington's views:

"As Mankind becomes more liberal, they will be more apt to allow that all those who conduct themselves as worthy members of the community are equally entitled to the protections of civil government. I hope ever to see America among the foremost nations of justice and liberality."[13]

George Washington's promises to America were full of grandeur and genuine passion, but what he gave America was equally grand. In the few years following the Revolution, he managed to lay the foundation of a country who could boast economic growth and full independence, which would make it genuinely successful in every way there is.

---

[13] From George Washington to Roman Catholics in America, 1790. Accessed:
https://founders.archives.gov/documents/Washington/05-05-02-0193

The doubts that sprung from George Washington's humility are now buried in the sands of history because he over-delivered with every occasion and because people never lost faith in him.

As a leader, you have to over-deliver. You have to set targets that are high, but feasible, and then push everyone to *want* to do more. True leadership does not happen when you keep pushing people over the edge in an attempt to achieve things that are *too* far away from what they are now. It happens when you give them the peace of mind that their goals are achievable and when you inspire them to do more and be more.

Understanding The Context

It would be terribly unrealistic to expect *anyone* to know everything about everyone and every single possible situation.

Yet, great leaders have the unique talent of being able to grasp the meaning of what is going on around them and make decisions that will lead everyone else to success.

George Washington had this quality, even though he was not the most educated leader in history. But, somehow, his desire to truly understand what was going on and make the best judgment of a situation pushed him further.

He was not a legislator, an engineer, or even truly a politician, yet he still managed to *win and build* his new country.

This is largely because Washington always wanted to expand his knowledge. His home education was lacking, and he had only learned the basics, but, throughout his life, he always strived to fill in the gaps in his knowledge by testing, experimenting, and learning.

As a farmer, he was one of the first to test the rotation of his crops with the purpose of rejuvenating the soil and helping it stay healthy year after year. This was a good choice from an environmental point of view but is also had the potential of helping Washington's crops yield better, healthier, stronger plants. To him, it was a win-win situation, but he would never have arrived at this conclusion if it weren't for his inherent inclination towards researching, testing, and adapting situations until they were *optimal*.

The same diligence was applied to his leadership. He may not have always fully understood the issues he was facing, but that is why he put men in charge who did and who could relay situations to him as they were, with the same honesty and straightforwardness he believed in.

The financial future of America, the very core of its economic evolution, and the social changes that occurred in that first mandate were all decided between George Washington and the various people who helped him.

Because he was honest with himself, he never dived into a decision without first analyzing its pros and cons. He took the time to fully understand every aspect of a decision, so that he could make the decision that would benefit *everyone*, not just move the process forward.

It was this ability to make sense of multiple bits of information that pushed him to become the first President of the United States of America. Everyone believed in him. Everyone expected him to be everything.

And he was.

But nothing would ever have happened the way if it wasn't for Washington's sheer desire to learn, study and experiment and to take decisions based on what we would nowadays call *data* and *experience*, rather than hunches and inspiration.

As a farmer, a military leader, and a political leader, George Washington sought to surround himself with those who would best help him make sense of what was happening. Most of the time, these diverging opinions helped him understand precisely what needed to be done and which course of action was best.

True leaders know exactly what they are leading their team into. They know the upsides and downsides, the context, and they know what could go wrong. They take the time to research with religious adherence to the rules. They take their time to speak to everyone and gain a full bird's eye view.

You can only make great decisions when you have all this information at your disposal. Without it, you are blindly walking into every decision, making choices that rely on instinct rather than knowledge.

Relying on instinct was bad back when Washington led the country, and it is even worse today, in the age of Big Data and ultra-information. Take the time to learn the facts and only act when you feel that you have grasped their full implications!

Knowing How To Present Your Ideas

By all standards, George Washington was a presentable man. He was tall and handsome, and in his military suit, it is really no wonder that Martha took a liking to him. She was rich, whereas he was far more modest.

George Washington was handsome, but more importantly, he behaved with dignity and honesty, he constantly sought to know more and be more, and he always wanted to prove himself.

Of course, when he was spending time in the high social circles of Virginia, George Washington couldn't have dreamed what significance his character would have not only in the lives of his friends and family, but also in the life of a nation itself.

Although he was a man who was capable of moving past first impressions and stereotypes, George Washington was, himself, a man who made a real first impression. It would have been hard not to, with his height and the dignity of his presence.

As a young man, Washington learned that presentation matters. Yet he was more than willing and able to move past this presentation and give anyone else who did not look the part a chance. We have already shown how he did this on numerous occasions.

Beyond this, however, Washington knew the world he lived in and he had experienced, first hand, just how powerful a good first impression and presentation can be.

For this reason, he always strived to make his outward appearance as appealing as possible. Even as he grew older, his impeccable image was striking in every room. When he sat for a portrait, he always chose to wear his military clothing -- this might be due to many reasons, but undoubtedly one of the most persuasive ones was the powerful symbolism behind that livery.

In his manner of speech and the way he delivered his speeches, George Washington was every bit a modern leader who inspired and motivated, lifted up downtrodden spirits, and managed to push past the self-imposed boundaries of people and make them *believe*.

If you look at any of the letters he wrote and any of the speeches he gave, you will see just how much he valued a pretty turn of phrase. You would think a man with his background education and military expertise would be minimalistic with the flourishes he used in speaking and writing. But, in fact, the way he spoke and the way he behaved was all a carefully constructed act of *presentation*.

Call it marketing, if you wish, or call it being civil and nice, but George Washington definitely knew how to motivate people and how to make them follow him.

And that is the mark of a great leader -- someone who could truly move past simple communication to transfer meaning and power into every single word he said or wrote.

Great presentation matters because human beings are wired to be impressed by it. We are programmed to analyze people and situations based on our first impressions, because that is how our brains are able to process the tons and tons of information that hit us every day.

Fortunately, the duality within George Washington played out for the best. He believed in the power of presentation for himself, yet, he was also able to recognize that many people might not *appear* to be great for a role on face value, but that their background and experience were far more important.

This is precisely the kind of balance you should also strive to achieve as a leader!

Conclusion

It's hard to find someone in the history of mankind as unique as George Washington was, which is perhaps why his legend lives on beyond the borders of the United States and the historical paradigm.

We could be talking about George Washington, the historical character, the military man and the politician that freed and shaped America -- and nothing more. We could talk about him in technical terms, how he used his advantages to win the War of Independence, the tactical tricks he used to defeat the British, and the specific approaches he used to lay the foundations of the new country.

Instead, we believe it is more important to talk about how George Washington was and is a role model, and a very relatable one at that. You probably struggle to relate to Napoleon or even Marc Antony, and you almost certainly can't relate to Alexander the Great. But when it comes to Washington, there's something very human about his education and the way he was brought up that makes you feel *close* to him.

Don't get us wrong, he was extraordinary in every point of view. His appearance is said to have been extraordinary, not to mention his character, personality and the behavior associated with them.

And yet, there is something genuinely relatable about George Washington. He was the son of a landowner -- a quite well-off one, but not a social star. He did not grow up in a modest family, but even with all of this, nobody could have predicted a future as bright and as remarkable as the life he lived.

Washington should have been a landowner, just like his father. And he was, but his diligent nature pushed him into being more. He wanted to be a military man, and he excelled at it, leading the colonies of America into battle against the British and winning their independence. He then went on to be the first President of the United States of America, the best first President America could have asked for.

Back on the lands of his father, nobody would have thought that little George Washington would become as preeminent a figure as he did. And yet, he did not allow his own education or the biases of the background in which he grew up to affect his decisions. He constantly pursued *more*, and when he felt he had done everything he could, he retired back to his land, away from the buzz of the political life.

'Tis well" were his last words. And well it was, for he left behind more than a story, he left behind a legacy we still look up to today. He left behind the written history of those first years of America, and if that is not *grand*, nothing else is.

Just like America itself, George Washington came from a modest background but just like America, George Washington was a self-taught leader. He learned how to lead, how to take the best decisions, and how to be more than anyone would have ever guessed he would be.

The destinies of George Washington and the United States of America are strongly connected to each other. In many ways, America has mirrored the evolution of its very first leader: a man who became everything and used his potential to the maximum.

George Washington left behind a country that was independent, with a political and economic system that gave it all the chances in the world to succeed. Sure, the United States still had a long road to travel before it reached the 20th century but nothing that America has ever done would have come about if it wasn't for that one man who shaped its fate and sealed it irreversibly into a story of grandeur, freedom, and power.

It's hard to pinpoint if there is anyone in our modern life as influential as George Washington was, for he not only shaped

America, but through this, he changed the world. We would dare to go as far as to say that everything we aim for today as human beings living in the United States has its roots in the aims of one visionary man who believed his land of colonies could be something more. Therefore, the history of the 20th century would have looked very different if it wasn't for America.

We keep stating that George Washington shaped the future, yet it still feels like an understatement. He wouldn't have made it without those amazing people that surrounded him those first years, but even so, he was always the one to *seek* them, knowing full-heartedly that he needed their input.

We don't know what Washington was thinking when he was battling the British in the trenches, when he was surveying the land as a young man or when he was growing up under his mother's protective and loving care.

We do know, however, what Washington thought of the dreams he wanted to achieve with his country. And we know that they came true.

Modest and humble to a fault, George Washington was never a man to bask in his own glory. As we have mentioned in the book, he was the only President who never set foot in the White House, as it hadn't been fully built by the time that he ended his last term. Instead, he lived as modestly as possible, together with Martha Washington and the few servants who helped her run the house.

It would be wrong to say that George Washington was perfect. Nobody is. He made mistakes. He learned from them. And even in relation to the biggest flaw of his life, that of being a slave owner, he learned that the ideals of the country he dreamed of building were incompatible with those of the Old World he had left behind.

Despite his flaws, George Washington remains a figure of importance and grandeur. He remains in history as a genuine visionary. He was not someone who would go on about his dreams and do nothing about it, but someone who knew when to take action and how to make sure the results were exactly what he was aiming for.

In terms of leadership, America could not have asked for a better role model and, regardless of whether or not you are an American, we strongly advise you to look up to Washington as a model of leadership. We are more than certain that most business leaders of the modern have borrowed, at least partially, from George Washington's points of view on leadership.

He was a man ahead of his times, with dreams that surpassed his own condition and the condition of the country he was living in. He saw beyond the imposed standards of his time and dreamed of *more*.

He was a brave man who was not afraid to run into battle even later in his life, after he had already reached the point where he could have stayed back to strategize.

He was an honest man. Anecdotes of his childhood show us that he had always been like this and the words and actions of his adulthood prove it without doubt. George Washington was a man who stayed true to himself and true to everyone else around him.

There were many occasions when he could have just given up and retired to his farm in Virginia, together with Martha, to live a far simpler life than that within the political limelight. And yet, he held onto his goals and when he was elected as President, he went on and became the President his country needed.

George Washington did not receive a very advanced education as a kid, yet he sought education and believed in it with all his power. He read and he surrounded himself with people who were better than him in specific areas he knew he would never master. As a consequence, he was always able to make judgment calls based on facts and logical thinking processes, rather than mere hunches.

Washington was inherently flawed. As a young man, he had been arrogant and quick to make decisions and he was uneducated for a man that would eventually hold the position he did. And yet, he moved past his mistakes, learned from them and internalized the lessons to the point where they became part of who he truly was.

Despite all his achievements, Washington was a humble man. He had faith in God, he had faith in the people who surrounded him, and he had faith in the country he was shaping and its people. He could have boasted and basked in his own glory but instead, he chose humility over arrogance and modesty over bragging.

Washington was a mentally agile man, who knew how to absorb a lot of information, synthesize it and then make the most out of it. This is perhaps the main reason why he set such high expectations for everyone around him. He did not want to lie in any way, shape, or form and he wanted to exceed people's expectations and over deliver, rather than make vain promises and not adhere to his own words.

George Washington was a presentable man who looked imposing, and yet, was also humble. He believed in the power of presentation, as we have already shown throughout the book, and that is why every single letter and every single speech he ever gave was so powerful and so capable of surviving the sands of times and still be relevant today, in 2019.

He was, without doubt, one in a million. He was the kind of leader you genuinely want to look up to, not because he is described in such detail by the history textbooks, but because his life and his words inspire and transcend history.

We hope this book has managed to do more than just merely teach you about George Washington and his life. We know you will have already come across facts related to him at some point in your life and that you know the basics of his storyline.

Instead, we hope this book has managed to help you understand that there is a very good reason he is so appreciated and so beloved. We also hope that this book has helped you understand the true value of genuine leadership - - the kind that fights in the trenches with the common soldiers and knows how to lift up spirits and inspire the public.

We hope this book will help you become a better leader yourself, regardless of what you do for a living or what position you hold within your company. The lessons are universal no matter what your goals are or how compatible your own personality is with that of George Washington.

We hope you will take his leadership as a model to hold onto for the weeks, months, and years to come. If more people were like George Washington, the world would be a more productive, humbler, and, ultimately, a more peaceful place.

Ulysses S. Grant

Table of Contents

Introduction

A lot can be said about Ulysses S. Grant. He was the 18th president of the United States, a clever and open-minded military man, a national hero and a highly scrupulous individual. But, at the same time, he is known for his scandal-filled and corrupt administration, failures in business, and his love of alcoholic beverages. These contradictory ways of describing Grant make him an interesting and complex historical figure that lived a tumultuous life.

In this book, we will take apart the legend of Ulysses S. Grant in hopes of finding and understanding the man behind it, Hiram Ulysses Grant, the man who fought for what was right in an era of racism and slavery. Something that you should know about Grant from the very beginning, to give you an idea of his character and evolution, is that he did not wish to be a military man. He was more inclined towards literature, arts, and horsemanship. He was a scrawny teen that delved into mathematics and even hoped to be a teacher after he was done with his mandatory military service. Despite that, he excelled in his military endeavors and became interested in the action and turbulent lifestyle. Although he held his military days as a pleasant memory, he himself detested war and saw it as something "wrong" that was only meant to further increase the territories and influence of America. The most notable wars he took part in were the Mexican-American War and the Civil War. During the later, he took command of all U.S armies and managed to put an end to the deadliest conflict the U.S had ever faced by accepting the surrender of the Confederate forces.

Throughout his life, Grant had many business ideas that fell short due to his tendency to put his trust in the wrong kind of people. This tendency of his also put its mark on his presidential days. At the time, Grant was the youngest president to take the reins of the country, and he had no political experience to back him up, which in a way explains why he followed the advice of people of bad character. His two terms were riddled with scandals and corruption, although Grant himself did not encourage or delve in illegalities. A closer look at his administration will show the admirable goals that Grant had in mind: innovation, acceptance, and unity.

He believed in civil rights for freed slaves, pushed for ratification of the 15th Amendment, attempted to improve the living conditions of Native Americans, and tried to limit the activity of terrorist groups such as the infamous Ku Klux Klan (which pushed an extremist racist agenda and heavily discriminated against people of color). Grant as a president focused a lot on Reconstruction, establishing both the National Park Service and the Department of Justice and on improving relations between the United States and the United Kingdom - a venture that proved to be successful. But even his attempts to "make America a better place" are seen by both historians and the general public as either a violation of the rights and laws of the states or as a weak and feeble attempt at equality. While we cannot deny that Grant's administration was far from perfect, it did manage to make a positive impact, and it brought the United States a step closer to being truly "united."

Grant the civilian was a family man. He remained loyal and dedicated to his wife, Julia Dent, and their four children, throughout his life. His failed business ventures and the time spent out of military service propelled Grant into a bad state of mind, which he medicated by consuming alcohol. However, he never let that method of dealing with life's hardships affect his character or better judgment, so it would be far-fetched to call him an alcoholic. The years after his presidency are marked by a two-year trip around the world, which cemented his image as "the hero of the Union." Financial problems prompted him to write his memoirs with the help of the famed novelist Mark Twain. Fortunately, his memoirs were a success and ensured the Grant family could continue to enjoy a comfortable life. As a last touch of bad luck, Ulysses Grant died before his memoirs were published, never realizing how appreciated they would be.

We can use many words to describe Grant: a great military leader, a compassionate husband, a person that put his trust in people with bad intentions, an advocate for civil rights, a skilled writer, and a man that had his fair share of both success and failure. Those that chose to focus on his mistakes in judgment forget that Grant was human. We all make errors, especially when we are inexperienced in a certain field of work. We all sometimes delve into bad behaviors that help us deal with disappointments. So, Grant was not perfect, but the feats that he managed to achieve are enough to set him apart from the ordinary.

So let's take a good look at the life of Ulysses S. Grant, the civilian, the war hero, the 18th president of the United States, and the historical figure that managed to put a mark on classical literature.

Chapter 1: Childhood and Family

Hiram Ulysses Grant was born on April 27, 1822. He was the first son of Jesse Root Grant, a skilled tanner, and Hannah Simpson Grant. The name "Hiram" was chosen by his father, as he considered it to be a suitable name for a Christian, while the name "Ulysses" came from his maternal grandmother's admiration for the ancient commander. Grant never liked the initials of his name (H.U.G) and in an attempt to escape it he would often put "Ulysses" before "Hiram." The initial "S" that is to this day attached to his name doesn't stem from anything. It was added by mistake when Grant joined the West Point Academy, and he chose to stick with it.

At the time of his birth, the family lived in Point Pleasant, Ohio but they moved a year later to Georgetown, where Grant spent most of his childhood. Jesse Grant was a clever businessman who had strong opinions on all fields of life from religion to politics, and who was not afraid to sustain said opinions via brawls and combative discussions. An item of note is that he had a distaste for the use of slaves, an ideology that he passed on to his son. Hannah Grant was a devout Methodist, often described as being good-looking, kind, family-oriented, and quiet, qualities that her husband cherished. Her dowry consisted of a substantial amount of land, something that ultimately sealed the wedding deal for the nifty Jesse.

Although his father had a big, strong personality, Ulysses chose his mother as a role model. Later in his life he would admit his moral compass and good sense came as a result of his mother's influence, and so did his deep respect for women. The kindness of his mother seemed to have no boundaries and she was the sort of person that trusted others way too easily, something that Grant himself would unfortunately practice. However, Hannah lacked the "warmth" of a mother, something that her son never forgave. Even in his memoirs, she is barely present, the focus being more on his boisterous dad, with whom Grant never really saw eye to eye, despite deeply caring about his father's opinions.

Their house in Georgetown had two stories and was made from bricks, showing the wealth of the family. In the years that followed, Jesse kept adding to the building in order to better accommodate his growing family. Grant had three sisters, Clara Rachel, Virginia Paine, and Mary Frances; and two brothers, Samuel Simpson and Orvil Lynch. The Grant family was very involved both in politics and in religion. They actively frequented and involved themselves with the Methodist Church and they were partisans of the Democrats – a political view that was widespread across Georgetown. In 1832, however, the head of the family, Jesse, gave up on the

Democratic Party and started attending Whig Party conventions. The Whig Party was a new and fresh political "force" which took a bold antislavery position that resonated a lot with Jesse's views. The Party also promoted the importance of the school system. It further warned against the dangers of alcohol, and it held religion in high regard.

Ulysses Grant was not the typical mischievous young boy. He was rather calm, had great self-control and never displayed a wide range of emotions, much like his mother, Hannah. He was brave to the point of neglecting the possibility of physical danger, and his father considered him to be the good-looking child of the family (although he was displeased with what he looked like once he grew up). Most of his relatives and acquaintances described Grant as being serious, earnest, and more mature than other kids his age. His behavior was suitable for the "proper family" he was raised in. The young Grant did not play card games, dance, or use curse words. He was very particular about swearing, even the harmless "darn" sounded horrible to him, and he deeply despised crude anecdotes and jokes that were popular in the military, as his respect for women made him unable to take part in such vulgarities.

Grant preferred harmless activities such as ice-skating and swimming and stayed away from hunting, as he did not enjoy taking the lives of creatures. Due to this sensibility of his, he was the target of bullying, which he was not afraid to stand up to. He did not actively seek conflict, but he was not afraid to interfere and help others in need whenever he could.

Because there were no public schools, Grant attended a small subscription school. He was an overall good student that had troubles with public speaking but excelled in mathematics. Although he was not devoid of ambitious qualities as a child, he was never the stand-offish type that strives to be the best, much to his father's dismay. Jesse wanted his son to achieve greatness and show everybody what he was capable of, while Grant preferred to lay low and let others discover his qualities. In a way, that was the son's way of resisting his father's power and influence, a way of imposing himself and defining his own character.

Having an overly present dad with high expectations and an emotionally absent mother left young Grant with a lot of suppressed emotions and a sort of internal suffering. One of his earliest joys was being around horses. He turned out to be a talented tamer and horse rider simply because he knew how to handle the wild animals with respect and an unbridled gentleness. The young boy dreamed of a future in which his horsemanship could bring in fortunes, but from an early age, he showed little to no affinity for the art of making, handling, and investing money. This had mostly to do with his shy nature and naivety, which would later haunt his adult life.

Grant was not the kind of child to dream of a spectacular future. He was very much content with having a simple life and wanted nothing to do with the family's business, which he perceived as cruel. He wished to remain a farmer or get a higher education rather than to thrive on the tannery business, that's how deep his love for animals went. His father prospered nonetheless, and in 1835, he even scored a contract with the Columbus Insurance Company. The money allowed Grant access to a better education at the Maysville Seminary private academy, where he continued to excel in mathematics but was an overall average student. In 1837, Jesse's business took a turn for the worse and he was no longer able to keep his son in Maysville. So, Grant was moved to the Presbyterian Academy in Ripley, an institution that preached abolitionist ideals. Although he was well-liked and he did not fail any subjects, he never stood out as a top student.

Because of his laid-back nature, his father had lost hope in Grant taking his future into his own hands, so he secretly arranged for the boy to attend West Point, a prestigious military academy. Grant was not pleased with his father's endeavor and he had little confidence that he would ever fit the academy's requirements. Through his father's influence, he was nonetheless listed as an applicant, as Ulysses S. Grant due to an error. The meaningless "S" will forever be associated with Grant's name as a grim reminder of his father's ambitions.

Chapter 2: West Point Military Academy

Grant was not happy about his father using his authority to get him a position in a sought-after academy and many believed that the country boy had no chance of making it there. In 1839, the young, frail-looking and too short for his age, Grant, left his hometown and embarked on the journey that would change his life.

His new "name" Ulysses S. Grant won him the moniker "Uncle Sam Grant," that spread like a forest fire. Soon enough, all the cadets knew him as Sam Grant, much to his chagrin. Despite not preparing for the tough entrance exams, he managed to pass them all, along with the physical tests and check-ups. The new cadets were then shaved and placed in summer encampment, a place known as "the Plain," where they lived in tents while receiving their initial training.

In September, the cadets were moved to barracks. At the same time, Grant signed his enlistment papers in the Army, a pledge that offered him an education in exchange for eight years of military service. This pledge to serve his country resonated deep in Grant's mind and heart. Despite his initial dread of going to West Point, he quickly took a liking to the academy's fields, and he admitted that his father's initiative was a clever one (from a business point of view). The academy had a very stiff and prim uniform and schedule that Grant never got used to. He was frequently reprimanded for his disheveled appearance and his tardiness. Albeit Grant was used to being mocked for his small frame and peculiar character, the cadets at West Point, which totaled only 250, were quick to discover his qualities. They admired his honesty, generosity, modesty, and his dedication to always complete his tasks correctly.

The barracks at West Point were simple and lacked unnecessary luxuries, giving the cadets a taste of a proper military life. Two cadets were to share a small room, and alongside the others, they were assigned to take care of the "house chores" such as scrubbing the floors and making their beds. Grant quickly got a reputation of always following the rules. A lot of his fellow cadets found him to be the perfect mediator for their disputes.

The curriculum at West Point was vast, with an emphasis on both typical schoolwork such as math, geography, history, and French, and on military tactics, artillery, and all kinds of basic military training. Much like his other experiences as a student, Grant was neither the worst nor the best. As usual, he shined in mathematics, but he showed the bare minimum interest in other fields, displaying a missing sense of competitiveness. His interest in mathematics was so integral to his character that he often dreamt about a future as a math professor. So for him, West Point was more of a trial that he had to endure in order to live an honorable life and not disappoint his father.

Besides being a "math nerd," Grant also showcased a love for reading and a tendency towards the artistic side. He loved the works of Sir Walter Scott and Washington Irvin, and he exhibited a raw talent in the drawing course that a popular painter by the name of Robert Walter Weir held at West Point. Drawing courses served the purpose of teaching cadets how to roughly sketch the topography of a battlefield and maps. Of course, Grant never forgot one of his first passions: horses. He was a skilled horseback rider, so much so that he was believed to be the best that West Point had at the time.

After his first two years at West Point, Grant and the other cadets were offered a two-month furlough. By that time his father's business was prospering again, he managed to expand his Bethel tannery and even become the mayor of Bethel.

The Ulysses Grant that returned home was no longer a boy. His frame was muscular, his slouch gone, but on the inside, he remained the same modest, shy individual - the exact opposite of his father. The locals took a liking to him and happily listened to his West Point stories. In the short period of two months, Grant had his first experience with infatuation, taking a liking to a woman named Kate Lowe. Their feeble link, however, never went further than a "liking" and was forgotten as soon as Grant went back to West Point. His return was marked by an unwanted promotion to Sergeant, a position that did not last long, as Ulysses kept accumulating demerits which led to his demotion back to private in the spring of 1842.

The last two years at West Point took a toll on Grant's mental and physical health. He suffered from depression and once again was a slim, scrawny looking guy (although he was now a lot taller). He had also developed a cough that worried him, as two of his uncles had died of consumption. Even in this bad state, Grant retained his status as "the most proficient horseback rider" and he established a record that stood for years to come. At his graduation in June 1843, he demonstrated a mounted exercise that amazed the crowd. James B. Fry, who was one of the spectators, described the performance: "When the regular services were completed, the class, still mounted, was formed in line through the center of the hall, the riding-master placed the leaping-bar higher than a man's head, and called out 'Cadet Grant!' A clean-faced, slender, blue-eyed young fellow, weighing about 120 pounds, dashed from the ranks on a powerfully built chestnut-sorrel horse and galloped down the opposite side of the hall. As he turned at the farther end and came into the straight stretch across which the bar was placed, the horse increased his pace, and, measuring his strides for the great leap before him, bounded into the air and cleared the bar, carrying his rider as if man and beast had been welded together. The spectators were breathless. 'Very well done, sir!' growled 'old Hershberger,' the riding-master, and the class was dismissed and disappeared; but 'Cadet Grant' remained a living image in my memory."[14]

The day of graduation from West Point remained one of Grant's most cherished memories throughout his life. He still had some dim aspiration of becoming a math professor, but he also contemplated a military career (since he still had military time to serve) in the cavalry branch. Rejected by the cavalry because of competition, Grant received his first assignment: brevet second lieutenant at the Jefferson Barracks as part of the Fourth Infantry Regiment. Before going on his first military assignment, he spent one more summer in Ohio, where he was the target of many people's envy and mockery.

An important aspect about Grant's time at West Point is the fact that he got the chance to personally meet a lot of cadets that would go on to join the Confederate Army (including Thomas J. Jackson and even Robert E. Lee, the general

---

[14] Ron Chernow, 2017 "Grant", page 54

himself). He never understood why they chose to break their oath of serving their country.

Chapter 3: Jefferson Barracks and Julia

The Jefferson Barracks represented one of the largest military outposts in the States, and it mostly served as a "shield" against vicious Indian raids for the Great Plains. The outpost itself was not only impressive but also a cherished military post, and it was commanded by Colonel Stephen Kearny, whom Grant admired. Grant arrived at the Barracks in the fall of 1843, and he still harbored thoughts of becoming a professor, spending most of his time going through math studies and pleasure reading.

During this time, Grant rekindled his friendship with his West Point roommate, Fred Dent, and he was encouraged by Fred to visit his family (who lived in White Haven, a plantation close to the Barracks) despite him being dispatched elsewhere. The Dent family, who had plenty of daughters of all ages, took an instant liking to the young lieutenant. It was not long until Grant spent more and more time in White Haven - a habit that brought multiple reprimands from Captain Robert C. Buchman. The Captain, who oversaw the Fourth Infantry, did not hold Grant in high regard and would later become an obstacle in Grant's career.

Because Julia Dent was at a boarding school in St. Louis, a major city to which officers were frequently dispatched because of its proximity to the Barracks, she met Grant at the beginning of 1844. She was four years younger than Grant and she shared his love of literature. Julia was no exceptional beauty (according to her, her biggest problem was her congenital strabismus, which made her extremely self-conscious) but she had her fair share of admirers. Regarding her childhood, she would go on to describe a picture-perfect scenario of a happy, kind family, where even the slaves at the plantation seemed content to her. She never let go of her belief that slaves were necessary, not even when her soon to be husband actively made efforts at abolishing slavery and giving slaves rights.

When Grant first laid his eyes on Julia, it was love at first sight. Grant saw her as the perfect woman, not only for her attractive features but also for her lovable personality and charm. And to Julia, Grant was the knight in shining armor from the romance stories she loved to read. Their relationship moved slowly but steadily, and soon the pair was inseparable. Their love was genuine, and they enjoyed each other's company. Julia was his rock and main supporter throughout Grant's life, and they remained loyal and faithful to each other.

Julia's father Colonel Frederick F. Dent never liked Grant, and their relationship only worsened as the years went by because of the old man's pride of being a slave owner. Despite her father's disapproval, Julia accepted and became Grant's fiancée (albeit their engagement was kept a secret) before he left for Camp Salubrity, which was in Louisiana, in 1844. Their marriage would have to wait as Grant was walking right into his first serious experience as a military man: war.

Chapter 4: The Mexican American War

Because President John Tyler wished to annex Texas (which at the time was an Independent Republic) a general fear of the extension of slavery strained the relationship between the North and the South. Grant's regiment was sent close to Texas' borders to ensure that Mexico wouldn't meddle in the proposed annexation, since Mexico considered southern Texas to be part of its territory. Grant understood that the whole purpose of the annexation was to increase the number of slaves in the Union, and he perceived the possible war between the States and Mexico as "a stronger nation going against a weaker nation." But he could not go against his orders as he had pledged his loyalty to the Union.

During his time in Louisiana, he sent numerous letters to Julia, frequently expressing his worries about her father not accepting their relationship. In February 1845, due to Democratic influence, the resolution to annex Texas passed and was signed by the President, marking the start of the conflict between Mexico and the United States. Before hostilities began, Grant managed to go back to White Haven and coerce the Colonel into promising a future marriage with Julia.

Mexico believed that the southern border of Texas was the Nueces River while Polk, the chief of the Democratic Party, believed it was the Rio Grande - which almost doubled in size the new annex of the United States. The Union was looking to provoke Mexico, and have it start the war, that's why military forces were stationed so close to the border. Grant's regiment was called the "Army of Observation." Texas' vote to agree with the annexation only stirred the pot faster. In this time of strain when war seemed inevitable, Grant was still more interested in his future with Julia and of possible advancements in his military career, rather than the conflict that was brewing.

In September of the same year, Grant's regiment (which consisted of thousands of soldiers) was moved to Corpus Christi, a small Mexican village, meant to accommodate only about a hundred people. He felt pity and kindness towards the Mexican people, as he believed that they opposed the Americans simply out of fear. General Zachary Taylor was impressed with Grant's style of commanding his men, as the young officer was not afraid to do the dirty work and show them exactly what he wanted. Grant himself observed Taylor closely, making him an example of a great leader. Thanks to his wit, Grant was soon promoted to full second lieutenant. Since he had a lot of experience with horses, Grant specialized in taming wild horses so they could sell them for profit. He still hoped that a peaceful solution could be found to avoid war. His father, though, understood the situation and tried to no avail to convince his son to resign and take on a math professorship that he arranged. Met with his son's refusal, he arranged for him to be moved to a different regiment, one of the mounted riflemen, through his connections.

Meanwhile, the small village of Corpus Christi was buzzing with all sorts of people, from soldiers to smugglers, murderers, and other bad apples. Out of fear that the military men would be corrupted, two theaters were built. The first play chosen was Othello, and because of his stature, Grant was cast to play the heroine Desdemona, an endeavor that did not work out. Soon Grant's regiment was moved further into the disputed territory, as now, President James K. Polk wanted the crisis to end. Grant later called his relocation an "invasion" that to him was shameful.

General Taylor split his people into four columns that marched relentlessly through the uncivilized, arid lands. When they arrived at their destination, the Rio Grande, they got a full view of Matamoros, a Mexican city that was visibly ready for war, with a small fort and artillery in plain view. The sight of the city made Grant understand that war was inevitable. In April 1846, General Taylor was warned by the Mexican General, Pedro de Ampudia to withdraw his forces but Taylor declined. This response led to the Mexican troops ambushing the American forces, killing and wounding over 16 men. The ambush gave President Polk exactly what he wanted: the Mexicans made the first move. Congress voted and the decision was almost unanimous. Mr. Polk's War started.

On the 8th of May, Taylor's men fought the Mexican forces at Palo Alto - a prairie that offered the American troops a fighting chance against the much larger enemy forces. Due to Taylor's ingenuity as a General, the Mexicans were drastically outmatched. Nonetheless, Grant had his first taste of the horrors of war: the mutilation of a soldier from a cannonball. He never forgot that haunting image. Despite that, he managed to keep calm during his first fight, and he even managed to sleep after the dreadful occurrence. The American forces won with minimal casualties, a victory that did wonders for Taylor's career.

Right after Palo Alto, the Mexicans made their next move. They formed a line behind Resaca de la Palma, a pond with swampy terrain. The topographical conditions rendered the American artillery useless, so the infantry stepped in. As two seniors from Grant's regiment were sent ahead as scouts, Grant had his first experience at leading a company. He showed extraordinary self-control and the ability to make quick decisions. However, he would go on to declare that his presence had nothing to do with the victory at Resaca de la Palma.

On the 18th of May, Zachary's troops entered Matamoros. During the lengthy time the troops were stationed in the Mexican city, Grant renewed his desire to speed up his marriage to Julia. He also spent a lot of time observing the situation in Matamoros. He disagreed with the custom of patronizing people from a city that was already conquered, and he despised the way in which the wealthy people treated the less fortunate ones, especially the slaves.

After they finally left Matamoros, Colonel John Garland appointed Grant to be the assistant quartermaster of his regiment, to Grant's chagrin. He saw the post as a tame administrative duty, one that kept him away from the "action." But this appointment ended up helping Grant understand what war consisted of and really was. The logistics were a crucial part of it, and as assistant quartermaster, he took care of all the essentials except for weapons and ammunition. The experience as a quartermaster would prove useful to Grant's future career. Even though he could "skip" the fight, he chose not to and was always on the battlefield alongside his people. Grant had a strong grasp of strategies and Thomas Hamer (who helped him get to West Point as a favor to his dad) was genuinely surprised by the young soldier's capabilities, foreseeing a great military future for him.

The Battle at Monterrey

Grant's talents shone as Taylor's army marched west. Everything was always ready and prepared for the troops that arrived at each encampment. The army's destination was Monterrey, a city with thick stone walls that was shielded by mountains, and where the Mexicans had a strong position. Besides the topographical advantages, the Mexicans also built a fort outside the city, making it the ultimate structure ready to withstand relentless attacks. The first American attack was an absolute failure, marked by multiple losses. Grant temporarily became regimental adjutant (taking the place of Charles Hoskins who lost his life during the fight) and during the fight, he lost one of his old friends from West Point, Robert Hazlitt, whom he considered to be an intimate and confidential friend.

On September 23, during a fierce fight, Grant volunteered for the dangerous mission of bringing ammunition, as their supplies were dwindling, and the American forces were in a very precarious situation. The young soldier hopped on Nellie, an agile horse, and against all odds, managed to make it back in one piece with the much-needed supplies. The next day General Ampudia asked for an armistice, a requirement that General Taylor answered graciously, showing mercy and kindness when setting the terms of the surrender. There is no doubt that Taylor's attitude inspired the young Grant, as he would also show kindness when he found himself in a similar situation years after the Monterrey fight. Only Polk, who sensed a future rival candidate in Taylor, was not happy with how the Mexican situation was handled.

For Grant, the Mexican American War was a pivotal moment of his life. He learned not only how a war is fought, but also how politics are the driving force behind it. The whole purpose of the Mexican War was to gain capital to satisfy Polk's greed. But, because of the Monterrey victory, Taylor became a threat, as his popularity was rising. So, Polk replaced him with Winfield Scott without even informing the General. It was Scott himself that informed Taylor of the demotion. Scott had big plans for the Army of Invasion. Instead of pushing onwards from Monterrey (which was Taylor's strategy) he wanted to lead the troops further down the coast and take Mexico City, an ambitious move.

Grant took Taylor's betrayal as a hard lesson: talented generals could be replaced at any time if politics demand it. Regarding Winfield Scott, the new General, Grant never grew to admire him as much as he did Taylor, mostly because of his tendency towards being vain and always seeking glory. He did, however, praise Scott's intelligence and courage. As mentioned before, his plan to march straight for Mexico City was a daring one. The troops were to travel from Veracruz, going through miles and miles of dangerous mountain terrain, only to then face the capital of their enemy - a fortified giant with plenty of manpower and resources. A lot of the officers assembled for this difficult task (George Thomas, Joseph Johnston, Robert E. Lee, Joseph Hooker, and many others) would later take part in the Civil War, both as allies of the Union and as enemies.

Scott's Campaign

In February 1847, Grant's regiment was put under the command of General William J. Worth, who boarded them on *North Carolina*, a ship that barely handled the weight of the four hundred soldiers and had been built for transporting cargo. And so began their journey on the Rio Grande. Meanwhile, Zachary Taylor had managed to gain a victory at Buena Vista, which helped maintain his good reputation and ensured a future nomination for the upcoming presidential election (he did go on to become the 12th President of America, succeeding Polk).

On the 9th of March, Grant's regiment made it to the beaches of Veracruz. Scott's strategy was to siege the city, rather than storm in at full force. They pounded the city using big guns and patience until March 29, when the Mexicans finally surrendered. Much like Taylor, Scott offered the Mexican soldiers mercy, paroling them and allowing them to leave with both their dignity and their goods (including horses and weapons).

But Scott wanted to venture forth into the hinterlands, confident in his and his army's ability to take on Mexico City, and thus leaving the army's base behind, rendering them unable to fall back into a safe position if the situation called for it. This plan made it very hard for Grant, a full-blown quartermaster now, to do his job, as the troops had to rely on the land for supplies. The countryside was beautiful but treacherous, and Grant had to attend to the soldier's needs while also being unable to write to Julia or his family (who grew very distressed over Grant's fate, with his mother allegedly going white from worry and his father monitoring Grant's every move with the Army Register).

The troops kept advancing until they reached a standstill: Cerro Gordo, a precarious mountain road across which the Mexican army stood their ground, prepared to fight. Going straight through was not an option. Lee was sent as a scout and managed to find a secondary road that bypassed their enemies, allowing the American forces safe passage and a great opportunity for a flanking maneuver. The Mexicans surrendered yet again, suffering great loses from the surprise attack. Grant, as attentive as ever, took note of the importance of quick thinking on the battlefield, a lesson that he wouldn't soon forget. As much as he "registered" everything that happened during this war, Grant also fought feelings of melancholy and depression because of his tendency to get lost in the beautiful scenery and his capacity to empathize with his enemies' motivations and social problems.

After this victory, Scott's army pushed forward on the National Highway to get to Mexico City, but they were held back waiting for reinforcements, giving Santa Anna (the Mexican General) a chance to improve the capital's defenses. While encamped at Puebla, Grant studied the maps of the field and came up with his own ideas of how the fight should happen, showing early signs of the desire to lead. He considered that the best route was to approach the city from its northern side and was disappointed when Scott chose to go the other way around, on a south path, following Lee's suggestion. Life at Puebla was not easy, and dysentery was rampant. Scott chose to go against the rule books of war once again and march onwards to the city, leaving supply lines behind. The army managed to surpass the outer defenses of the Mexican capital by sheer force, reducing Santa Anna's army considerably. Grant was genuinely impressed by Commander Scott's ability to strategize and how much he was admired by his troops.

On September 2nd there was an attempt to negotiate a peace treaty, coming from Polk's emissary. The terms of the treaty were not very flattering towards the Mexican side. They would not only lose their "part" of Texas, but Mexico City and California were also to be transferred to the United States (albeit, for these two the Mexicans would receive payment). To no one's surprise, Mexico refused.

On the 8th of September, Scott attacked a mill, Molino del Rey, not expecting any enemy forces to be there to protect it. He was mistaken. A whole Mexican division fought against four American companies to protect the mill. Fred Dent, Grant's friend and Julia's brother, was wounded in the fight, but Grant managed to bring him to safety. However, Grant did not use his compassion only on Dent. He tended to a lot of injured soldiers on the battlefield, many of said soldiers owing him their lives. Grant received the honorary grade of brevet first lieutenant for his heroic actions. The fight at Molino del Ray was won by the American forces, but the casualties they suffered were horrendous. Eight hundred American soldiers died on the field.

On September 13th, Americans took Chapultepec, a true fortress that acted as a military school. To fend off the Mexican forces, Grant managed to take over a church and use the steeple as a sniping spot. Grant gave a short description of how he managed to get into the church in his *Memoirs*: "When I knocked for admission a priest came to the door, who, while extremely polite, declined to admit us. With the little Spanish then at my command, I explained to him that he might save property by opening the door . . . and besides, I intended to go in whether he consented or not. He began to see his duty in the same light that I did, and opened the door, though he did not look as if it gave him special pleasure to do so."[15] Thanks to Grant's initiative and the idea of using the church, General Worth managed to take the San Cosme gate (which was the city's link to their water source), dealing a hard blow to the Mexican forces. For his actions, Grant received the honorary rank of brevet captain, allowing him to temporarily perform the duties of a captain.

On September 14th, Winfield Scott, ornate in his military fineries, entered the National Palace of Mexico City. The town was empty apart from prisoners that Santa Anna released before leaving the city. Unfortunately, one of these inmates managed to take a shot at Lieutenant Sidney Smith, Grant's friend, who did not survive the wound. As a grim reminder of the death of a friend, Grant received his permanent rank as a first lieutenant (which also made Grant realize that without this sudden loss, he would have gone back to being only second lieutenant after the war, despite the abilities he had shown multiple times).

Because the members of the Mexican government were nowhere to be found, the troops stayed as an occupation army, until a peace agreement was signed. The occupation

---

[15] Ulysses S. Grant, 1885 from "Memoirs", Volume 1, Chapter 9, page 241

was tumultuous, but ultimately Scott was a generous winner, which made the city a "law-abiding place" according to Grant. The infantry was stationed in Tacubaya, a small city, where Grant attended his duty as a quartermaster while also having plenty of time to indulge in pleasurable activities, such as riding and playing cards. He also showed pity and compassion over the fate of the poor Mexican masses, never displaying the belief that they were his inferiors in any way, shape, or form. He attended a bullfight to learn more about their customs and traditions, but the experience disgusted him (he remained all throughout his life an avid animal lover that hated cruelty). Some experiences that he did enjoy were the ascent on the volcanic mountain Popocatépetl and the exploration of the Valley of Cuernavaca.

Because they were devoid of any engaging occupation, Grant would indulge in drinking (something that he never did when he oversaw something, or when he had responsibilities to take care of). His relationship with alcohol was an episodic one, whenever he was bored or depressed, he would lapse back into it. But this bad habit never ended up negatively affecting his performance in the military or his personal life. Alcohol for Grant was more of a coping mechanism, that nonetheless came with a bad reputation.

The war finally ended with the Treaty of Guadalupe Hidalgo, which was as expected, extremely favorable for the

Americans, with plenty of new territories added to the Union (such as New Mexico, California, Nevada, Utah). However, this conquest raised fears of conflicts between plantation owners and abolishers. So, in the summer of 1846, David Wilmot, a congressman, introduced a measure that made slavery illegal in the territories gained through the Treaty. This act made slavery a central issue in American politics, with the southerners protecting it and the Whig party wanting to abolish it.

While the Mexican American War was over, a state of unrest reigned over the United States. Later, Grant would declare that the Civil War was just an extension of the Mexican War.

Chapter 5: Post War Struggles

In the late summer of 1848, Grant's regiment was transported to Camp Jefferson Davis in Mississippi, and Grant wasted no time in getting a leave of absence to go to St. Louis, where the Dent family spent their summers. Pressed by Grant, Julia agreed to set the date for the wedding to the 22nd of August, making it a very rushed celebration. The wedding was simple, and the social occasion rendered Grant to be extremely shy and awkward. Also, of note is that all the members of his groom party, consisting of James Longstreet, Cadmus M. Wilcox, and Bernard Pratte, would go on to join the Confederate Army, and thus fight against Grant's forces in the Civil War.

During his leave Grant also visited his family in Bethel, and after the wedding, he returned with Julia to introduce her to his side of the family. Although the Grant family never treated Julia inappropriately, they also never liked her, due to their personal feelings regarding the Dent family (with whom they had multiple altercations). In November of the same year, Grant had to report back to duty in Detroit. His leaving led to a final conflict with the Colonel, Julia's father, who wanted to keep his daughter with the Dent family and only allow Grant to visit his wife once or twice a year. But Grant imposed himself and managed to free Julia from her father's influence. So, Julia accompanied her husband to Detroit.

Because of his numerous leaves, Grant lost his quartermaster position and was instead sent to the Madison Barracks, a post close to the Canadian border. Despite initial worries regarding the harsh weather and the scarce winter supplies, Grant and Julia had a great time at the Barracks, making friendships and enjoying their life as a married couple. In March 1849, he was sent back to Detroit and resumed his post as quartermaster (because he appealed the decision to let him go and won). The move to Detroit benefited the couple's life, and his military position during peacetime held few responsibilities. In 1850, Julia gave birth to their first child, which she chose to name Frederick Dent Grant, to honor her father. They both turned out to be kind, loving parents. In the summer of 1851, Grant's regiment was transferred to Sackets Harbor (were the Madison Barracks where) much to the delight of the Grant family.

While in Sackets Harbor, Grant got involved in the organization of the Sons of Temperance, a lodge that advertised the danger of alcohol consumption, mainly as a way of dealing with his own unhealthy use of spirituous beverages. The idle life in Sackets Harbor was not meant to last, as the Fourth Infantry was moved to the West Coast, to keep in check the ruckus created by the Gold Rush. Grant had to make the journey alone as Julia was pregnant with their second child and was physically unable to safely cross Panama. As Julia and their family were the main elements which set Grant's mind at ease, the departure was hard on the young man. The whole trip ended up being harsh on the troops, with bad weather and travel conditions, diseases running rampant and plenty of injuries. A lot of men lost their lives during the passing. He was also in bad relations with the commanding officer, Colonel Benjamin L. E. Bonneville, who tried numerous times to strip him of his quartermaster position. Grant's only joy at the time was finding out that Julia safely gave birth to their second son, Ulysses S. Grant Jr., in the summer of 1852.

Ultimately, after a few stops along the way, the Fourth Infantry arrived at the Columbia Barracks (later renamed Fort Vancouver) in Oregon, in September of the same year. During his stay here, Ulysses would go on to pursue numerous business ventures affected by Gold Rush mania like many others (he also tried a farming venture). Because he put his trust in scoundrels and con artists, and of his lack of experience, none of his ventures brought him any profit, the failures deepening his depression (which led to him falling back into his drinking problem).

Lost Opportunity

In the summer of 1853, the opportunity for a change arose: Captain William W.S. Bliss, who was stationed at Fort Humboldt, California, had died, leaving a vacant post. But Grant was not that happy about the promotion, as Fort Humboldt was supervised by Colonel Robert C. Buchanan, the same man that frequently reprimanded him during his stay at the Jefferson Barracks. Nonetheless, he arrived at the location at the beginning of 1854, after a long and tiring journey. The Fort was a beautiful destination but also extremely secluded, worsening Grant's feelings of solitude and loneliness. He had little to nothing of importance to do and he frequently clashed with Colonel Buchanan. Alcohol again was his only solace. Only a few months later, Grant resigned from the army, allegedly of his own accord and due to his desire to be reunited with his family. Whether he truly left voluntarily, or his alcohol addiction had something to do with it, we may never know. What we can say for sure is that the hasty resignation made Grant the subject of a lot of talk and assumptions, which ate away at his reputation, even in the years to come when he would command the Union Army. Grant avoided telling his father, out of shame or fear of disappointing him. When Jesse Grant found out, he tried to use his influence to get the decision revoked, but Jefferson Davis (who was the United States Secretary of War at the time) considered the situation already settled.

The journey home was once again problematic, as Grant had used his money in an unwise manner, having handed big sums to people of bad character, leaving himself with a meager sum that would never get him back home. It was thanks to the kindness of an old West Point friend of his, Simon Bolivar Buckner, and with the help of his father who sent his brother, Simpson, to get him from New York and settle his debts, that Grant made it back. He stayed with his parents in Covington for a while before reuniting with Julia and his children at White Haven. The meeting was an emotional one, Grant having been anxious about the status of his relationship with Julia after his long departure.

The family moved to Covington (which created a whole new conflict between Julia and the Grants who wanted to control her expenses) to start their life together, as Grant was trying to figure out what he should or could do to support his loved ones. His father offered him a job alongside his brother Simpson, he could supervise their store in Galena. But the offer was only available if Julia and the kids would live with Jesse and Hannah, something that would most likely put an end to Grant and Julia's marriage. Therefore, Grant refused and brought his family to White Haven, where his father-in-law had given Julia sixty acres as a wedding gift. They initially lived in the main estate alongside the Dents, but in 1855, they managed to escape the Colonel's watchful eye by moving into Lewis' (Julia's brother) house, a villa that allowed them some privacy and accommodated their growing family. The family now had a third child, Ellen (named after Julia's mother) who quickly received the nickname Nellie (which stuck with her throughout her life).

The Life of a Farmer

Left with no other options, Grant decided to farm the land in hopes of making a profit. As he got more used to life as a farmer, his desire for independence led him to build a house from scratch, a new house to serve as a family estate, made by his own hand. He called the construction Hardscrabble, a rustic and homey two-storied house, that unfortunately Julia never liked (albeit she did not tell her husband that, so as not to hurt his feelings). The married couple's bond strengthened at Hardscrabble, and they continued to be united and loving parents, despite any troubles that arose in their lives. Multiple accounts from his old friends seem to show that in this part of his life, Grant was free of the influence of alcohol. During this time, he also expressed clear anti-slavery views even though he lived in a state in which slavery was still blooming, and Julia herself had four slaves. For his fieldwork, Grant chose to hire and pay black men and work alongside them, rather than govern them.

At the beginning of 1857, Julia's mother died, and the Colonel suffered so much that he pleaded with his daughter to move her family back into the main house to keep him company. By that time, Grant's farming venture was already failing due to lack of funding, and he barely survived by selling firewood in St. Louis. When the economic depression hit in the same year, Grant lost all hope. He did, however, try another business, a real estate partnership in St. Louis with Harry Boggs (a relative of Julia's father). This partnership did not last long, as Grant was not only inexperienced but also generally bad at everything that the job represented, from collecting rent to organizing documents. The stress and depression this caused affected his health, and he experienced horrible headaches and became sick with "fever and ague." Tuberculosis and malaria also roamed, and Grant lived in fear of getting them or seeing his loved ones suffer from these illnesses. His fears became a reality when Simpson, his brother, got a bad case of tuberculosis.

Because his middle son was in such a bad shape, Jesse Grant beckoned Ulysses to come with his family to Illinois and take over the store in Galena, something that Grant had to accept, now that his business attempts had failed. He took the farming failure so hard that he did not even mention the four-year period in his Memoirs. Also by the time that he left to take on his father's business, he was severely in debt due to him losing money on his businesses and using his money to make a point (for example, he bought a slave from his father-in-law just to go and declare him a free man). It's fair to say that the Grant that left for Galena had little hope of a good future and had his confidence shattered multiple times.

Store Clerk

In the spring of 1860, Grant and his family arrived in Galena. They moved into a simple but comfortable brick house on High Street, and Grant found Galena to be a good place to raise his kids as it offered education opportunities and a good Methodist church. He tended to the leather store, performing multiple duties from serving customers to handling the paperwork. Although he was not as well-built as in his military days, he still possessed an admirable strength that allowed him to transport numerous hides effortlessly. Grant managed the store alongside his younger brother, Orvil, who was more of a rascal than a gentleman. Mary, Orvil's wife, was also a malicious type of woman that had no qualms about bad-mouthing her brother or sister-in-law whenever she got the chance. Grant's life in Galena was a quiet, resigned one.

While Grant was doing his job as a businessman, in the political world, trouble was brewing. The Democrats and Republicans were going head to head for the presidential election. While Grant's family voted for Abraham Lincoln, a former Whig that was the Republican's nominee, Grant himself was conflicted on the matter. He was torn between his anti-slavery views and those of his wife's family. He remarked his support for Stephen A. Douglas, who was a Democrat but was known to be open-minded and reasonable, but when the fight settled on Lincoln versus John C. Breckinridge (a Southern Democrat with very stern pro-slavery views), Grant admitted that Lincoln should win. As Grant was a new citizen of Illinois, he was not allowed to vote, so his support was just declared.

On the 6th of November 1860, Lincoln was elected president with troubling results as in the Deep South his name did not even appear on the ballot. The North backed him ardently while the South was unconvinced of his abilities to be a good leader. For the Southerners, Lincoln was more of a threat, an obstacle that would restrict slavery and thus affect their businesses. Merely a month after Lincoln's election, on December 20th, delegates in South Carolina voted to leave the Union, a decision that laid the ground for the bloodiest war that America would ever face: The Civil War.

Grant rapidly became a militant supporter of unity. In his mind, leaving the Union was an act of treason, and he rallied the people in heated conversation regarding whether the North would win a future civil war against the South. In January of the next year, other southern states, such as Florida, Alabama, Georgia, and Louisiana, departed from the Union. The cherry on top came in February, when delegates of the southern states gathered in Montgomery and consecrated the Confederate States of America, with

Jefferson Davis acting as president. They adopted the American Constitution but made it very clear that they protected slavery and the rights of the people. Grant was infuriated by this turn of events, while President Lincoln still held on to the hope that the "unionist" spirit would prevail, even in the south. Despite Lincoln's beliefs, the south would not yield. War became the single way of resolving this dispute.

Chapter 6: The Civil War

On April 12th, 1861, the Confederate Army led by Pierre Gustave Toutant Beauregard made the first move, attacking and taking over Fort Sumter. Most southern officers believed their loyalty to their states was in a higher place than that for a government that they were unhappy with, so they joined the Confederate Army. The loss suffered by the Union Army was so great that it gave off the impression of dissolving, and they remained heavily understaffed. At this point, both sides still believed that the war could be won with a single, well-placed move and without too much bloodshed, and part of that was because both sides truly believed that their "way" was the correct one and that they were doing the right thing.

Lincoln would emerge as a strong-willed, focused leader, despite southerners painting him as a tyrant. As a result of the formation of the Confederate States, only four southern states remained in the Union: Maryland, Kentucky, Missouri, and Delaware, a dreary situation. Grant's loyalty to his country awakened in him the will to fight and make a difference. When Lincoln called for volunteers, Galena answered by deciding to form two military companies. The first company was named Jo Daviess Guards, and Grant was chosen as chairman due to his experience in the Mexican War. He lectured the recruits on what being in the military meant and he answered their questions. However, he refused to act as their Captain, hoping for a higher post that would allow him to make a difference in the fight that was coming. He still trained the people and helped the appointed Captain, Augustus Chatelain, get a hold on his function. He also traveled to the nearby towns in hope of rallying more people to join their cause.

Determined to Be Part of the War

Led by his patriotism, Grant decided to leave the family business in Orvil's hands and join the military. Grant left Galena on April 25th, going in the same direction as the Jo Daviess Guards (Springfield) but not as one of them. He went alongside them as he was promised a meeting with Governor Richard Yates that could give him a regiment to command, as his ambitions were not that high. But his reputation and appearance (he was not young anymore and the mental toil he went through left marks on his bearing and poise) did not do him a favor. Close to going back home after his pleas were not answered, Grant finally got a commission from Yates: he was to join the adjutant general's staff. This turned out to be an administrative position, in which he was tasked with filing reports and requisitioning food supplies - tasks he was familiar with from his quartermaster days.

Through the intervention of his old friend, Captain John Pope, Yates let Grant act as temporary commandant for four days, a time that Grant used disciplining the new soldiers and showcasing his true potential. Yates took note and realized that Grant had the ability to do way more than what he had initially believed, so he let him supervise the mustering of ten new regiments. This assignment allowed him to visit his father-in-law, as he wished to have Julia and the kids stay with him. But when he arrived in White Haven, what he ended up meeting was a devout Confederate that wanted nothing to do with the Union or their ideals. It's no secret that Grant was not saddened by his father-in-law's fate: in the years to come most of his slaves fled, damaging his business. Grant also rejoiced at the fact that St. Louis was one of the first cities to be captured by the Union forces (led by Francis P. Blair Jr. and Captain Nathaniel Lyon), thus saving an impressive arsenal from the hands of their enemies. He managed his assignment remarkably well and he was saddened when he had to go back to Springfield, to his monotonous desk job (Yates did not wish to give him command over anything because he believed Grant to be a Democrat).

In the late spring of 1861, the Confederate States chose Richmond as their capital city, making it clear that the bulk of the war was to be fought on Virginian land, and placing Washington in a very precarious position. During this time Grant tried numerous ways to get himself into action. He wrote a letter to Washington, he tried asking for favors from old friends that were in high positions, but nothing seemed to work, and Grant remained dejected. When all hopes of being actively involved in the war almost left Grant, on June 16th, he received a letter from Yates appointing him colonel of the 7th Congressional District Regiment (shortly renamed Twenty-First Illinois). He was to replace Colonel Simon S. Goode (who did not manage to discipline his troops and engaged in excessive drinking). This news radically changed Grant's life.

Colonel Grant

Due to his fair and tough nature, Grant quickly gained the respect of the troops, who initially did not think much of him. Now in a leadership position, Grant drastically changed, regaining not only his energy but also his confidence. While disciplining the unruly soldiers, he also made time to go through William J. Hardee's manual of tactics and reports to further study the art of war. In need of money to buy a uniform suited for his military position and a horse, he had to borrow money from the Galena bank (after his family refused to aid him). When it was decided that Grant's men were to switch from short-term service to three-years of federal service, none of them wavered as they believed their commander to be the very best.

The first assignment of the Twenty-First Illinois was to travel to Quincy, a journey that Grant chose to make on foot rather than by train. He also took Frederick, his oldest son, along to experience military life. Once they got to Quincy, Grant's men received the mission to save an Illinois regiment that was under rebel attack in Palmyra. Grant sent his son home and prepared his men for the fight, which ultimately never happened as the rebels fled, freeing the Illinois people. The next mission of the Twenty-First was to arrest a small Confederate army located in Northern Missouri and led by General Thomas A. Harris. Yet again, the fight was not to be, and Grant would later declare in his Memoirs that General Harris was afraid of a confrontation, as much as Grant was. These two instances told Grant about the importance of understanding the enemy's psyche and how much it mattered to project yourself in their mind as an unbeatable force.

On July 22nd, the first major confrontation between the Union and the Confederate forces (later known as the battle of Bull Run) took place in Manassas, Virginia. The Union Army was led by General Irvin McDowell, who replaced the old Winfield Scott, but who also had little to no experience commanding troops in the field. His inexperience showed, and the Union forces were forced to flee back to the capital, defeated. President Lincoln was shocked with the result of the battle at Bull Run and quickly signed two bills to enlist new volunteers, as he understood that the conflict was becoming a full-blown war that required all their resources.

Brigadier General

Grant now had power over three infantry regiments and a section of artillery (assigned to him by Pope), and he did his best to settle the troublesome situation in Missouri, a place full of rampant Confederates, while also making sure that his men did not abuse or harass the common people. In August, Grant was promoted to brigadier general thanks to Elihu B. Washbourne's influence in the Lincoln cabinet. Funny enough, Grant found out through the newspaper *Daily Missouri Democrat* about his new assignment. Grant was amazed at how his life had turned from a store clerk to a person that had four regiments under his command, and all that without him ever leading his troops in a fight. The new brigadier general took under his command the military district of Ironton, which was being threatened by Confederate forces. Meanwhile, on August 10th, the Union forces were defeated again at the Battle of Wilson's Creek, where General Nathaniel Lyon lost his life. The news of another defeat made Grant wonder about the fate of the war, and marvel at how far the rebels were prepared to go.

Grant's time as a commanding force in Ironton was short, as he was replaced by Brigadier General Benjamin M. Prentiss without even being given notice about the replacement. He was then assigned to take command in Jefferson City, a town that was heavily harassed by Confederate forces led by

General Sterling Price. The situation in Jefferson City was dreary, to say the least, and Grant was more than happy when he was called to St. Louis to receive special instructions while Colonel Jefferson C. Davis came to replace him. At St. Louis, thanks to Major Justus McKinstry who spoke favorably of him, Grant was given command over the District of Southern Missouri, and he was ordered to relocate to Cape Girardeau, where he would fight against the Confederate state Tennessee and try to take hold of the neutral state Kentucky.

He decided to make Cairo his headquarters, as it gave him great opportunities for massive operations near water that could bring his troops into the deep south. But, because of its closeness to the Ohio River, Cairo was flooded and suffered from mosquitos and rat infestations, making it a breeding ground for malaria and dysentery. Grant had to act as a brigadier general, quartermaster, and commissary, putting a lot of stress on the freshly appointed man. Because he was bad at handling paperwork and documents, he appointed John Rawlins, a young lawyer, to be his assistant adjutant general, making Rawlins Grant's chief of staff. Rawlins also took on his own accord the mission to ensure that Grant, and all the military men that served under him, would not touch a drop of alcohol until the war ended. Because of his good character, Rawlins became Grant's closest friend and he would often take the lawyer's opinion into consideration whenever making important decisions.

President Lincoln was very apprehensive about Kentucky's position and he made it very clear to his military forces that they must respect the laws of the state and not impose an adhering to the Union. The Confederate forces were not that wise, and they attempted to invade Kentucky, ultimately making the undecided state pledge its allegiance to the Union.

On the 5th of September, Grant found through a Union spy that the Confederate forces wanted to move to Paducah, a town that was close to Cairo and a strategic point that would secure the position of the Confederate Army. Grant decided to act fast and assigned two regiments and one artillery to go with him and seize the city. They managed to arrive before the Confederate forces, taking Paducah (a city that was already ornamented with Confederate flags, waiting to succumb to its fate) peacefully by convincing the people of his good intentions. To reassure the people that he indeed meant them no harm, he made the "Proclamation to the citizens of Paducah:"

"I have come among you, not as an enemy, but as your friend and fellow-citizen, not to injure or annoy you, but to respect the rights, and to defend and enforce the rights of all loyal citizens. An enemy, in rebellion against our common government, has taken possession of, and planted its guns upon the soil of Kentucky and fired upon our flag... He is moving upon your city. I am here to defend you against this enemy and to assert and maintain the authority and sovereignty of your Government and mine. I have nothing to do with opinions. I shall deal only with armed rebellion and its aiders and abettors. [...] The strong arm of the Government is here to protect its friends, and to punish only its enemies." [16]

Belmont Victory

Lincoln himself was impressed by Grant's talent for managing delicate political situations. After this political victory, Grant yearned for action and wished to move to Columbus but was momentarily held in place by his responsibilities in Cairo. While he waited for the order to go, he found out that Simpson, his brother, has succumbed to his illness and died on September 13th. Since he could not attend the funeral, his father gave him Simpson's watch as a keepsake, which he promised to forever hold on to, in his brother's memory.

By late autumn, he sent some of his men to Missouri to aid the Union forces that fought to protect the state. At the beginning of winter, he chose five of his regiments and marched alongside them to Columbus after hearing that the Confederate forces there planned to move some of their

---

[16] Excerpt from General Grant's "Proclamations to the citizens of Paducah", Kentucky, 1861

troops to Belmont. The purpose of the assignment was to simply make a "demonstration" for the Confederates, but that plan fell flat and Grant's men were shortly involved in a battle for Belmont, which they surprisingly won. The victory was short-lived as reinforcements from Columbus soon arrived, forcing Grant's men to flee. On a last-minute notice, the Union forces also received reinforcements, securing Belmont as a Union city. Although they suffered great casualties, this mission allowed Grant to show his men that Confederate soldiers did not possess any special powers or strengths, helping them gain confidence in their own forces and get a taste of real action. Also, by cleaning Belmont of rebels, Grant's forces managed to ensure the safety of Missouri, a feat so great even the *New York Times* praised the "brilliant movement" of General Grant and his troops.

While he was idle from battle, Grant made a great effort to fight corruption and discover disloyal people that chose to collaborate with the rebels. Because Grant was now an influential individual, many people, including his father, tried to use him to get business opportunities for acquaintances, but Grant stood strong and refused all requests. His honest and incorruptible character won him many enemies. These enemies sought to see Grant depleted of his military rank and in order to do that they preyed on Grant's past problem: alcohol consumption. Lincoln himself received a letter of concern regarding Grant's sobriety, about which he asked

Washbourne for clarification. The one that answered these claims and cleared Grant's honor was Rawlins, his good friend and "sobriety watchdog." His response was a touch over-dramatic (by stating each and every instance where Grant drank, as part of social situation and never abusing the beverages) but nonetheless honest, settling the matter once and for all.

Fort Henry and Fort Donelson

Fed up with the fact that his troops only had a defensive and sometimes diversionary role, in January 1862, Grant went to see General Henry Wager Halleck to ask for permission to conquer Fort Henry (that would offer Union forces a river pathway) and Donelson (that would ensure that Nashville would fall). Although Halleck originally refused, on the 30th of January, he endorsed the campaign, prompting Grant to start with Fort Henry. Grant proceeded eagerly but in a secretive manner (which was one of Grant's characteristics), only letting his most trustworthy people know about the objective of their mission. On February 2nd, he alongside fifteen thousand of his men left Cairo and started the Fort Henry campaign.

By the 4th of February, an entire division landed close to Fort Henry, while the transporter was to go back and bring on the rest of his troops, so large was his personal army. Grant wanted his people to stay in an area that shielded them from enemy fire while still offering easy and fast access to Fort Henry. Unfortunately for the Confederate forces, Fort Henry was not the best place to use as a "fortified citadel" as its topographical position made it vulnerable to attacks and dangerous for the people within (as it was close to the Tennessee River which flooded frequently). The fort also had old military equipment, and the majority of it was not safe to use. Grant's plan was to attack them from their vantage point while General Smith made sure to neutralize the nearby fort that could send reinforcements, Fort Heiman, and General McClernand blocked the escape route to Fort Donelson, trapping the Confederate forces.

On February 6th, Grant started the attack. Faced with a strong approach, both on land and on water (the naval force was, in this case, the asset that secured the victory of the Union forces), Fort Henry was left with no choice but to surrender. The North was ecstatic with the news of the victory. Finally, the Union flag was firmly plunged in Tennessee soil. On the other side of the barricade, Confederate forces wept at the loss of such a strategic position, and they made the erroneous decision to send reinforcements to Fort Donelson instead of calling back their troops. On February 10th, Grant was already devising the plan for Fort Donelson, asking his council of war whether to attack or wait for new forces. The final decision was to commence towards Fort Donelson without further delay. While Grant was already marching towards another victory, Halleck was plotting from the distance to replace Grant, seeing him as a threat and having little to no trust in his ability to lead.

Unlike Fort Henry, Fort Donelson had the topographical advantage and a lot of work was put into fortifying it. There were trenches, heavy artillery, and plenty of manpower to defend it. Grant wasted no time in getting familiar with the terrain and concocting the simplest yet most efficient way to conquer the Fort. And indeed, his final plan was very straight to the point: the infantry was to take care of the Confederates from within, while his naval forces (represented by gunboats, a new advanced technology of naval warfare by that time) bombarded Fort Donelson at close range. While Fort Henry was won with the usage of the naval fleet alone, this time Grant's naval power abandoned the fight earlier on, leaving the hardship of conquering Fort Donelson on the infantry. Even so, the Union forces were slowly eating away at the Confederates, forcing them to resort to a suicidal plan: launching a surprise attack on Grant's troops, hoping they could create a path towards safety.

Shocked with the intensity of the Confederate attack, the Union forces temporarily retreated. Managing to keep his cool in this dreary situation, Grant quickly realized that the goal of the enemy was to create an escape route, not to stand and fight. He made use of his battered naval force to aid and motivate his infantry with long-range attacks. Grant's movements and push toward gaining back the lost terrain made the Confederate forces vulnerable. The enemy was now convinced that an escape to Nashville was too much of a risk. When Grant realized that he had them where he wanted, he doubled the attack. Out of the three Confederate generals that protected Fort Donelson, two fled (Floyd and Pillow) leaving their men behind.

On the 16th of February, Buckner, the remaining leader, sent his letter of surrender to General Smith, who promptly delivered the good news to Grant. He was now the only Union General to capture at least thirteen thousand men, but he did not wallow in his glory. He showed compassion to the defeated soldiers, treating them well by feeding them, allowing them to keep their weapons, and not publicly shaming them in a "victory parade." He also made sure that the wounded were taken care of, no matter what side of the barrier they were from, and he prevented the "sport" of trophy hunting from the battlefield as he believed it was barbaric and devoid of dignity. The battle at Fort Donelson also signaled the start of the era in which fugitive slaves were accepted as Union soldiers, safe from their former masters.

The campaign of Fort Henry and Fort Donelson marked the first Union victory in the Civil War, breaking the chain of defeats and giving the people of the North hope once again.

He was nicknamed "Unconditional Surrender" Grant (he required the confederate forces at Force Donelson to surrender unconditionally, giving them no benefits whatsoever), which went nicely with his initials. His reputation quickly skyrocketed, with both newspapers and civilians buzzing about the esteemed General and his accomplishments. In light of his recent endeavors (and with Halleck's approval), President Lincoln nominated Grant as Major General of Volunteers, placing him above any other northern General except Halleck. With this rank, Grant's confidence would no longer falter in the face of his father or father-in-law. He had proven what he was capable of, and now the world had all eyes and ears on him.

A Man of Action

Thanks to Grant's efforts, the North now had Kentucky, portions of Mississippi, and western and central Tennessee, a feat that also weakened Alabama's ties to the "Deep South." Grant's strategy was to quickly follow up victories in order to not give the enemy time to regroup their forces. We can say that Grant was a man of action, while most of the generals or people in command preferred to stay back and wait for the enemy to make a move, not willing to risk their positions. With new forces under his command, Grant marched to Clarksville, winning more territory back for the Union. Now that he had Cumberland in the palm of his hand, the next step in Grant's plan was Nashville, a capital city of the Confederation. When they reached Nashville on February 27th, they found an empty town (except for the now-liberated slaves). Grant realized that the enemy was fleeing in fear, while some of his generals believed that the Confederates were plotting to come back and try to take the city.

While Grant was planning his next move, Halleck tried to make use of his success to gain more power in Washington. Even if Halleck wished to bask in Grant's glory, he also wanted to undermine him. Halleck tried his best to denigrate him and make him seem like a negligent general that was receiving glory for other people's merits. He, alongside McClellan, accused Grant of misconduct and other disciplinary issues, without even giving him the chance to defend himself. Despite being innocent, Halleck made him give up the command to Major General Smith and ordered him to go back to Fort Henry to await new orders. However, by mid-March, the White House was made aware of the situation and presented with proof against Halleck's claims. Lincoln pressed Halleck to give Grant back the command of the troops, which he did on the 17th of March.

The focus of the Union Army was now to conquer Corinth, which was near the Tennessee border. While on road to Corinth, on April 6th Grant repelled a surprise Confederate attack at Shiloh Church. The situation, however, turned out to be highly controversial, because some younger generals refused to admit that the attack was indeed a surprise. So there were newspapers describing a grim situation in which Union soldiers were killed with bayonets in their sleep, while other accounts spoke of men abandoning their positions and running for safety, all stories painting the image of an inexperienced, untrained military force. Whatever actually happened at Shiloh, one thing cannot be denied: it was a massacre. The losses were so horrendous that Grant's reputation as a leader was damaged (albeit it was only thanks to Grant's abilities as a leader that the Confederate forces were defeated), and on April 11th, Halleck ended up taking control over the army in Grant's place. Even with all the slander and doubts regarding Grant's leadership, Lincoln never really lost faith in him, keeping Grant in high regard and "saving" him for future battles.

Grant was dejected about the situation. On top of being dismissed, he also lost his trustworthy friend, General Smith, whom he knew from his West Point days, and showed great military talent. When Halleck arrived to take on the command, he wasted no time in admonishing Grant for his sloppy leadership. In reality, Halleck had little to no experience on the battlefield and was more suited to the bureaucratic life. It's fair to say that when he was called back to Washington in July of the same year, Halleck was overjoyed with being as far from the battlefield as possible, and with being promoted to being Lincoln's military advisor and general in chief. Grant was given back the command, and his first thought was to make the freshly conquered Memphis his headquarters. But he was forced to go back to Corinth to reassemble the troops that Halleck had left, and made it his headquarters instead of Memphis.

The Vicksburg Campaign

Meanwhile, the Virginia campaign had failed, and despite the unfortunate situation, Grant felt relieved the attention as not on him anymore. Instead, Robert E. Lee was rising to fame as an admired Confederate General, beating the Union forces in the Second Battle of Manassas. Halleck's career suffered from the loss at Manannan, and he never truly recovered. While in Corinth, Grant managed some defensive missions but also sought to improve his military position by abiding by Lincoln's policies and lobbying for more troops and supplies. By the end of the year, he began advancing with his troops to Vicksburg, a city that represented the last major Confederate stronghold on the Mississippi River.

Being stubborn and determined, Grant marched directly to Vicksburg, aware of the imminent danger that awaited him. However, it was his signature style to opt for an aggressive approach, rather than a defensive one. Now, more than ever, when the Virginia loss still was fresh in people's minds and when politics were at wars again regarding the slave problem (with Democrats naming Republicans "Nigger Worshipers"), there was a need for a new victory to raise morale and calm spirits.

While the Vicksburg campaign was being fought, Grant had to deal with the rising problem of cotton trading, which proved tricky to control and represented a real danger of intelligence being sold to Confederate forces. He went hard on the traders, especially the Jewish ones, because his own father tried to vouch for two Jewish brothers in order to get their trading permit. Lincoln himself had to get involved in the situation to calm the offended Jewish community.

Because of political schemes, McClernand was placed alongside Grant as commander in the Vicksburg campaign. However, Grant knew how to manipulate the situation to his own advantage, and soon enough, he continued his mission with the troops that were under his command, starting a "race" with the other commander. Due to the telegraph wires being damaged, Grant lost contact with his naval force led by Sherman and had no means of alerting his general of the troubles he encountered along the way (he had to retreat due to destruction at Holly Springs). So on December 29th, Sherman attacked alone, an operation that caused massive casualties to the Union Army.

In January 1863, Lincoln signed the Emancipation Proclamation, adding abolition to the focus of the Civil War.

By that time, Grant fully supported the liberation of slaves and even Julia relented and freed the four slaves that she had since her childhood. This also meant that black people now had a reason to rise against their masters and join the Union Army.

Vicksburg was a real challenge for Grant, as it was a "strongly garrisoned" city with fortifications that were almost impenetrable. But he was not the man to feel intimidated by such situations. He chose to put Vicksburg under siege, approaching it from the east. He used plenty of ingenious contraptions: digging canals to allow gunboats to approach the city, demolishing a levee that protected the northern side of Vicksburg, creating a water passage that would allow his gunboats to bypass enemy fire, attacking during the night, and other such marvelous ideas. Finally, on July 4th, 1863, the city, led by General Pemberton, surrendered (Grant asked again for an unconditional surrender). Grant did not doubt even for a second that the town would submit, although the Vicksburg campaign was a tumultuous one, mixed with multiple other affairs and new rumors of Grant's inappropriate behavior (related to his drinking problem).

Only a few days after Grant's victory, Port Huston also fell to the Union Army forces, led by Nathaniel Banks. The Confederacy suffered massively from the loses, being effectively cut in half, while the Union regained its thoroughfare for commerce (Mississippi). Many rebels saw the fall of Vicksburg as the start of the end of the Confederacy, and they were not entirely wrong. Vicksburg was for Grant the moment in which his full capabilities were put on the table for the world to see, and Lincoln's respect for this honest and efficient general grew stronger. The President was so elated with the victory that he even wrote a personal letter to Grant, acknowledging his talent as a military strategist. Now no one could doubt Grant and slander his name. On July 7th, Grant was named major general of the regular army, a post that practically put his military career in his own hands.

A Northern Victory

Coincidental with the Vicksburg victory was Lee's defeat at Gettysburg, signaling that the war now leaned towards the Union side. But while the war situation was beginning to look better for the northerners, they still had internal conflicts that were becoming more heated with every day that passed. There were riots in New York, opposing the black emancipation (which also led to the death of many black citizens) and protesting a government that allowed for wealthier people to escape the draft by paying a sum of money or sending someone else in their stead. These riots once again showed the importance of black recruitment, which Grant fully supported (not only due to his own views, but also because now he directly corresponded with the President, who's views deeply influenced Grant's). During these times of idleness, he managed to visit Julia and spend some family time together, while also shyly receiving the admiration of others. Due to a horse-riding accident, he was bed-ridden for a couple of months, during which he was nursed back to health by his family. Fortunately, there were no battles that required his presence during this time of convalescence.

Lincoln's happiness was not a long-lasting one, as on September 20th, the Union forces lost the Battle of Chattanooga, which led to massive numbers of soldiers and ammunition being captured. In October of the same year, Grant was called to Nashville to supervise the transfer of troops from the west. However, his plans changed when he was called to Louisville for a meeting with a War Department Official, Staton. He transmitted direct orders from Lincoln: to lead the new military division of Mississippi and to replace Rosencrans (the general behind the loss at Chattanooga) with George Thomas. Both Lincoln and Staton were sick of their bad luck with appointing generals. Things needed to change. After another victory that solidified the Union Army's position in the south once again (the Battle of Missionary Ridge, that took back Chattanooga), it didn't take long for Grant to be appointed lieutenant general (in March 1864) making him the commander of all U.S. armies (he received the new rank at Washington, during a meeting with the President).

Lincoln wasted no time, just after Grant received his new military assignment, he wanted to know his strategy for fighting the war. Grant gladly obliged. His plan was to pin down the Confederate forces led by Lee close to Richmond (their capital in Virginia) while General Sherman, his loyal and trustworthy man, was to lead the Union troops through Georgia and defeat Johnson, having a two fronted battle. As simple as it sounded, Grant's plan turned out to be extremely efficient. Only a few months after becoming lieutenant general, Grant's forces already had Lee stuck in Petersburg. Georgia was rampant with Union troops and General Sheridan neutralized the Virginia supply line of the Confederate forces. By late June, Grant wanted the entire army to focus on the two Confederate generals, Lee and Sherman, while also making sure that Washington was being protected.

After long months of constant fighting, on April 2nd, 1865, Lee had to give up on his Petersburg defense line, ultimately surrendering a few days later (April 9th) at the Appomattox Court House. The terms of the surrender were discussed in private by Grant and Lee, and once again, Grant showed great compassion for his fallen enemy, going against his nickname "Unconditional Surrender" Grant. He chose to parole the Confederate soldiers, allowing the men to return home without any punishment or prosecution (they had to surrender their weapons, but they could keep their horses and sidearms). He also allowed Lee to keep his sword and abstained from any practice that would humiliate the General and his men. Grant provided food for the hungry soldiers that fought valiantly for the cause in which they believed.

This surrender marked the end of the Civil War. It's not a stretch to say that Grant's versatility, intelligence, ability to learn from mistakes, and openness to technological innovations, were the tools that led to the Union Victory.

Chapter 7: General of the U.S Army and Secretary of War

Celebrations were underway at Washington, and Lincoln wanted Grant to be present. The President was also very eager to reinstate peace amongst the states even as he made the decision not to recognize the rebel governments that were in place. However, Reconstruction was to be the goal of future presidents, as Abraham Lincoln was mortally shot on the 14th of April, at the Ford Theatre (as a side note, Grant and his wife were invited to accompany the Lincolns, but they refused because they wished to be reunited with their family), by John Wilkes Booth (a Confederate sympathizer). On April 15th, the news of Lincoln's death shook the entire north. The Grant family took the news to heart, as, during the years of the Civil War, Grant developed a deep and sincere love and admiration for the gentle President, and he saw Lincoln as a dear friend.

The death of Lincoln was not only a tragedy but also a strain on the newly found peace. While Lincoln understood the importance of mercy and kindness, Andrew Johnson (who was in line to succeed him) was rather hostile toward rebels. Grant returned to Washington as quickly as he could because his services were needed. While on the road, Grant could not help but wonder whether his presence at the Theatre would have made a difference. Meanwhile, Staton lost no time in investigating the conspiracy and keeping the country in order, as the assassin was being pursued. The Grant family was moved to Georgetown, where officers and privates could be on guard in case other plots were in place. The ruckus created by the awful event was so great that Grant even feared a resuming of the Civil War, but the uproar calmed down when Booth was found and shot.

It wasn't until Andrew Johnson took the reins of the country that people started to understand what a remarkable man Lincoln was. Johnson was an ambitious man and a skilled debater, but he was not blessed with a likable character. He viewed slavery as beneficial and heavily discriminated against black men (which made southern plantation owners support him). Despite his racist views, Grant initially supported Johnson, being trustful of his abilities to bring the country back together. Of course, Grant's positive opinion of Jackson would drastically change when the President switched from being overly harsh to rebels to being overly accommodating to their needs.

Ordered by Johnson to tour the South and assess the situation, Grant discovered a land that lived in misery, where fear still lingered (except for a few isolated places where the rebels still lingered, but they were far too few to pose a real threat to the installed peace). Touched by the suffering of the people he advised Jackson to be lenient with his reconstruction policies.

Grant had a hard time adapting to life in Washington, but he had plenty of matters to attend to that made living outside Washington a foolish dream. Although he was the Hero of the Civil War, Grant did not drown in his fame. He dressed plainly and expected no special treatment from those who met him. Thanks to some kind donors, the Grant family got a house of their own in Georgetown, where Grant was not spared the presence of his still very determined, Confederate supporter, father-in-law.

A Rocky Bond

Grant's relationship with Johnson started off on amicable terms, as the new president seemed to take compassion on the poor southern whites and on the slaves' situation while justly punishing the rich. But he was easily swayed by the influential, Democratic slave owners, who soon enough had Johnson on a leash. He became the first American President to display open racist views, being an ardent supporter of white supremacist ideals. In May, Johnson's Reconstruction program was revealed: southerners who agreed to take an oath of allegiance would have their citizenship restored, and he outlined the steps that each state was to take in order to be taken back into the Union. His reconstruction was merely for show, as the south would just go back to its initial situation, where rich plantation owners held the power.

The first massive "showdown" that Grant and Johnson had was over the terms of Lee's surrender. Johnson wanted the Confederate officers prosecuted for treason, while Grant wished to keep his word and parole the soldiers. When Grant threatened to resign, Johnson finally gave in, aware of how much Grant's resignation would affect his presidential administration. Another preoccupation that Grant had was the spiky situation in Mexico. which was seemingly occupied by imperial French forces led by Maximilian. He opted for a hands-on, forceful approach while the Secretary of State, Seward, believed that if the French were left alone, they would eventually retreat from Mexico.

Around the time President Johnson refused to give black people the right to vote when confronted with five of their leaders (including Frederick Douglass), the strain in his and Grant's relationship was starting to show, but they kept up the appearance of a partnership. By the time Grant's oldest son was admitted to West Point, Radical Republicans that no longer supported the President introduced a bill that gave the right to citizenship to anyone born in the United States, no matter their race. The bill was short-lived as Johnson vetoed it, on the count that it was trespassing on states' rights. Johnson sought Grant's support for this decision, even if the general made no secret of his abolitionist views. The Radical Republicans wasted no time in also trying to get Grant on their side.

To swoon Grant, on July 25th, Johnson created the new rank of "General of the Army of the United States," which he bestowed upon Grant, giving him the "full" general title. Grant was very aware of the situation he was in, and of the Republicans' plan to have him as a presidential nominee, but he made no claims regarding a future presidential candidacy. After the riot in New Orleans, Grant's distaste for Johnson's ideals only deepened, yet he was frequently manipulated by the President into taking part in social events meant to show the world that Grant fully supported his President. One example of such, is when Johnson dragged Grant along for his "swing around the circle" which was a speaking tour of northern states in which the President wanted to boast his pro-southern policies. The tour ended up being a real disaster that dwindled the ranks of Johnson supporters and triggered a rise in those that supported Grant.

Johnson did his best to encourage southern states to deny the Fourteenth Amendment while Grant believed it was necessary for them to abide by it before they were let back into the Union. Grant also complained about the mistreatment of black people, a complaint that was quickly put away by Democrats. Meanwhile, the Republicans were slowly but surely gathering strength in their movement that sought to impeach the President. Congress (represented by Republicans) and the President were engaged in a quiet show of power that many officials feared would become public. In order to protect the black people from Texas, Grant urged Stanton to place the state under federal law, in January 1867.

As Republicans gained more power, they managed to get the Reconstruction bill to pass, which invested former slaves with full civil rights, along with the Tenure of Office Act (which ensured that no cabinet member could be dismissed without the Senate's approval). However, Johnson soon went against the Tenure Act, dismissing Station from his function as Secretary of War and appointing a reluctant Grant as interim in August of the same year. But when Congress insisted on reinstating Staton, Grant resigned (in January of 1868), infuriating the President, who took it as a personal betrayal. Johnson's anger ruined all that was left of his relationship with Grant, unwillingly pushing him towards the Republicans that wished to have him go against the Democrat Horatio Seymour in the elections that were to come.

Sure enough, thanks to the Republican backing and to the black voters that favored him, Grant won the 1868 election by a narrow margin, becoming the 18th president of the United States. The last line in his letter of acceptance, "Let us have peace" became a motto for his presidential administration.

The phrase would later be used as an epitaph on Grant's Tomb.

Chapter 8: Presidency

On March 5th, his first day in office, Grant efficiently formed his cabinet, which consisted of people that he considered trustworthy. The Cabinet of President Ulysses S. Grant had Elihu Washbourne as head of State, George Boutwell managing the Treasury, John Rawlins (later changed to Hamilton Fish) as War Secretary, Adolph Borie to supervise the Navy, Ebenezer Hoar acting as Attorney General, and Jacob Cox takng care of Interior. In short, it had intelligent men that believed in equality and civil rights, views that matched Grant's own. However, the Senate looked down on the inexperienced man and resented him for forming a Cabinet on his own without consulting anyone.

Used to military thinking, Grant was quick to appoint people and just as quick to dismiss them, a strategy that could be life-changing during a war but in the political sphere, all it did was ruffle the feathers of sensible politicians. He was a headstrong man that tended to treat his Cabinet as if they were his war generals, with the only difference being that Grant was severely inexperienced in the finery of politics, which is why he gave leeway to his "political general." His leeway often came out as naivety, and indeed Grant let himself be swooned by dreams of peace and quiet, and perhaps gave the wrong type of men too much power. Some good examples of men with disputable characters are Adam Badeau, an opportunist that gained several diplomatic posts and Orville Babcock, who ultimately became a layman between Grant and other people, his loose morals influencing Grant's administration.

Showing his honest nature, Grant initially abstained from offering favors to members of his family, whether they were Grants or Dents. However, he allowed his father-in-law, Colonel Dent, to live at the White House with his family, showing great compassion for the man who never gave up on his Confederate views (although he was smart enough to keep them to himself). Whether it was because of Julia's influence or other reasons, Grant ended up offering some posts, mostly small ones, such as bank examiners, collectors, and marshals. On a more positive note, Grant also named a great number of minorities (Jews, natives, and blacks) in federal positions. The American Government was changing greatly after the Civil War, having to expand at such a rate that Grant could barely keep up. New business and industrial advances required governmental supervision. A national currency and a tax system had to be put in place. It seemed like the entire country was booming with the need to produce money (as it offered plenty of opportunities for doing so), a period which was called the Gilded Age.

On the 18th of March, Grant signed his first law, a conservative decision that pledged to redeem in gold the currency issued during the Civil War. For that, he appointed the first Civil Service Commission. Unfortunately, he quickly abandoned his support for the group when faced with the congress' refusal to accept it. Grant was again faced with the congress' denial when he tried to annex the Dominican Republic (which he was convinced held strategic importance, as it offered the opportunity to create a canal that could connect the Atlantic and Pacific Oceans). But, on a sunnier side, his involvement ensured the settlement of the Alabama claims against the British Government (the British forces initially declared their neutrality regarding the American Civil War, but they went against their initial claim and ended up helping the Confederate navy, making them liable for any destruction caused by rebel ships that the British provided). Britain ended up offering $15,500,000 in gold.

During his first term, Grant witnessed the transformation of Washington, from a simple village to a modern town that sported paved sidewalks, a sewage system, as well as gas and water sources. To further improve the city, streetlights were installed, "green spots" were fixed up and legislation was signed for the construction of the Washington Monument. Surprisingly, Grant had a keen eye for architecture, a trait that has left his mark on governmental buildings. The White House itself was completely refurbished for the Grant family's stay, as Julia expressed discontent at the state of the place. Many took this as the Grants living a lavish life, but it was more a case of Julia trying to make the White House feel like a home for her family. Another role that Julia happily attended to was entertaining her husband's guests (as he never managed to leave his shyness behind). Despite her physical disability (that made her insecure), most visitors were pleasantly impressed with the First Lady. Grant was not one to follow etiquette to a tee, so he frequently visited his cabinet members and old army friends, preferring the carefree atmosphere to the formal one implemented at the White House.

He took the safeguarding of the freed slaves as one of his most important missions as president. He worked for ratification of the Fifteenth Amendment which ensured that no citizen of the United States could have his vote denied on account of race, color or former condition of servitude, and doubled down his efforts by actively encouraging African American people to vote and giving them political positions. Another way in which Grant sought to protect the black people was by passing the Ku Klux Klan Acts, in 1871. Also known as the Force Acts, they consisted of four acts that sought to protect the constitutional rights of the freed slaves, which were guaranteed by the 14th and 15th Amendments. The most important provisions of these acts gave federal authorities the right to enforce penalties upon whoever interfered with said constitutional rights such as voting, registration, jury service, or officeholding of African Americans. Also, of note is that the

Force Acts gave the president the power to use military forces to make summary arrests and place states under martial law (several counties of South Carolina were placed under martial law because of severe mistreatment of black folk that went rampant). Although the acts were bold and well-intentioned, they proved mostly inefficient and it did not take long for the Supreme Court to assess various sections of them as being unconstitutional.

Grant was re-elected in 1872, defeating his adversary Horace Greely (who was the candidate of the Democratic-Liberal Republican coalition) by a big margin. However, during the electoral campaign, it was discovered that many Republican politicians that held high functions were involved in the Crédit Mobilier of America. Crédit Mobilier was the perfect example of post-Civil War corruption. It consisted of illegal manipulation of contracts, by a company (that dealt with constructions and finances) associated with the building of the Union Pacific Railroad. Veteran railroad organizers knew a lot more money could be made from construction contracts than from operating the railroad, especially since the Union Pacific Railroad (which had federal support) traversed the bare regions between Omaha and the Great Salt Lake. So, a few men contracted with themselves or their associates, and they reaped huge profits while the railroad was impoverished. One of the biggest names that marked the scandal was Oakes Ames, a congressman from Massachusetts. After the House of

Representatives investigated the issue, Ames and an associate were judged and condemned, while other big names, such as the Vice President, Schuyler Colfax, were absolved of blame.

Second Term

During Grant's second term, scandals escalated, and they reached deep into the President's inner circle of officials. For example, in 1972, Grant signed into law an act that sought to eliminate private tax collector contracts, but an attached amendment allowed for three more contracts after the law came into effect. Williams Adam Richardson, who acted as the head of Treasury in Grant's second term, hired John B. Sanborn, a lawyer and politician, to go after corporations and individuals who presumably evaded taxes. Supported by Richardson, Sanborn collected a hefty sum of $427,000, which were supposedly delinquent taxes. When Congress found out about Sanborn's action, Richardson was condemned and forced to resign. Grant, however, gave him a post as a judge in the Court of Claims, but he also signed another law that managed to abolish this system. Grant replaced Richardson with Benjamin Helm Bristow for the function of Secretary of Treasury, because of Bristow's honest character. His anti-corruption campaign would only go on to expose even more high officials that chose to dabble in illegal practices. Grant encouraged him to "Let no guilty man escape," words that he would later regret when faced with the condemnation of close friends.

The Secretary of the Interior Department, Columbus Delano, was one man that was not afraid of fraud. He had corrupt contracts put in place to benefit his son, and he had plenty of corrupt agents going about doing his dirty work. Once Grant found out about the situation, he forced Delano to resign and appointed Zachariah Chandler in his stead. Chandler managed to clear up the corruption and completely reform the department. Attorney-General George H. Williams was also fired, due to an extortion scandal involving his wife, and Grant replaced him with Edwards Pierrepoint.

Perhaps one of the most notable scandals was that of the "Whiskey Ring," which was discovered by Bristow in 1875, as part of his anti-corruption campaign. The so-called Whiskey Ring consisted of a group of whiskey distilleries that conspired to defraud the government of taxes. They bribed Internal Revenue officials and other political accomplices from Washington so they could keep the liquor taxes for themselves, instead of paying them to the government. They mostly operated in St. Louis and Chicago, and their operations were exposed through a secret investigation orchestrated by Bristow. The investigation resulted in 110 convictions, but a more pressing matter was the allegations that stated that the illegally held tax money was used by

Republicans to have Grant re-elected, which created public outrage. While Grant himself was not found guilty of foul play, the investigation showed that his private secretary, Orville Babcock, had received kickback payments and even advised the ring's mastermind, McDonald, of the upcoming investigation. Grant refused to believe the allegations against Babcock and was willing to testify in his favor, even if that meant going against a case that was prosecuted by members of his own administration. Instead, Grant gave a deposition in Babcock's defense, expressing his confidence in his secretary's innocence. Thanks to Grant's implication, Babcock was acquitted, but there was enough evidence against him to convince Grant to dismiss him from the White House (although he allowed Babcock to keep his position as Superintendent of Public Buildings).

The scandals only multiplied when Democrats took control of the House in 1875. They found that Secretary of War William Belknap took kickbacks from the Fort Still traders (which was part of the Indian Ring, in which governmental agents passed out allowances and treaty goods to Natives). Grant accepted his resignation, and thus Belknap avoided conviction because he no longer was a governmental official. Congress also discovered that the Secretary of the Navy, George Roberson, received bribes from a naval contractor, but there were no convictions drawn up. Perhaps the nail in the coffin for Grant was the fact that his own brother, Orvil, was guilty of setting up partnerships and received kickbacks from several trading posts.

Sickened by all the scandals and corruption, on December 5th, 1876, Grant publicly apologized to the entire nation and admitted that mistakes were made during his presidential years, albeit he maintained that the errors were ones of judgment and not of intent.

Grant had no desire to participate in the 1876 elections, but his involvement indirectly influenced Rutherford's victory. The "fight" was between the Democrat Samuel J. Tilden and the reformist Rutherford Hayes. Because of voting irregularities in some Southern States, the election remained without a conclusion. Grant came up with the proposal to have the matter settled through legislation, ensuring that military force was not to be used except for the purpose of curbing violence. In January 1877, Grant formed the Electoral Commission, which ruled that the disputed votes belonged to Hayes. In order to avoid protests from the Democrats, Republicans called back the troops that were settled in the Southern capitals. Rutherford became the 19th President of the United States, settling the Civil War divisions and putting an end to the Reconstruction.

Chapter 9: Last Years

Fresh out of the White House, the Grant family was not in their best financial situation. During his days as President, he spent a lot of money on entertainment and saved very little. His financial saving grace came in the form of the money that he received after the war from admirers, and that he had invested in a mining venture which gave a small but substantial profit. Grant wished to spend most of his money on traveling. In May 1877, Grant and Julia left for England, and soon enough their journey transformed into a full-blown world tour, with the Grants visiting Europe, India, and Africa. He was also the first President to visit the Holy Land, Jerusalem. Besides admiring the scenery, Grant also met important dignitaries such as Pope Leo XIII, Queen Victoria, Emperor Meiji, and Otto Von Bismarck. They were often received with celebrations and official greetings, out of respect for his "War Hero" status.

Let's go through some notable moments of the trip. While in England, the Grants stayed at the Windsor Castle and dined with Queen Victoria, an event that strengthened the Anglo-American alliance. Grant was the first American President to visit Scotland, something that he deeply wished as his ancestry was Scottish from both sides of his family. There he was well received and even greeted as a member of "Clan

Grant" a Highland Scottish Clan. In Belgium, Grant met King Leopold II who gave him a tour of the Alps. He had some quarrels with members of the French aristocracy while visiting the country, but he overall enjoyed his stay, especially taking a liking to the Louvre Museum. While in Egypt, the Khedive Ismail the Magnificent allowed Grant to stay at his palace, and the war hero spent his time in Egypt visiting the ruins of the Karnak Temple (the Egyptian villagers saw Grant as the "King of America"). The voyage through the Holy Land ended up being quite depressing for the Grants, as it showcased the bad living conditions of Jews under Ottoman leadership. But still, he was flattered by how well the Ottomans studied his military campaigns, and he praised their Arabian stallions and had a cordial relationship with the Sultan. While in Italy, Julia had her cross blessed by Pope Leo himself.

Grant showed great admiration for the Nordic countries and their honest people and efficient school system, but he came to appreciate the American government more after he saw how much European countries taxed their people in order to keep military forces well supplied. The Grants were mesmerized by India's beauties, but could not turn a blind eye to how badly women were treated there and how much power the European countries had over their conquered land. While in China, he agreed to act as a mediator of China's dispute with Japan over the Ryukyu Islands, a promise that he kept, thus becoming the first American ex-president to get involved in foreign affairs (Grant managed to defuse the situation but he did not convince the Japanese to give up on the land, and, shortly after Grant's departure, Japan annexed the Ryukyu Islands).

Most of the Grants' transportation during their two-year-long trip was ensured by the Hayes administration, which encouraged the former President to assume an unofficial diplomatic role and represent the United States, strengthening America's foreign relationships (and for some countries to even help them solve internal issues). Grant's campaign as an American delegate was successful in showing the world that the United States was slowly rising as a notable world power. The Grants reached American land on September 20th, 1879, where they were greeted by enthusiastic crowds.

With Grant's popularity rejuvenated by his diplomatic endeavors, Republicans saw that as an opportunity to regain power and wished to nominate him for the 1880 elections (which would have been Grant's third term, violating the unofficial two-terms rule). Although Grant did not say anything publicly, he wanted to be President again, and he encouraged his men to campaign for him, although he admitted that he would be happy if any Republican candidate won. In order to receive a nomination, Grant had to win against James Blaine and John Sherman and to collect 370 votes. After the first voting session, no candidate was close to the 370 requirements, and a second ballot led up to the same result. Neither Grant nor Blaine (Sherman barely had a few votes) won. The Republicans compromised on nominating James Garfield, who Grant whole-heartedly supported and gave speeches for while abstaining from criticizing his Democratic opponent, Winfield Hancock. Garfield ultimately won, but his fate was a bitter one, as only a year after he assumed the role of President, he was assassinated.

Now that his dreams of another presidency were done and dealt with, Grant found himself again in financial distress. With the aid of some of his wealthier friends, he got a house in Manhattan, New York and started making plans for building a railroad from Oaxaca to Mexico City. The railroad, just like most of Grant's business ventures, failed after only a year. Simultaneously, Ulysses Grant Jr. opened a Wall Street brokerage house in partnership with Ferdinand Ward. As Grant & Ward seemed promising, Ulysses Grant the father also joined the business, investing most of his money in it. Because of Ward's schemes, the firm was soon facing impending failure and it ended up going bankrupt, despite Grant's efforts to keep it going. Grant felt betrayed and testified against Ward in 1885, which led to Ward being convicted of fraud.

Because the financial situation of the family was extremely grim and he did not wish to venture into another business that would only end up eating away at his almost nonexistent fortune, he decided to write articles about his Civil War campaigns and sell them to *The Century Magazine*, for $500 apiece. The articles were so well received by both the public and the critics, Grant was advised to write his memoirs, as other military men have done. While struggling to make money, Grant ignored his physical health and put off seeing a doctor for his everlasting sore throat. When he did finally see a specialist, Grant found out that he had cancer, a great blow for the Grant family. In light of Grant's diagnosis and wishing to honor the former Hero of the Civil War, Congress restored Grant to his rank of General of the Army, which gave back his military pension (that he had to forfeit when he was elected President).

Even with the pension, Grant lived with the anxiety of having to ensure that his family would have a suitable amount of money to live on after his demise. Understanding his dreary situation, Mark Twain, his friend, made him an offer for his *Memoirs* which gave Grant a 75 percent royalty, a percent so high that it was unheard of. So, Grant started working frantically, with the help of his former staff member Adam Badeau and his oldest son Frederick. He managed to finish them only a few days before his death on July 23rd, 1885, at the age of 63, surrounded by loved ones. *The Personal*

Memoirs of Ulysses S. Grant was an utter success, both commercially and on a literary level, and was considered one of the most significant works of American non-fiction and one of the best military autobiographies.

In Grant's honor, President Grover ordered a nationwide period of mourning, which lasted thirty days, and the General of the Army ordered a day-long tribute on all military posts. Grant's coffin was visited by over a quarter of a million people in the short period of time (two days) before the funeral. The funeral procession included both Union and Confederate generals, the two former presidents, Hayes and Arthur, Grover along with his entire Cabinet, and members of the Supreme Court. The New York funeral was attended by a staggering 1.5 million people, and ceremonies were held in many other major cities around the country. Grant's body was temporarily placed in a tomb in Riverside Park. It was moved twelve years later to the "General Grant National Memorial" (also known as Grant's Tomb), the biggest mausoleum in North America.

Conclusion

Regarding the way Grant was seen through time, we can certainly say that he was a controversial figure. At his death, he was a hero and an honorable man who represented the American spirit. But shortly after, in the late 19th century, the national view regarding the Civil War started favoring the Confederate sentiment and more focus started to fall on his rocky presidential years, which brought about negative feelings towards Ulysses S. Grant. However, more recently, historians have started pointing out that his work as both a military man and as president brought about a lot of significant changes.

He recognized slavery and racism as wrong in a time when others saw African Americans as nothing more than business investments. Despite having corrupt people in his cabinet, he did his best at replacing them with honorable men, even if that meant going against intimate friends. His military genius was undermined time and time again, but the young general never gave up on the fight. He wished for peace and he was not afraid to fight for it in a military world where "playing it safe" was the generally accepted consensus. He fought to protect the rights of those that were powerless, and he did not discriminate.

Regarding his character, most historians agree that he was an honest, headstrong, intelligent man, that learned from his mistakes and was not afraid to stand for what he believed in. But Grant was also shy, naive, and quick to trust people, which was his downfall in the business world and in Office. Stories about his alcoholism followed him all throughout his life, and there are way too many accounts regarding his delicate problem for anyone to deny its existence. Grant had the tendency to use alcohol as a means of lifting his spirits whenever he felt down (especially when he was away from his family) and as entertainment in times of boredom. Yet Grant never indulged in alcohol consumption when he was in a leadership position with responsibilities on his hands, even if malevolent people tried to paint him as an inebriated general. His quick decision making, present in all his military campaigns, is a clear testament to his sobriety in the times when he was needed.

Grant was a devoted family man who always put the good of his loved ones first. He was also merciful and compassionate, traits that can be seen in the way he treated his father-in-law, as well as his enemies on the field, and the freed slaves.

Was he without fault? No. But he was a man with good intentions that always did his best, and nobody can take that away from him.

Bibliography

1. Chernow, R. (2017). *Grant*. New York: Penguin Press.
2. Grant, U. (1886). *Personal memoirs of U.S. Grant.* Montreal: Dawson Bros.
3. Simon, J. (2019). Ulysses S. Grant | Biography, Presidency, & Facts. Retrieved 7 August 2019, from https://www.britannica.com/biography/Ulysses-S-Grant
4. Ulysses S. Grant. (2009). Retrieved 7 August 2019, from https://www.history.com/topics/us-presidents/ulysses-s-grant-1
5. Hutchinson, S. (2019). 13 Things You Might Not Know About Ulysses S. Grant. Retrieved 7 August 2019, from http://mentalfloss.com/article/547771/ulysses-s-grant-facts
6. Ulysses S. Grant. (2019). Retrieved 7 August 2019, from https://www.biography.com/us-president/ulysses-s-grant
7. Brophy, A. (2018). 10 fascinating facts about President Ulysses Grant - National Constitution Center. Retrieved 7 August 2019, from https://constitutioncenter.org/blog/10-fascinating-facts-about-president-ulysses-grant

Napoleon Bonaparte

Table of Contents

Introduction

Napoleon Bonaparte, also known as Napoleon I, is considered to be one of the greatest military leaders in history. He is also among the most celebrated persons throughout the history of the West. His gradual rise to fame through his contribution in various wars makes for spectacular records in history, and his story is one that continues being told one generation after another.

Napoleon is undoubtedly not one of the regular war veterans. His tact and skills made him among the best military geniuses that ever existed, enabling him to win several wars and attain the status of emperor. His journey to the top of the military ladder began when he enrolled in military school, with some of the unfortunate occurrences, such as bullying, propelling him to gain courage and strive to always defeat anyone who was against him.

Napoleon is known for his contribution to the European army through the providing of modern and professional conscript armies. Unlike many leaders who are selfish and self-centered, Napoleon's ideology was always inclined to ensuring that the needs of the people were always put first. As you will find out from this read, Napoleon had many challenges, particularly when it came to the wars and the many people in authority who attempted to silence him since they were afraid of his skills. However, it was his determination and constant drive to excel in the face of adversities that made him one of the greatest warriors that ever lived, and the world knows his name. From a poor simple military boy, Napoleon grew to become one of the most notable emperors that France ever had. This biography will provide a detailed analysis into the life of Napoleon—from his personal life to the many wars that he fought and won, and the decision-making process that guaranteed him constant victory.

Chapter 1: Early and Personal Life

Early Life

Napoleon Bonaparte (August 15, 1769–May 5, 1821) was the second surviving son of Carlo Bonaparte and Letizia Ramolino, born on the island of Corsica (Thompson, 2018). His father was a well-renowned lawyer, and the family was relatively well-off. In addition to his law career, Carlo also served in the French administration. The Bonaparte lineage was considered to be noble, and the family was counted as being among the few elites in the port city. Despite their status, the family lived frugally, and Napoleon admitted that at one point, he felt very disappointed with his parents. Their quest for a simple and gentle life was too much, and Napoleon felt that they could have afforded to provide him and his siblings a much better life. Living together crammed in a few rooms that were in a very old house was not really what most noble families would choose. Much later, Napoleon would admit that he eventually became accustomed to the lifestyle and that he even grew a little too fond of it than he anticipated.

Where Carlo Bonaparte lacked in terms of giving his children a robust and affluent livelihood, he compensated with pushing his sons and encouraging them to aim for greater heights. Napoleon did not need much pushing, as he was very focused and determined to prosper on his own accord. The passion lived on despite the many challenges that he faced, one of them being the constant bullying that he faced when he enrolled in a military academy at the age of nine.

The military school was based in France, which automatically made Napoleon an outsider among all the other students. Also, social barriers became evident. During his time, most people who enrolled in military academies were from affluent and noble families, of which Napoleon was a part of. However, unlike him, the other participants came from families who lived in a manner that highlighted their nobility and high social status. Since Napoleon's family lived frugally, the schoolmates dubbed him dubious and constantly taunted him. Also, the fact that Napoleon grew up speaking Italian gave him an accent that came out with his poor French, further making him a subject of ridicule.

Napoleon's experiences in the military school, although terrible for a young boy, ultimately came to serve as one of the factors that largely shaped his character, as shall be seen throughout this book. First, the fact that he was a loner made him stronger on his own and devoid of relying on anyone for anything. Also, Napoleon developed a very defensive arrogance, which was evident in his interactions in the course of his duties. Most importantly, since he was always subject to ridicule and had to defend himself, Napoleon continually developed tactics that aimed at outsmarting the bullies. The tendency continued, and throughout his fights, Napoleon was always very open to the ideas that could help him outsmart his enemies. In 1785, Napoleon graduated. In the same year, while still in France, his father passed on, and Napoleon had to assume the role of head of the family, a factor that resulted in imminent financial hardship. Still, Napoleon was stronger than ever. The military positions that followed established his career as one of the most prolific military experts in history, and soon Napoleon Bonaparte was a household name.

Personal Life

Marriage to Josephine

Napoleon Bonaparte might have been an expert when it came to war, but that did not mean that he had no heart for love. In 1795, he met a widow who had just lost her husband and was the mistress of one of the most powerful men in France. The man, Paul Barras, was seemingly unresponsive to her love, and when Napoleon expressed interest, he encouraged it. Josephine, the mistress, gradually responded to Napoleon's pursuits, although it was just for convenience. Since Barras had discarded her, she just wanted security as well as financial support for herself and the children. Napoleon, on the other hand, deeply loved the woman and showed her compassion and empathy. He was delighted to be with her and did not care that she potentially did not love him as much. Napoleon was a hopeless romantic who illustrated signs of constant fantasies. In one famous romantic letter addressed to Josephine, Napoleon asserted how he always awoke full of her and how the memories of the pleasures they shared left eternal rest to his senses. In 1796, Napoleon proposed to her, and they were married on March 9.

Napoleon's affection toward Josephine was not only unrequited but was also immensely eventful. While Napoleon wrote many letters when he was away on official duty, Josephine rarely wrote back. Further, the lady began an affair with another man the same year that she got married, and Napoleon eventually got wind of what was happening. It is said that his feelings changed in entirety soon after realizing what she was doing, and the burning flame that was once there was wholly extinguished.

It took two years for Napoleon to come to terms with the fact that his wife had cheated on him. As revenge, Napoleon began an affair with a beautiful married woman in 1798, the woman popularly known as Cleopatra. Cleopatra showed Napoleon a deep and intimate kind of love to a level that Josephine had never even been close enough to experience. As a result, Napoleon's marriage to Josephine dwindled even more, and he stopped sending love letters or even attempting to show Josephine any kind of love. Notably, Cleopatra wasn't his only mistress, although she was the first woman that Napoleon had developed an affair with after his failed marriage. Soon after, Napoleon is known to have had even more sexual relationships with several other women.

Despite the rampant infidelity and problems in his marriage, Napoleon proved to be a man of class and stature when he remained true to his role as a husband. Without a doubt, there is a very high possibility that he would have been faithful had Josephine not been unfaithful to him in the first place. So seemingly committed and true was he that when he was elected emperor in 1804, he allowed his unfaithful wife to be crowned empress.

Though committed, the relationship never healed, and Napoleon continued being unfaithful right until the time when the two divorced in 1809. The basis of the divorce was not infidelity, but rather that Josephine had failed to conceive a child, and Napoleon was in dire need of an heir. Surprisingly, the divorce was entirely amicable, and Napoleon even allowed Josephine to retain the title of empress for good. In his words, Napoleon wished for Josephine never to doubt all the sentiments that he had given her earlier on when they were happy. Also, it was his wish that, even with the divorce, Josephine would hold him as her best and dearest friend.

Marriage to Marie Louise

Marie Louise was the second wife of Napoleon Bonaparte who reigned as the empress of the French beginning in 1810. The main reason as to why Napoleon chose to marry her was not out of deep love, as it had been in his first marriage, but rather as an attempt to sire an heir. Initially, Marie was not even his first choice, and he had only decided to marry her when he got tired of the delay in marriage approval from one of the leading royal families in Europe. At the time of the marriage, Marie Louise didn't know who Napoleon was in-depth, and the only reason she married him was so she could fulfill the wishes of her family and elders. The wedding brought very favorable inferences as France and Austria ended up developing solid ties.

Marie and Napoleon got married in an Augustinian church in 1810, and their wedding was not only full of color but also involved some of the most affluent people in the community. The wedding party was so magnificent that it ranked among the most brilliant festivities that had ever been conducted in the community. Marie was only a teenager, but she handled her affairs so well that Napoleon began admiring her. While their marriage was not based on love from the onset, their romantic relationship soon began to grow, although it was not half as profound as the affection that Napoleon had shown to his first wife. Also, there was no infidelity, as Marie remained faithful to her vows. However, the marriage was not without its own set of issues, as Napoleon consistently regarded Marie as being too shy in comparison with his first wife—sentiments that hurt her. Also, the fact that he was still in constant communication with Josephine always upset Marie, threatening the marriage.

In July 1810, Marie realized that she was pregnant, much to the delight of many people, and most especially Napoleon. In 1811, a boy was born and he was named Napoleon Francoise Bonaparte. Since he was royal, he was automatically given the title of the King of Rome. The birth had been very sensitive and difficult, and Napoleon felt that he was not ready to have other children if Marie would suffer so much. The fact that she had given him a son made him soften more towards her. The two remained married up until his death.

Chapter 2: Military Career

Initial Role as a Second Lieutenant

As soon as Napoleon graduated from military school, he went on to become a second lieutenant in the artillery regiment. For some reason, Napoleon was not quite assiduous in the service as a second lieutenant, and at the end of his service, he had accumulated thirty-eight months of absence in comparison to just thirty-three months when he was present.

During the period when Napoleon was serving as second lieutenant, there was an outbreak of a revolution that saw the end of military occupation of Corsica, a military operation that had begun in 1769. Notably, Napoleon was an avid Corsican nationalist, and he vowed to fight for his country of origin (de Bourrienne, 2012). During the early stages of the revolution, Napoleon spent his time fighting a complex struggle that was among the royalists, revolutionists, and the Corsican nationalists. Between the three groups, the Corsican nationalists have the least number of fighters because the nationals were not only more disadvantaged than the rest but also because most of the qualified army officials were fighting for the other groups. Despite the shortcomings, the biggest advantage was that there were plenty of volunteers who were ready to fight for Corsica, and all they needed was a leader.

Napoleon took on the role of commander and was intent on helping the volunteers win the war.

One of the reasons Napoleon was so against the French invasion of Corsica was the administration and absolutism that was bestowed upon the Corsican as well as the disregard to their preferred way of life. Before the invasion, Corsica had been an independent nation and had its system of governance. Since Napoleon had grown up in the country, he was greatly fascinated by its history and the stories he read about how his country used to operate before the invasion. Napoleon was very passionate about restoring the lost glory of his country, hence the determination to fight the war. Ultimately, not only was Napoleon successful in helping win the war, but he also gained wide accolades and status among the military officials. By the end of the war, Napoleon had already been promoted to commander in the French army.

Rise to Power

It was while Napoleon was a commander in the French army that he proved his skill and expertise. In 1792, there was an increased revolution between France and various nations in Europe. The military conflicts and tension had always been in existence, but it is only in 1792 that the war became mainstream and absolute. Napoleon made preparations with the army under his command, and in 1796, he made advances that began the war. During this time, the major rival was the Austrian army, and Napoleon was able to defeat it quite easily. The war had not been easy, and Napoleon had to face the opponents in a series of battles, particularly in Italy. By 1797, Austria had conceded defeat, and the result was a signed treaty with the French that resulted in territorial gains and a win for the French. This battle was very revolutionary, and it marked the stepping stone in recognition of Napoleon as an exceptional commander.

So exceptional was Napoleon's commandeering that he was approached by some of the senior-most commanders in France to lead an invasion in England. The senior commanders comprised of a group of five top-notch individuals that had governed France for several years. This directory was very oblivious of the risks a sudden invasion held, and Napoleon was able to change their minds by explaining how the sudden invasion would work against them. At the time, the French army had just won a battle against Austria, and it was not strong enough to fight another battle just yet. Also, there was not enough workforce for such an extensive war, and Napoleon knew that if they invaded England at the time, they would be highly outnumbered and defeated. Such trivial information turned out to be quite beneficial for the overall French army, and Napoleon was able to study war plans extensively and come up with a better strategy that guaranteed the French army even more success. In this case, the best strategy was to conquer Egypt first and wipe the British trade routes to weaken the European forces. The directory was impressed with the analysis and decision-making skills showcased by Napoleon, and they agreed to follow his strategy.

Napoleon in Egypt

Napoleon's expedition to Egypt was aimed solely at achieving two critical things. The first was to re-establish the expected wars that had been put on a temporary pause between the French revolutionary army and the European forces. At that time, Napoleon had already foreshadowed an imminent defeat where they had to advance towards the European army, seeing that they neither had the workforce nor resources required to fight a winning battle. The second critical thing was to secure their position by blocking Britain's trade route to India, which would leave them devoid of the necessary resources that they required to finance a war.

Notably, one of the reasons why Napoleon was so hard-pressed to fight the battle in Egypt successfully was that it had always been his dream to lead a war in the Middle East and come out of it victorious. The battle through Egypt provided the perfect opportunity, and Napoleon was determined to prove that he could win any war that he set his mind to. Not only would the conquest in Egypt enable the French to get a hold over the Mediterranean, but it would also serve as the perfect route to attack Britain when they were least aware of what was happening.

Notably, the directory was not as happy about Napoleon's vigor and courage as one would have thought. Since Napoleon was a great army commander and had amassed the support and admiration of thousands where he was known, these leaders knew that he posed a very serious threat and that eventually he could oust them easily and take up the leadership position. While these leaders wanted victory over the British, their selfish interests took precedence, as they valued their positions in government more than retaining a skilled war leader such as Napoleon. Therefore, when they sent him out to the war, they were sure that it would keep him busy for a while, making their positions more secure. Further, there was always a possibility that Napoleon could be killed in the war, and experts believe that the directory secretly hoped for that outcome.

On July 1, Napoleon landed in Egypt with a large army of around 40,000 fighters, and multiple ships. Napoleon's strategy was very well-defined and clear. First, they had to capture all the vital towns one by one, and soon they would have what was needed to defeat the British army. Alexandria was the first town the army came across, and they conquered it effortlessly. The next target town was Cairo, and Napoleon was determined to do more than conquer it. In addition to the army of fighters that he had brought, Napoleon also brought with him a large number of civilian scientists whose role was to establish a learning institution in Cairo. With the institution, Napoleon hoped to win people over through the provision of civilization in the form of education. Also, Napoleon constantly asserted that he was there to defend Islam and the Egyptian interest, and he soon gained their favor. While his assertions may have been true to some extent, Napoleon faced a lot of resistance, and rebellions soon began against his army.

The Battle of the Pyramids

This was the very first battle that Napoleon fought after his entry in Egypt, and it was against the Egyptian army. As stated, the Egyptians were not happy about the presence of Napoleon in the country, and they had immense reservation over his assertions that he was there in the best interest of the people. Initially, Napoleon did not have the desire to fight with the Egyptians, as his target was the British. However, when the clashes began, Napoleon led his army to war and had an easy win. Cairo was occupied immediately upon the defeat, and Napoleon took over the leadership of the same. Soon after the win, Napoleon wasted no time as he installed a new system of governance that ended feudalism and serfdom.

Also, he imported some of the critical French structures, and soon, Egypt began adopting the new system of operations. Notably, Napoleon was not oppressive and was genuinely concerned about the needs of the people. It was his genuine resolve that with the new system, the people would be able to lead better lives.

The Battle of the Nile

With any conquest, there is undoubtedly bound to be some form of resistance, regardless of how beneficial the new system of governance is. The resistance is exactly what Napoleon faced when he took over Cairo. As soon as Napoleon landed in Egypt, the British got wind of what was happening, and they decided to stop him. While Napoleon had already captured Cairo, the one weakness that he had was that he could not command at sea. Therefore, he was hit by surprise when the British army attacked him, something that he had not anticipated. The British army came on strong and destroyed the entire fleet of ships that the French army had come with. Notably, the ships contained some of the most vital war resources that Napoleon has organized. Therefore, the sudden destruction imminently weakened his position.

The defeat was immense. Napoleon did not even have the resources to take his small surviving army back to France. Conceding defeat, Napoleon decided to March to Syria with the few survivors with the hope that he could get the Syrian army to take his side and drop any alliances that it may have had with the British army. The plan failed, and Syria even collaborated further with the British in an attempt to wipe out the small surviving team in its entirety. It was at this moment that Napoleon's will and courage were tested to the maximum. Even when he knew that he had potentially been defeated, Napoleon was still determined to prove a point, and he captured the first Syrian city he came across, which was known as Jaffa, and had 3,000 prisoners executed. He aimed at sending a message that he was still strong, with the hope that they would consider him an ally and help defeat the British. However, Syria was not welcoming in the least, and they responded by sending a 20,000-troop army to fight Napoleon. Luckily, Napoleon had already gotten wind of what was about to happen, and he quickly led his army back to Egypt before the British troops arrived. It was a lucky escape, and there is a very high likelihood that he would have been defeated and the remaining army wiped out had they stayed longer in Syria.

Leaving Egypt

Perhaps one of the most controversial decisions that Napoleon made was to leave Egypt after the embarrassing defeat. To many, Napoleon turned from a hero to a coward since he left his army behind, more or less abandoning them. Napoleon felt that he had lost everything, and even the rebels who had taken his side turned against him. To many, this seemed like the end of Napoleon and his leadership.

However, there was a clear motive and strategy behind this. During this period, Napoleon was unhappy with the French regiment and, to some extent, felt that they betrayed him since they did not send any backup the entire time he was in Egypt and Syria. He traveled back to France with one clear motive of taking over the government and saving his situation. Note that Napoleon traveled alone, which meant he knew the opposition he would face as well as possible elimination by the current government. However, Napoleon was unafraid and ready for any eventuality. During this time, his strong character started to show, affirming his legacy as one of the bravest people that ever lived. As it turned out, it was the defeat in Egypt that served as the defining moment for the onset of the Napoleonic wars.

Chapter 3: Napoleon as the French Emperor

The Coup of 18 Brumaire

When Napoleon left Egypt, he had mixed emotions—disappointment in the French government for seemingly abandoning him and the rest of the army, and anger due to the poor leadership displayed. He was determined to overthrow the government through a coup, although he was not the chief instigator. At the time, Sieyes, another disgruntled military official, felt that the government was not performing as it should, and he resolved to overthrow it. Napoleon found the situation already dire with the coup imminent, and he decided to capitalize on the situation.

Napoleon, being the skilled plotter and analyst that he was, thought about the many ways through which he could achieve the coup without getting killed in the process, and soon he had a clear strategy that he was sure would not fail. The first thing he needed to do was get the most powerful men in France on his side. These powerful men were the landowners in France, and their influence was immense. At the time, the landowners felt that their needs and rights were not being taken into consideration, and they were highly charged and motivated to attempt to change the system. Further, in the prior revolutions, a lot of lands had been stripped away from churches and many aristocrats and sold to the landowners. Since there was a possibility that the land would be stripped away from the landowners and restored to the rightful owners, these powerful people were living in constant fear, as having their land stripped would render them poor.

Napoleon took advantage of the situation and convinced them that he would be the one to instigate the changes they desired. Further, he assured them that as soon as he got into power, he would legalize the acquisition of the land, and no one would be able to take it away from them. Since his track record was solid and he had earned the admiration of many, convincing the people was quite easy, and he soon got the support he needed. Further, Napoleon drew a constitution that gave the landowners power and assured them that as soon as he was the emperor, the constitution would be legally binding. With such assurance, all the landowners and powerful people in France gave him their full support.

With the support of people of power, Napoleon was able to lead a coup that overthrew the government, making him the people's leader. The main government officials that were overthrown were the five directors who had advocated for Napoleon to lead the war against the British and who were greatly anxious that his popularity would soon work against them. Their fears soon came to pass as Napoleon took over the leadership and ousted them, much to the delight of all the citizens. Napoleon began acting fast, getting rid of all the former government officials and recruiting the ones that he wanted in power.

In 1804, the government officials, all of whom had been chosen by Napoleon, passed a law that made him the French emperor. Notably, Napoleon rejected the title of King, as he felt that it was too mainstream and not ambitious enough. Also, he wanted something different because he had always viewed himself as unlike any of the other leaders that had even been at the forefront of the French leadership. During the crowning, he was still married to Josephine, and she was consequently crowned empress.

In addition to his crowning, Napoleon extended his ambition to his family members, ensuring that a law was passed that recognized heirs and demanded that they come from his family tree. At that time, he did not have any children, but it was okay since there were other Bonapartes who could take a leadership role in case anything happened to Napoleon. The people were seemingly so happy about Napoleon's leadership that they supported his bid immensely. Of the official recognized votes that were cast, 3.5 million were in support of Napoleon's ideology, while only a meager 2,500 were against him. The support was a great stride on his part, as it showed the immense belief that the people had in him.

The Napoleonic Code

One of Napoleon's greatest legacies was the development of a modernized system of governance, one that still lives on and is referred to as the Napoleonic code. The Napoleonic code was established soon after Napoleon became the emperor, and it served as the alternative to the continental laws that had been in existence in the previous regimes. As is already evident, Napoleon was very vocal about feudal laws, and he was determined to eliminate them at all costs. Among the factors that led to the determination of changing the system was that Napoleon considered himself to be elite, and he could no longer stand the primitive governance that was majorly inclined toward oppressing the minority in society as well as taking advantage of their inferior status. Further, the fact that France did not have clearly defined laws meant that it was challenging to distinguish between right and wrong and the ordinary people did not even know how to seek justice for the wrongs they felt were being done against them.

Napoleon was also determined to change the existing laws that gave the feudal lords control over people's personal lives. As Napoleon noted, most ordinances, including marriage and family life, were significantly imposed upon by the kings, and the people seemingly had no control over any aspect of their lives. Worse, the laws kept changing each and every day, and this was how the lords managed to ensure that everything that they wanted came to pass. Whenever these lords desired anything to work in their favor, they changed the law, and the people had no option but to oblige. One example of such a situation was the lords passing a law that stipulated that the commoners had no right to refuse to work in the fields of their masters for free. Once it was passed, the commoners' suffering increased while the lords continued amassing wealth.

Napoleon began changing the legal system right after selecting a team of four that made up his jurists, and they came up with a set of legal doctrines and tenets that served as a replacement for the previous laws, which were vague. The jurists worked with Napoleon on the codes, and by 1801, they were done. It, however, took time for their publication, as Napoleon was still leading wars at the time and unsure if he could successfully impose the stipulations on the other nations. However, he commanded his jurists to begin educating the people about the changes they should expect from the new system of governance as well as the ways in which it would differ from the previous laws.

The primary tenets that formed the basis of the code were as follows:

1. Equality among all men

For the first time in history, a law based on rationale would be established, and it would be free from all the past prejudices that the people had already became accustomed to. One of the most significant aspects of the rationale was coming to terms with the fact that all men were equal and that no one had authority over anyone else. Through this code, Napoleon aimed at getting rid of all social classes, nobility, and the privileges that were only accessible to a small segment of the population.

Scholars assert that the desire to abolish the social classes had its basis from his childhood, given the fact that Napoleon was severely bullied due to his family's status and background. Therefore, Napoleon knew the effect that such groupings had on people, and he was determined to abolish them for good in his country. Going through school was definitely one of the toughest periods Napoleon experienced in childhood, and he was determined to save as many people as possible from such situations.

2. The law of persons

The law of persons dealt with all aspects of human rights and the protection of personality, guardianship, and relations. Napoleon knew how many people suffered from circumstances they could not control for the simple reason that it was what was widely accepted. People got accustomed to the worst of times, and they rarely made an attempt to change, as it was considered to be the usual and acceptable way of life. To overcome such laws, Napoleon required all laws that elevated some people while undermining others be disbanded entirely. A majority of the laws were in line with ownership of property as well as the guardian having absolute authority about what their children could and could not do. For instance, many people had arranged marriages, and the result was a life of dissatisfaction in a loveless marriage. According to Napoleon, every adult had the right to choose whomever they wanted to stay with and the person that they wished to marry without the interference of the broader public. Also, issues pertaining to divorce and marriage annulments would be handled by the relevant parties as they pleased, and nobody had the right to dictate what was supposed to happen in another person's life.

Further, customary and traditional laws would not have any influence on the new law, and moral justification would be based on its conformity to the decrees of reason and common sense. For example, beating up workers was considered to be a customarily regular occurrence. However, common sense dictates that all people are equal and should be respected, and the law would protect them henceforth. This is precisely what Napoleon was aiming at achieving.

3. The law of things

The law of things deals with the aspects relating to property rights, ownership of assets, and all issues relating to inheritance, succession, obligations, and any marriage settlements. Basically, all persons were allowed to own any property they acquired through legal means, and no person had the right to take it away from them on the basis of superiority or authority. Through this code, Napoleon ensured that all persons had equal rights and that all hardworking persons would get what they deserved. With the system, not only was there an increased sense of satisfaction among the people, but it also served as motivation. Eventually, France would be able to amass more resources.

Influence and Jurisdiction of the Napoleonic Code

The Napoleonic code was first introduced into the areas and countries that were under French control. These areas included Belgium, a few parts of Germany, Italy, Monaco, and Geneva. Later, Napoleon continued spreading the jurisdiction of the codes into the areas he gradually occupied and controlled, such as the Netherlands, Switzerland, and Western Germany. Eventually, there were significant changes, and the people boasted of better living standards as soon as the code was in full effect, and Napoleon was determined to spread it wherever he went.

A few years after the first introduction, countries surrounding France were in awe at the level of development that accrued from the adoption of the code. So impressed were they that they voluntarily adopted the law and began changing their systems of governance. European and Latin American countries were the first to adopt this code willingly, and within no time, it had spread to multiple nations, some of which did not even have any level of acquaintance with France.

Currently, the Napoleonic code is still rife and alive in a significant section of the world. Napoleon had been amazed at the transformation to both his and other nations, and he always asserted that his real glory was not in the wars that he had fought and won, but the development of the civil code. True to his word, the code still lives, and nothing can destroy it.

Napoleonic Wars

The Napoleonic wars represent a series of battles that began when Napoleon took leadership of France, and they are considered to be the most defining battles Napoleon ever fought. It is not clear when the wars began exactly, but many historians believe that they commenced in 1803, a very short time after Napoleon succeeded in his coup (Connelly, 2012).

The wars occurred at different times, and they are often categorized into five distinct coalitions.

The War of the Third Coalition (1803–1806)

The War of the Third Coalition was the first Napoleonic war that occurred after Napoleon's rise to emperor status. Before this war, there had been two other minor preceding wars—*the War of the First Coalition*, which occurred between 1793 and 1797, and *the War of the Second Coalition*, which took place between 1799 and 1801. These two wars were all in an attempt to defeat the French army, and they failed drastically. Ultimately, France and Britain reached a peace agreement in what is popularly known as the *Peace of Amiens*. This peace treaty involved Britain relinquishing all the control that it had previously taken on some of the French territory as well as other nations, such as Egypt. France, on the other hand, agreed to leave Italy and give up all the control it had on some of the cities therein. This peace treaty was among the highest points in time for all the nations, and it resulted in tranquility and respect that was previously unavailable. The peace would not last, as the War of the Third Coalition soon ensued.

In May 1803, two years after the peace treaty had been signed, hostilities suddenly erupted again. It was at this time that the Third Coalition was formed, comprising of England, Russia,

Sweden, and Prussia. To a large extent, Napoleon was largely to blame for the formation of this coalition, as he had just recently started a military quest in Europe. Also, Napoleon had seemingly gone against the peace treaty by invading Italy, a factor that necessitated a coalition to stop him. At the time, Napoleon had already occupied a part of Switzerland and was at the time contemplating a re-invasion in Egypt. Even worse, he began disrespecting Britain because he felt that its army was weak. All of these nations were angered and they came together to stop him.

Notably, the fact that multiple nations formed a single coalition in an attempt to beat Napoleon affirms how strong he was. Napoleon was fearless, and he was ostensibly unaffected by the thought of the nations rallying against him. The fact that he had already strengthened the French army gave him confidence that he could defeat anyone, further affirming his position as one of the most robust and fearless leaders of all time.

How the Coalition Formed

The coalition formed to fight Napoleon took time, with the nations involved highly set and determined to ensure there was no way they lost. The first meeting was held in Vienna, and it was attended by some of the topmost and highly-sought leaders in the Russian and Austrian armies. The two nations were well aware of the power and strength Napoleon had, and they set aside 250,000 Austrian fighters and 180,000 Russians and began training them in preparation for the war. Both nations had the highest number of fighters, with the others comprised of the following:

- 100,000 Prussians

- 35,000 Germans

- 20,000 Neapolitans

- 5,000 Englishmen

- 16,000 Swedes

- 16,000 Danes

The teams began preparing with their various officials, and the leaders were already getting acquainted with each other in preparation of the Great War. When the training was complete, it was estimated that over 437,000 military members were selected to participate in the war. Around 100,000 military members from the Austrian army were kept at bay, and they would serve as reinforcement in case help was needed during the war.

Once the training was complete, the contingent got ready to advance and begin the war. Notably, there were military operations at both sea and land since the military knew that Napoleon was intelligent and would attack when they least expected. The military operations at sea were necessary since they would ensure that Napoleon had no way of reaching the British shores while the operation at land was meant to secure all the entry points that Napoleon could possibly use to attack. England played a major role in the operations at land and secured its border.

When the coalition formed, the major objective was to corner Napoleon at all sides and to ensure that he had nowhere to run to. Since the French army was concentrated in the north, the military coalition felt confident in defeating Napoleon if they attacked from all sides and cornered him at the middle. Unknown to them, Napoleon was not threatened in the least, and he was busy preparing his army.

The first army in the coalition to attack was the Austrian military. The army was made up of 72,000 strong fighters, and they invaded Bavaria. Napoleon heard about the invasion and left for Bavaria, where he defeated the army in no time. Defeated, the Austrian army was forced to retreat. As the war was taking place, the Russian army was heading to Bavaria to help the Austrians. When the commander heard about the defeat, they were no longer bold enough, and they resorted to retreating. Napoleon surged into the Russian territory and took the city of Vienna with no resistance.

The Austrian army soon converged with the Russian army and decided to approach and fight Napoleon as a single unit.

Once they had prepared enough and recruited other fighters into the army, they approached Napoleon, and soon a battle erupted. Napoleon fought with gusto and easily defeated the combined army. The Russians and Austrians soon retreated, having suffered a crushing and severe defeat.

The outcome of this battle was better than Napoleon had even anticipated. After the Austrian army's defeat, the nation seemingly became more afraid of Napoleon since they had seen his strength. They swallowed their pride and agreed to sign a peace treaty with France. Napoleon wanted a number of Austrian territories handed over to him, and the Austrian government agreed with little resistance. Therefore, Napoleon became richer than he previously was and had the Austrians at his command. The Russians were against bowing to Napoleon and they continued with their military operations against him. While they did not attack him again at this point, it was clear that they would when another opportunity presented itself.

The War of the Fourth Coalition (1806–1807)

Soon after the defeat and surrender of the Austrians, a disgruntled coalition that largely consisted of the Prussians and the British was formed. The two nations had heard about the defeat of Napoleon, and they were actually adamant about approaching and fighting him. However, they knew the more Napoleon continued to be in charge and at the helm of the military, the more likely he was to take over more land and resources that belonged to the other coalitions. Ultimately, a total takeover was imminent, and Napoleon would be the overall king. None of the nations wanted this, and they came together to form another coalition to attempt defeating Napoleon again.

At the time of the convergence of the Third Coalition, Napoleon was still in Vienna, and he appeared to be quite isolated and alone. While the coalition thought the isolation was a sign of weakness and that they would have a very easy time defeating him, the truth was that Napoleon was strategizing about his next move; he knew there was an impending attack that could potentially be bigger and more serious than all the other battles he had fought. True to his thoughts, the Third Coalition struck, and Napoleon fought and won what is considered to be his most impressive battle in history.

Many historians have focused on the eventualities and nuances of this battle and the ways in which it shaped the reign of Napoleon. The one thing that stands out is that, unlike the many battles that Napoleon fought and won, in this case, he was not the instigator. The coalitions that were formed of the different nations were the aggressors, and all

Napoleon did was retaliate and protect himself. Also clear is that Napoleon was fighting solely with the French army only while the coalitions had even more resources at their disposal, as they were behind many nations.

The War of the Fourth Coalition resulted in one major eventuality—Napoleon taking over the whole of Prussia. Note that Napoleon already knew there was an impending war. Being the fast and smart thinker he was, Napoleon decided to attack Prussia before the coalition attacked him so he could weaken them by taking over the entire nation. At the time, Prussia was still in the process of training with the other coalitions' armies, and it was their belief that Napoleon was doing the same. Consequently, being attacked caught them by surprise, and it was a very easy takeover on Napoleon's end. But he didn't stop there. He went on to fight and defeat Berlin, and in less than ten days, a total overthrow had already been completed. Just like what had happened in the War of the Third Coalition, Prussia conceded defeat, and they surrendered once again.

Napoleon knew better than to waste any time. At the time he was taking over the nations one by one, he knew that he had instilled some level of fear in all the other nations that were in opposition to him. Since he knew how easy it would be to defeat people who were already fearful of him, he immediately moved into Russia. Note that the fact that

Napoleon was winning the wars one after another does not mean his army was not getting harmed to some degree in the process. As with any war, his army also suffered a lot of casualties, and it took Russia by surprise as they expected the two battles to have weakened France to some extent. They were even more fearful of the French army as they did not know how they managed to succeed at the levels they did.

Fear was imminent in the Russian army; they continued to retreat as Napoleon moved in. With the retreat, Napoleon captured city after city, beginning with Warsaw. With each city captured, Napoleon replenished his horses and got even more volunteers to join his army. The need and human desire of being associated with the winning side saw very many young men join his army, and soon, Napoleon had one of the largest armies the world had ever seen. By the time he took over Warsaw, Napoleon had an estimated 60,000 good horses and hundreds of thousands of foot soldiers.

Napoleon continued to go deeper into Russia until he arrived at a place called Eylau, and the army set up camp. Winter had already set in so the army decided to stay since the unrelenting winter conditions were unforgiving outside. It was too cold to continue moving, and Napoleon had no intention of launching an offensive at the time. This may have been the one time Napoleon underestimated his enemies, thinking that no one would launch an attack in such extreme weather. He was wrong, and Russia charged unexpectedly, leading to one of the biggest and most extreme wars Napoleon ever fought.

The Battle of Eylau

As has been stated, Napoleon had no intention of fighting in the winter period once he took over some of the cities in Russia. However, Russia decided to launch an offensive, and Napoleon had no option but to retaliate as fast as possible. Naturally, fighting in the cold was not a good idea, and neither of the armies would be able to fight as efficiently as they would have had they undertaken the fight during a period with more favorable weather. Since Napoleon was already used to the wars, he knew that if the entire Russian army intercepted him, there was a chance he would be defeated. Thinking fast, he ordered part of the team to head west, away from the camp. This strategy was aimed at confusing the Russians into thinking the whole army was headed west, and the rest of the French team would have an easier time attacking them from behind. Unfortunately, the Russian commander was also smart, and he knew that if the plan worked, there would be a very high likelihood that he would be cornered. The strategy also confused him, and he decided to fall back for a while so that he could read the French army and the exact tactics they could potentially use.

Seeing the Russian army fall back, Napoleon knew he had succeeded in scaring the Russians, which meant they would fight with little confidence. These were the chances Napoleon lived for. Therefore, he instructed his army to chase after the Russians and launch an attack. The army set off, chasing the Russians until they had no alternative but to turn back and fight.

Notably, the war was not as easy as Napoleon had anticipated. The Russians fought fiercely, and it was apparent that the French would not be able to take them down as easily. The war began at around 2:00 p.m., and both sides fought gallantly in the freezing weather. As the hours passed, neither army was surrendering, and the result was a bloodbath that had never been seen before. As the war raged on, the control of the city passed back and forth between the two sides, and both armies were determined to gain victory. When night approached, the Russian team decided to fall back, giving the French army a temporary belief and assurance that they had won the war.

The reality of the war was imminent the following morning. Thousands of fighters had been killed, with most of the dead being from the French army. Even worse, some of the soldiers who had been injured were freezing in the cold weather, and Napoleon was certain they would lose even more people to the weather. Of the over 100,000 military fighters that had set up camp, Napoleon had only around 45,000 able fighters. This number placed him at a serious disadvantage, considering the fact that the Russian army had around 67,000 troops. Napoleon was not shaken, and he immediately called for reinforcements. His many years of war had taught him that this was not the type of war that he could be confident was over. Russia was undoubtedly going to attack again.

True to his belief, Russia launched an attack early the following day. This was not the typical war where only swords and knives were used. Both armies had cannons and heavy machinery, and they did not shy away from using them on their enemies. The war was intense, and even the injured were commanded to join in. At that point, Napoleon needed all the help he could get.

As the war advanced, Napoleon realized that the Russians had stronger weapons than he even thought was possible. An entire team that had been sent out west to try and corner the coming Russian reinforcements came head-on with blazing guns, and they were wiped out in an instant. The loss of the gallant men presented even more trouble for Napoleon, and for the first time, he may have been shaken. The Russian army continued pushing deeper into Eylau and started showing signs of more strength and imminent victory. Napoleon stepped back to think and soon came up with the plan that managed to save his quickly weakening army.

First, the weather was very humid and the visibility was poor. If he could capitalize on this weakness, he would be able to turn the tables and France would have dominion over the Russians. Calling out to some of the fiercest fighters, Napoleon commanded them to try their best to take over the Russian machinery and weapons as he commanded the remaining army to fight the best they ever had at the field. The Russians realized that some of the French men were falling back, and they were confused, as they did not know whether it was a sign of surrender or if something else was going on. Even more confusing was the fact that the army on the ground was seemingly fighting even more strongly, and they did not know whether this team would fall back as well. Napoleon was counting on that confusion, as it would reduce the efficiency of the Russians by sending them mixed signals. True to his belief, the team that had broken off was able to take over all the major weapons as the troops had already been told that the French were apparently surrendering, which made them less vigilant. As soon as the French army took over the weapons, the bloodshed that followed among the Russian troops was unlike any other. Thousands more died and the Russians were weakened. Prior to that, Napoleon had called for reinforcement, and when they finally arrived, the Russian army was further massacred. By the time nighttime approached, the Russians had already conceded defeat, and the few military men that survived fell back. By 10:00 p.m. that night, the war was over.

The extent of the casualties and death was clear in the morning. The white snow was covered in blood, thousands of bodies scattered everywhere. Napoleon was saddened at the turn of events, and he asserted that he did not feel victorious. Of all the wars that he had been in, this was one that had cost him thousands of good men. In his words, Napoleon was disappointed at the extent of the massacre, and he felt that it had all been for nothing.

War of the Fifth Coalition (1809)

Napoleon's frequent victories against the coalitions that formed against him did not stop them from making more plans to defeat him. Austria was among the nations that were at the forefront of advocating for the wars, and they did not stop with the defeats they constantly suffered. During this period, many of the nations in the previous coalitions had already accepted and conceded defeat, and identified Napoleon as among those whom they would not be able to defeat easily. Therefore, they refrained from joining the coalition, leaving only Austria and the British in the fight against France.

When Napoleon heard that the Fifth Coalition was training and just about to attack him, he decided to change the tides and stop Austria before they were even strong enough to fight him. During the moments preceding the war, Austria came on strongly and even led an invasion into Bavaria. The army came out strong, and the few French militants that were there at the time were gradually forced to retreat. Napoleon got wind of what was happening and decided to stop the Austrian army once and for all. What followed was a smaller war known as the Battle of Eckmühl.

Battle of Eckmühl and Abensberg

The Battle of Eckmühl took place in April 1809, and it marked the beginning of the War of the Fifth Coalition. While Napoleon had heard there was a Fifth Coalition that was forming in an attempt to stop him, he was oblivious of the fact that Austria would attack that fast and by themselves. Markedly, the first attack against the French militants took place at a location where neither the French nor the Austrian army knew the surroundings well, which placed both groups at a disadvantage. Napoleon was determined to end the Austrian army, and he led troops in two different places. The first troops were reinforcements, and they helped beat the Austrian army. Napoleon knew the first group might have been just a distraction, so he led the other group west and in a different location, sure there would be other Austrian militants that would attempt to attack him therein. He was right, and he found an Austrian army on transit to France. The attack came as a surprise to the Austrians, and Napoleon defeated them easily. This war is known as the battle of Abensberg.

The aftermath of the war exhibited the severity by which the Austrian army had lost its militants. Over 12,000 Austrian militants were killed at the cost of just 5,000 French militants. Once again, Napoleon had established himself as among the greatest war leaders the world had ever known. It is alleged that this was among the most fulfilling wars that Napoleon had ever fought, rumored that he mentioned it was the finest of plans that he had ever conducted. After the victory, Napoleon moved into Austria and occupied the capital.

The victory against the Austrians made Napoleon more confident and significantly less empathetic against the Austrians. The result was the drafting of a peace treaty that is considered to be incredibly harsh. The treaty was meant to keep the Austrians grounded and also reduce their strength in case they ever decided to attack Napoleon again.

The main tenets of the treaty were as follows:

1. Austria had to surrender the Duchy of Salzburg to Napoleon. The city was the main access to the Adriatic Sea, and the surrender meant the Austrian army would be trapped in the country without a way out unless they

went through the French. Therefore, it would be very difficult for them to interact with other nations that were against France, and they consequently couldn't use the sea as a means of transport anymore. This was the one tenet that really destroyed the strength of the Austrian army, as without the sea they were stuck. Many other cities also surrendered, and Napoleon ensured the choice was strategic. The only cities he took over were the ones that had something to offer, since Napoleon knew he needed capital and resources more than anything else.

2. The Austrian army had to replace the able militants they had killed in the two wars. The indemnity was duly paid, and the Austrian army was reduced to just 150,000 men. With such a number, Napoleon was sure the Austrian army was crippled, and they could never engage in any other war unless they had the help of outsiders.

3. The Graz fortress, which was significant in the resistance against the French, had to be demolished. For a long time, the fortress inhabited persons who were against the French, and multiple coalitions against France were created therein. Therefore, Napoleon viewed it as a sign of resistance, and it had to go down. The Austrian army conceded, and the

building was duly pulled down.

Austria had to disband their mode of governance and use the French continental system. The continental system largely encompassed a decree and allegiance to the French army through the avoidance of British trade. Therefore, Austria had to forbid any importation of British goods and the severance of any communication and interaction between them, including mail communication.

While the Austrians knew they had no choice but to abide by Napoleon's stipulations, they made one last attempt to eliminate him. On October 12, as Napoleon was preparing to sign the treaty with the Austrian officials, a young man requested an audience with the emperor so he could present a petition. The French army guarding Napoleon refused him and pushed him into the crowd. Later, Napoleon was watching a military parade when the French army noticed the same man pushing through the crowd and getting closer to where Napoleon was. Having been trained by the best, they knew there was a possibility the boy presented some level of threat, and they arrested and took him in. When they stripped him, they found a large knife hidden well in his coat. After a lengthy interrogation, Staps, the young man, revealed that he had the intention of getting close enough to Napoleon to kill him. Staps retorted that Napoleon had brought nothing but misery to Austria and that the lives of the common people were more miserable because of him.

Napoleon was a tough fighter, but the words of the young man struck a chord with him. So deep were the words that instead of being angry his life was threatened, he was willing to show him mercy. Attempting to create rapport and somewhat changing his impression to the young man, Napoleon asked him what he would do if he was pardoned. Categorically, Staps affirmed that he would come back and attempt to kill him at a later date. Napoleon was wise enough to know determination when he saw it, and he concluded that the young man was better off executed. The army shot him outside the palace in a public execution that drew wide and mixed reactions. In the end, people considered Staps to be among the bravest and most confident to ever challenge the French army, and to date, he is regarded as a martyr.

Crossing the Danube

The defeat of the Austrian army was both a blessing and a curse. It was a blessing in the sense that it affirmed Napoleon's character and status as a powerful person, and a curse in that it filled him with pride and a very false and misguided sense of security. Napoleon was determined to take up even more Austrian cities, with the first in line being Vienna. Note that, even though Austria had signed a peace treaty, they were very angry at the fact that Napoleon had taken over the majority of their cities, and they were still determined to take him out. As it turned out, the Austrian army was perhaps one of the forces that Napoleon seemingly underestimated too much, and it would affect him in more ways than he could even imagine.

Napoleon marched toward Vienna, expecting no resistance since he had already weakened the Austrian army and a peace treaty had already been signed. As Napoleon approached the city, he came face-to-face with the Austrian army, and he was sure he could defeat them easily. The only problem was that his intention was to cross a river, and if he responded to the Austrians by engaging in war, there was a possibility they would run into the nearby Bohemian nation.

The biggest problem with this occurrence is that Napoleon would undoubtedly be tempted to pursue them in a foreign land, and he knew of the possibility of it being a trap, which meant that he would be beaten in a foreign land. Also, Napoleon had not been in the nation prior, and he knew that this was a disadvantage on his end as it would give the Austrian army a competitive advantage and ultimately better chance of winning the war. Napoleon decided to be wise and avoid losing more of his army through another war as much as possible. Therefore, there was only one thing to do at this point. Napoleon decided to turn back and attempt to cross the river from a different location—a place known as the Danube.

As fate would have it, the Austrian army had already prepared for this eventuality, and they were waiting for Napoleon at the Danube. This army, led by an Austrian leader known as Charles, would be the most memorable and humiliating for Napoleon. Once the two armies met, it was evident that a war would soon erupt. By midday, the war had already begun, and both sides fought their best. By the end of the day, Napoleon won and pushed the Austrian army out of his way.

One major factor that made this war stand out from the other wars was the way in which the Austrian army had fought. Even though it was a win for Napoleon, it was not the typical war he had been used to. For starters, the Austrian army fought more gallantly than they ever had, and Napoleon's army was more overwhelmed than they ever had been in the past. This was a sign that Napoleon's performance was going down and an affirmation that the other armies were getting stronger by the day.

The battle drew a lot of mixed reactions from Napoleon's supporters and militants. Most of them were of the opinion that Napoleon would have performed much better had he chosen to destroy the Austrian army at the first chance he had, while others were unsatisfied with the manner in which the team had fought. However, Napoleon still maintained that he had managed to take over Vienna regardless, and the team prepared to start crossing the Danube as fast as they could.

Unknown to Napoleon, the resistance they had faced at the beginning was just a small portion of what the Austrian army had. Napoleon made his first major mistake during this time by believing that the biggest portion of the Austrian army had been left at Bohemia. The truth, however, was that the Austrian army had studied their defeats during all the other wars, and they knew how Napoleon operated. Napoleon had already gotten used to the idea that, whenever he won a war, the defeated nation fell back for a considerable amount of time. This time, he was wrong. The Austrian army had not even sent half of its army to the Danube the first time, and they had many more men awaiting Napoleon at the opposite side of the river. Napoleon knew there would be some form of resistance, although he expected them to be hidden and very few in total.

To affirm this, Napoleon sent out a few men to cross the river, and there was no counter-attack throughout the journey. For some reason, Napoleon's overconfidence clouded his sense of reason. When the men arrived at the opposite side, they only found a few Austrian militants who were not even interested in engaging them in a fight. Unknown to them, this was a strategic decision on the part of the Austrians. Well hidden in the hills, the Austrians wanted Napoleon to come with a sizeable army, as only then would they be able to weaken them. Killing a few French men would have no effect on Napoleon. However, if a large army was present, the Austrian army would use their newfound skills to kill as many as they possibly could, with the hope of bringing Napoleon to his feet.

When the first militants sent across were not attacked, Napoleon continued sending more men across, with the only challenge being that the bridge constantly broke as a result of the weight of the horses and strong men. Therefore, the militants would move in bits, allowing reconstruction whenever the bridge broke, and another team would cross. With time, the Austrians would realize the weakness with the bridges, and they chose to capitalize on the situation. Charles, the Austrian leader, came up with the decision to find a way of threatening the bridges so the French militants who had already arrived would be trapped alone and without the hope of receiving any reinforcements.

When Charles began to attack, Napoleon knew he could not hold them back. First, he was outnumbered by around three times in terms of weapons and militants. Also, the bridges were not yet complete, and he was sure that it would be a while before he received reinforcement. Therefore, the first instinct was to withdraw and escape from the imminent war. However, he decided to stay back and fight when he received the good news that the bridge was almost completed and the Austrian army had already launched an attack to French officials in the other parts.

Charles had learned from the previous wars, and he was slow to advance an attack. This time around, he was behaving like Napoleon by thinking about what he was doing keenly before actually implementing the strategies on the ground. Napoleon was still holding his ground, aware that he would lose if he chose to advance at the Austrian army first. He made a conscious decision to stay put and await the Austrian army to charge and attack him first. The advance was slow as each side was waiting on the other to charge, and soon, the Austrians realized the reason as to why Napoleon was not advancing was that he was greatly outnumbered. Therefore, it would be prudent to attack him at that point. A full-fledged battle soon ensued, and Napoleon fought quite impressively considering the fact that he was greatly outnumbered. At the end of the day, no one could claim victory, and the war raged on. At this point, the Austrian army kept breaking the bridges to prevent Napoleon from receiving reinforcements, and the battle at the river was also immense. Napoleon's army proved to be very effective as they were able to fight off the Austrians time and time again. However, it was not easy, and multiple times, the Austrian army was able to break the bridge. Nevertheless, the army that had already crossed at this point was handling the war well, and Napoleon was on the verge of winning.

Napoleon kept making the same mistake of underestimating the Austrian army even after the heavy fight. Similarly to what he had been accustomed to in the past, he expected the army to fall back and concede defeat as the dark approached, which would give him the chance to continue with his mission of taking over Vienna. However, the Austrian army was as strong as ever, and they fell back to strategize on how they would carry out attacks the next day.

The following morning, the war resumed and this time, Napoleon was the one who launched the attacks. The procedure was similar to what had happened the previous day. The bridge would be restored upon falling, allowing more French troops to cross and the process repeated in the case it fell. The major challenge, just like before, was that the Austrian army was also breaking the bridge purposefully, and the fact that they held a very protective and strong front meant the French had a very difficult time rebuilding it in the first place. As the war raged on, more troops entered to help Napoleon, and the Austrians were surprisingly better at war than anyone ever thought was possible. The battle was anyone's, as both armies took the lead at different points of the day.

Napoleon's army started relaxing when they realized they were receiving more reinforcement with every successful crossing of the troops. This was a mistake on their side, and it gave the Austrians a chance to do two major things that changed the course of the war. First, two large ships were commissioned to hit and break the bridge, and Charles commanded his entire army to engage in the war. The ships set sail and hit the bridge, breaking it at multiple points that would take days—even weeks—to successfully repair.

Even though some of the Austrian militants perished in the accident, it was worth it because it gave them the competitive edge that changed the course of the war. When the French army realized what had happened, they suddenly started panicking, resulting in making more mistakes and having decreased confidence in their skills. Ultimately, the French were pushed back, and they retreated, resulting in Napoleon's first defeat ever.

This battle was revolutionary since it resulted in three major eventualities:

1. First, the Austrians became even more confident they could stand their ground, having defeated a man that everybody considered to be undefeatable. There is something about confidence and the joy of winning an impossible task, and the result was that the Austrian people became even more confident in their militants as thousands more joined the army. Therefore, Austria was able to create an army that was unlike any other in the history of the country.

2. Second, the news about the defeat of Napoleon spread all over the world. Nations far and wide heard about

what had ensued in Vienna, and a new wave of revolution was imminent. As you may have figured, Napoleon had thousands of opponents, and his defeats restored their enthusiasm that they, too, could beat him and regain the cities that had fallen under French rule. Simply put, Napoleon was about to face the biggest revolution the world had ever seen.

3. Third, the defeat broke Napoleon. There was something about being the best, then suffering defeat from those least expected as being capable of victory over him. For the longest time, Napoleon had considered the Austrian army to be a non-threat, and he was sure that they could never beat him. In the course of the previous coalitions, Napoleon had defeated the Austrians more than five times, and to suffer a defeat from them was very humiliating. Further, he knew that the news about the defeat would spread and that all the people who had confidence in him would lose it, and his ego was severely bruised.

This War of the Fifth Coalition changed Napoleon like no other battle did. Many people assert that Napoleon was egotistic and that is why he was never able to recover from this defeat. As the upcoming wars showed, this was the beginning of the end of Napoleon.

War of the Sixth Coalition (1813–1814)

The War of the Sixth Coalition took place between March 1813 and May 1814 in Europe, and it is considered to be a war of liberation in Germany. The War of the Sixth Coalition was largely influenced by the War of the Fifth Coalition, where the different military associations had regained new confidence regarding the strength of Napoleon and their ability to beat him in the different wars. As soon as Napoleon was defeated by the Austrians, there was increased confidence from his opponents, and they were ready to come up to him once again and regain all that they had lost from him. In the previous wars, Napoleon had taken over many cities in different countries, and they were all ready to regain them back. Largely, this War of the Sixth Coalition was between the Prussians, Austrians, Portugal, Spain, Sweden, Germany, and many other small nations that had at one point clashed with the French army.

There are a number of battles that took place involving the sixth coalitions. Some of the notable ones included the following:

Battle at Lützen (May 2, 1813)

The battle of Lützen was the first battle Napoleon fought soon after his defeat by the Austrians in the Fifth Coalition. During this time, Napoleon was still embarrassed and angered by his defeat, and he was determined to reclaim his legacy as the greatest warrior that ever lived. Napoleon had lost many troops in the previous war and enemies knew it would take quite a while before he was able to rebuild it. However, Napoleon was a master at his craft, and he still retained the love and admiration of quite a number of his countrymen. With love and support, Napoleon was able to build back an army faster than his enemies could have fathomed, and soon he had a sizeable number.

Once Napoleon was sure that his men were well trained and could fight, he sought to advance into the north of Germany with the aim of capturing and seizing Danzig. This time around, he knew a lot of nations were already rallying against him, and the fact that he had already suffered massive defeat meant their confidence was over the top. Therefore, he could not afford to underestimate any of them. He considered all possibilities and potential eventualities, planning carefully until he was sure about what he was doing. First, he would concentrate the army at a location called Erfurt and advance on any attackers from any direction they came from. Also, the army would travel in groups so they could offer some form of reinforcement in case the main army needed it.

As the French army was advancing toward Germany, around 100,000 men made up of the Prussians and Russians intercepted them. Napoleon had already learned from his previous battle, and he used the first group as bait to see if there was any other army that would attempt to attack them from elsewhere. When the battle began, Napoleon realized there was no other attacker, and he drove the entire army into fighting off the Prusso-Russians. The attackers were defeated, and the Napoleon who won battles was back. Both armies had casualties in excess of 20,000, and the Prusso-Russians felt more pressure compared to Napoleon since they had fewer militants. Napoleon knew there would be more attacks, and he was ready to keep up the winning strides.

Battle of Bautzen (May 20–21, 1813)

Napoleon's victory in the Battle of Lützen sent both the Russian and Prussian armies into a frenzy. Napoleon knew the win would be short-lived and the combined army would make advances at him again in the attempt to defeat him. Therefore, he began preparing his army and had more men recruited so they could replace the thousands of militants that had been killed in the previous battle. The recruit went well, and soon enough, Napoleon had a well-stocked army.

Among the factors that always gave Napoleon an upper hand was able informants who kept him in the loop about each and every single thing that was happening in his country and nearby countries. Through such informants, Napoleon learned that a defensive line had already been formed by the combined army of the Russians and Prussians, which meant they had also resorted to recruiting more militants and fighters. So advanced was the military that they formed lines that were seven miles long. Immediately, Napoleon knew he could not wait for them to attack and that he was better suited to lead the advance. As had been apparent in the other fights, the show of increased confidence in one army served as a threat to the others, and Napoleon needed to make the enemies know that he was not afraid of them in the least.

On May 19, Napoleon slowly advanced with his army right to where the Prusso-Russian army was. As soon as he arrived, he realized he had no match. All throughout, Napoleon had the notion that the combined army would have more than 150,000 militants. However, the number was much less, so much that he was almost disappointed. The total number of his opponents did not amount to more than 96,000 men, while Napoleon had virtually double the number. The overestimation was, however, in his favor. Right there, Napoleon was convinced that it would take him less than a day to defeat the combined army.

Napoleon soon set his plan in motion. Since they had the numbers, they would attempt to surround their opponents, weakening them on every side before killing as many as possible. By surrounding the enemies, all Napoleon wished to achieve was preventing the escape and retreat of most of the fighters, which would make the combined army have a harder time recruiting more soldiers in case they desired to attack him at a later date. The fact that both countries had engaged in so much battle meant that recruiting was not an easy process, and they could not get militants and fighters as quickly as they would have been able to in the past.

By noon, Napoleon had sufficiently and strategically placed his fighters, and he got ready to attack. The French artillery fire opened at around 3:00 p.m., and Napoleon ensured that he was doing the minimum. By avoiding significant progress, Napoleon hoped he would weaken the Allied forces significantly, ultimately keeping them pinned and ensuring they had very little energy left to fight a full-fledged war as soon as Napoleon decided to attack. His plan worked, and by 6:00 p.m., his opponents were getting tired. Throughout the day, they had hoped that Napoleon would fully advance towards them, and when he failed to do so, they were confused. Napoleon counted on that confusion, and as dark fell, his army was able to take their positions unnoticed around these Allied militants.

At dawn the following day, Napoleon resumed with his slow advances, doing the bare minimum. When he was confident that his entire army was in position, he then began the full-fledged attack. Had there not been a violent thunderstorm, Napoleon would have defeated the military more than he did on that day. Many militants were able to escape, contrary to Napoleon's desire to have most of them killed so as to prevent the probability of another attack from happening in the near future. The rain, coupled with a few mistakes on the side of the French militants, allowed most of his opponents get away intact, making sure they would undoubtedly launch another attack soon.

Battle of Dresden (August 26–27, 1813)

The Battle of Dresden occurred two months after the previous major battle of Lützen, and it marked Napoleon's last victory in Germany. In the previous war, Napoleon had won, although far from his terms. While his desire was to have killed as many opponents as possible, rain and mistakes from his team members ruined his plans, and most of his opponents escaped. The Allied army spent two months recruiting and training more fighters, and by August, they had already doubled their first number. Napoleon, on the other hand, may have been a little lax when it came to the recruitment process, as he had 120,000 militants in comparison to the 170,000 troops that belonged to the Allied army.

At the time of the war, Napoleon was held at Dresden, and the Allied army knew if they could capture the area, they would have the upper hand since it was the French's center of operation. Not only did Napoleon's army train there, but the entire supply of their fighting weapons was located there. Therefore, successfully attacking it would render Napoleon helpless, and they could potentially defeat him. Napoleon had proceeded to Dresden with only a few men, no more than 20,000. However, Napoleon had formed a robust military base and he knew that reinforcements would arrive in the minimum time possible in the event he was attacked. When he learned of the vast army of Allied troops approaching Dresden, reinforcements were called upon immediately.

The loyalty of Napoleon's army was evident after the call for reinforcement. The rest of the military had been far off in France, over 190 kilometers away. As these were the on-the-ground fighters, they had to cover the entire distance on foot. The army was estimated to be 190,000, and it resulted in what is still one of the most significant marches in history. Within four days, the militants had arrived.

While the French army had been on their way, the Allied army was busy making fortifications so they would be safer when the war began. Napoleon knew the fortifications would hinder him from achieving a proper attack, but he could not do anything until reinforcements arrived.

The Allied army was the first to attack, and Napoleon was fortunate that all the reinforcements had already arrived at the time. This army was very strategic, and they used heavy weapons and cavalry in the attempt to intimidate Napoleon as much as they could. Napoleon, however, was lucky there was a lot of mud and some rain, which affected the other side's heavy weapons by making them relatively ineffective in the war. One of the most significant mistakes this army had made was to lay out the weapons openly, and they soon realized that a good number of them were not even working anymore. Napoleon, therefore, had a considerable advantage.

The leading French army began attacking at around 7:00 a.m., hours after the opponents had already started the attack. Napoleon had realized that the opponents' weapons were problematic, and he opted to wait until they had used up most of them so he could attack and destroy them with little resistance. His plan worked. By the time he began the attack, the Allied were already frustrated, and they could not fight as effectively as the French were doing. Ultimately, Napoleon defeated them, killing more than 30,000 of their men while he lost less than 10,000 himself.

A shift of events would soon occur when Napoleon became ill right after the victory. So sick was he that he could not lead his army anymore, and he sent the corps commanders to pursue the fleeing Allies. This was not a wise decision, and the military faced a massive battle. The Allied fought with skill, and the French army was severely defeated. Ultimately, the win at Dresden was canceled out, and the French could no longer claim victory.

The Battle at Leipzig, a.k.a. Battle of the Nations (October 16–19, 1813)

The Battle at Leipzig is also known as the Battle of the Nations, and it is the most massive Napoleonic war that ever took place. Prior to the First World War, the Battle of the Nations was singlehandedly the largest battle in history, involving more than half a million men. The war involved separate armies that were coordinated and fighting toward the single purpose of ousting Napoleon. These men consisted of the Russians, Prussians, Austrians, and the Swedes. Collectively, over 1,300 heavy guns were available and with the opposition troops while Napoleon had 717 guns.

While it is clear that Napoleon was at a disadvantage, it is important to realize he had no supporters and was fighting on his own. Therefore, coming up with 717 guns while a combination of more than five countries had 1,300 is an illustration of the extent of the resources that were available to Napoleon and how well prepared he was as a leader and militant.

Napoleon already knew the number of men that were intent on attacking him, and he knew the battle would not be like any other he had ever fought. Not only was he outnumbered by more than double, but his weapons also could not measure up with those of his opponents. Napoleon had already been in a similar situation at a previous battle, and he knew the best thing to do was to attempt to fight the nations one by one before they came together to fight as a single unit. Thus, he had to instigate the fight right before his opponents were even aware or anticipating an attack. There was only one major flaw in the plan. Attacking the different armies independently meant that all of his commanders had to act independently and attempt to provide the skilled leadership and quick decision-making that Napoleon usually accomplished. This presented a problem since the marshals and commanders available were not nearly half as good as Napoleon. Further, Napoleon had maintained an autocratic system of leadership, which meant he would tolerate no competition, and he had done little to train the marshals to be as good as him. Despite the weakness, the battle had to be fought.

On the first day of the battle, Napoleon sent a section of his army to the north at a place where he had heard a part of the Prussian army was advancing from. The Prussians were on their own, and the French army had a very high chance of fighting and winning that day. For the more substantial part of the battle, the Prussians were defeated and had even started retreating. This short-lived defeat gave Napoleon some sense of pride and even undue overconfidence, and he began making mistakes. First, his army already had clear instructions pertaining to how they were expected to proceed. Napoleon kept changing the instructions, and soon the army was confused.

It was while the instructions were still relatively unclear that the Allied nations had a chance of getting together, and they formed a front that was too much for even a confident and qualified man such as Napoleon. Napoleon kept redeploying reinforcements to help the trapped troops, and even they did not help. The Allied army was too strong. Withdrawing and pulling out was not an option since the major bridge that connected the French to Leipzig kept getting destroyed by the thousands of French men crossing. The army was trapped, and their best chance of survival was staying put and fighting off the attackers by all means. The fight waged on, and at the end of the first day, Napoleon had lost 73,000 men, compared to the 50,000 men that belonged to the Allied nations.

The battle of Leipzig marked the first occasion where Napoleon was clearly and indisputably defeated. This defeat was different from all others in the following sense:

- The Austrian victory in 1809 was more of a stalemate and not a clear win, and the supposed win was soon reversed when Napoleon beat the army in the war of Wagram in the same year.

- The Russian victory in 1812 was caused by Napoleon's flawed strategy of fighting and not the actual defeat of the army on the field.

The battle of Leipzig ended in Napoleon losing troops and being defeated in the field, something that had never happened before. At this point, Napoleon had no will to fight anymore, and he turned back and fled to Paris.

The Battle of Paris (March 1814)

The Battle of Paris signified the first major war that Napoleon was involved in right after his defeat in Leipzig. Just like the other war, the Allies of the Sixth Coalition were more charged than ever following the defeat of Napoleon, and they were determined to make him fall to his knees. Despite the defeat, Napoleon still held a number of cities in Germany, Israel, and across other small countries. The Sixth Coalition was not only determined to take back all the cities but aimed at ensuring that Napoleon abdicated and stepped down from power for good.

The coalition forces recruited more militants and troops, and it is estimated they had about 400,000 once they started marching toward France. The French army, on the other hand, was down to less than 70,000 troops, for multiple reasons. First, the people were no longer confident about Napoleon's ability to lead and win a war. As such, there were not as many volunteers as there typically had been in previous years. Further, the fact that Napoleon fought on his own meant there were even less available strong men in his country that could join and fight in the war.

Napoleon may have been disappointed and even had his ego bruised in the previous war, but he was not about to watch his city be taken away from him while he did nothing. Therefore, he organized the available troops and got ready for war. Notably, Napoleon had a big advantage over the other forces, which was that he was both fighting on a friendlier ground and that he was at home. He was able to prepare effectively and strategically place the army at positions that would give him the best advantage and a higher chance of succeeding.

Using this advantage, Napoleon was able to defeat the coalition forces that preceded the attack as they came independently. As more reinforcement came in, it was clear there was nothing much he could do, and a defeat was imminent. However, Napoleon still stood his ground and fought the armies as they arose, one after the other. The French citizens were immensely scared when the war was brought into their country, as it had been more than 400 years since a foreign army had entered France. Napoleon was counting on a revolution, which would have seen the populace stage a war against the attackers, and he hoped that maybe that would have helped them win the war. However, the coalition knew about this probability, and they sent ravens to the people with the assurance that none of the ordinary persons would be harmed as long as they kept away from the war. According to the coalition commander, the armies were against Napoleon and not the French people. This assurance, coupled with the fact that most people had already lost hope in Napoleon, resulted in an unnatural peace and calmness, and the commoners stayed away from the war. At this point, the defeat of Napoleon was imminent.

The coalition stayed true to their assurance, and they purposefully drove Napoleon as far away from the city as possible. Ordinary people were safe, as none of them would be harmed during the war. Soon, the marshals and the rest of the army surrendered when they finally realized they could not fight the coalition. Napoleon heard about the surrender and was angered. His first instinct was to turn back and lead the army that was with him to the city and fight, but the marshals and troops were already done. None of them were willing to fight anymore, and they pleaded with Napoleon to abdicate. On April 4, Napoleon finally abdicated in favor of his son. However, the coalition would not allow him to act on his terms, and they ensured that Napoleon abdicated unconditionally. The terms of the abdication spelled out that he would not be killed and would be exiled to the Island of Elba. These conditions were settled in a treaty known as Fontainebleau, and the War of the Sixth Coalition was finally over.

Chapter 4: The Fall of Napoleon

Napoleon was successful for very many years. Unfortunately, his tenure came to an end when he was defeated and overthrown from power in 1815. The downfall began soon after the defeat at the Battle of Paris, a fight that forced him not only to retreat but also to proceed to exile.

Napoleon's Exile to Elba

The Allied powers declared that Napoleon was the obstacle toward the restoration of peace in France. According to the treaty of Fontainebleau, Emperor Napoleon was to be taken by the Allies to exile in Elba, which was an island in the Mediterranean Sea. The Allies gave Napoleon sovereignty over the island and allowed him to retain the term *emperor*. While this may have seemed like a good deal, considering the fact that Napoleon was in exile, the truth is that Napoleon felt much disrespected and distressed. Initially, he had the dominion of over 70 million people, and the island only had 12,000 people. So distressed was he that he even attempted to take his life using pills he had obtained in Moscow after his defeat from the Prussians. However, the pills did not work, and Napoleon survived.

Napoleon was not imprisoned on the island, and he had chosen it as the preferred location for his exile. Not only did the island have crystal clear waters, but it was also very rich in minerals. Despite the fact that Napoleon initially felt disrespected and did not even want to stay there, he decided that the best he could do was to lead the people to the best of his ability, and maybe someday he would have the chance to go back to France and reclaim his title.

Gradually, the island became more united than it ever had been in the history of its existence, and a lot of developments took place at the time. To date, Napoleon is known as the only leader who managed to unite the territory, and it fell apart as soon as he left. To many observers, it seemed like Napoleon had the best life and was content with retirement. However, Napoleon was just strategizing, and it would only be a matter of time before he came up with an excellent plan to get himself out of that place.

Napoleon proved to be strong and dedicated to the military. After some few months in exile, he created a small army and navy, which affirmed his position as a born militant. Also, he led in the development of the iron mines, watched over the construction of new roads, and issued declarations about upcoming methods of agriculture. Being very vocal on civilization, Napoleon also revamped the island's legal and education system.

Napoleon knew the importance of being in the light and seeking as much information as he could concerning what was happening around him. Despite there being guards who constantly watched him, Napoleon was not in isolation, and he had access to multiple letters, newsletters, and publications from all over the world. It was while he was reading one of the newsletters that he got to learn about the demise of his ex-wife Josephine. The first empress had committed suicide under unclear circumstances, and Napoleon was greatly troubled. He locked himself in a room, wept, and did not leave for two whole days. Evidently, he still loved her very much. Napoleon's wife and his son went to Austria to seek refuge, and they were safe. Surprisingly, Napoleon was not as concerned about the current wife as he had been about Josephine. After learning about her death, Napoleon made up his mind to escape.

Napoleon's Escape from Exile

Napoleon knew there were guards whose role was to watch over him and report any deeds and misdeeds that he may have been involved in to the Allied coalition. Therefore, Napoleon had learned to be very careful in words and deeds, and he planned the escape alone. Since the army saw nothing suspicious in anything he did, they did not find it awkward when Napoleon began organizing an army, and they thought that he was merely performing his duty as the emperor of the island. Unknown to the guards was the fact that Napoleon had maintained secret communications with some of the marshals in France, and they awaited his return. The communications were dangerous to the coalition and were a time bomb, which had since relaxed.

Napoleon had intended to plan the escape slowly but soon changed his mind when he learned there were plans to move him from Elba to another island in the South Atlantic. The coalition had decided on the move, owing to the fact that an uprising had started against their rule, and they were worried that Napoleon would soon get help from his people if he continued staying in Elba, which was near France. Therefore, the only option was to move him further, leaving the people destitute. Napoleon could not allow this to happen, and the fact that he was sure of support back at home gave him the motivation he needed to run away.

At first, Napoleon desired to run unnoticed. Later, he decided the best course of action was to act boldly, and he even began telling more people about his intentions. So bold was he that he even met up with some of the Elba officials and bid them goodbye. He left with his army that consisted of around 1,150 troops that he had trained, and soon he was back in France. Having carried out sufficient intelligence, Napoleon was sure he would arrive in France faster than any plan would be devised against him. True to his words, this was exactly what happened. The people heard about the heroic escape and were elated. Within no time, he had the support of the French as well as the army he had left behind. The emperor of France was back.

On March 13, the powers of the Congress of Vienna declared that Napoleon was a fugitive. After about four days, the coalition army made up of Great Britain, Russia, Prussia, and Austria each provided 15,000 soldiers to end the rule of Napoleon.

Napoleon arrived in Paris on March 20 and ruled for a period that is now referred to as a hundred days. By early June, Napoleon had about 200,000 armed forces. He planned to attack oncoming Britain and Prussian armies. The armed forces of Napoleon attacked the coalition troop of Britain and Prussia, and the Duke of Wellington and Prussian Prince Blücher finally started preparing for one of the most defining battles—the Battle of Waterloo.

Battle of Waterloo

The Battle of Waterloo took place on June 18, 1815, in Belgium, part of the United Kingdom of the Netherlands. At the time, Napoleon had been back to power from March 1815, and many states were against him. Therefore, they formed the Seventh Coalition to mobilize their armies and attempt to defeat the French. Two major armies made up the coalition, headed by the Duke of Wellington from Britain and Field Marshal Blücher from Prussia. This battle turned out to be among the most decisive engagements of the Waterloo campaign and signified the beginning of the end for Napoleon.

The war was orchestrated by the British and Prussian militants, and it is clear they had a well-defined plan as to how they would beat Napoleon. The armies of the Duke of Wellington and Blücher were close to the northeast border of France, and Napoleon had already confirmed that they were approaching him. At this point, Napoleon had learned to be more vigilant, and he refrained from assuming his opponents were harmless. He knew the only way to stop them was early enough while they were still in their distinct countries and before they came together to fight as a unit. His plan worked.

Napoleon successfully attacked the large Prussian army at the Battle of Ligny with his main force on July 16 while another portion of the French army attacked the Anglo-Allied army at the battle of Quatre Bras. The defeat of the Prussians made the Duke of Wellington withdraw north to Waterloo on July 17, but Napoleon was not done with him. He sent his forces to pursue the Prussians that had withdrawn parallel in good order to the Duke of Wellington. This led to the separate Battle of Wavre with Prussian guards. The Duke of Wellington prepared another battle on Mont-Saint-Jean escarpment on July 18, where he managed to attack France together with the support of the Prussians, who had arrived as reinforcement at the time.

The sudden attack took a massive toll on Napoleon. While it is not clear what exactly led to poor performance, the French army was beaten thoroughly. Some schools of thought attribute the defeat of Napoleon to be a result of two critical things:

1. First, Napoleon had been fighting alone and without the help of any other nation ever since the First Coalition was formed against him. Therefore, while the other armies always had new, robust, and much healthier militants, Napoleon was always using the same fighters for all his wars. At some point, these militants were bound to get exhausted. The poor performance was illustrated at this battle.

2. There was a loss of confidence about how long Napoleon could keep fighting his enemies. In as much as he had won multiple battles, the coalitions kept cropping up year after year, and without the support of any other nation, Napoleon could not fight them off forever.

With these two significant shortcomings, Napoleon decided to run away and re-strategize. The powers at the Congress of Vienna heard about the escape and declared Napoleon a fugitive. On March 13, 1815, the United Kingdom, Russia, Austria, and Prussians mobilized their armies to defeat France. Napoleon had known that his attempt to stop his opponents from invading France had failed. The only way for Napoleon to succeed was to destroy the existing coalition forces. Just like before, his plan was to attack them before any coalition had materialized. Previously, Napoleon had succeeded in destroying an alliance in Brussels, which made him confident that he could also drive off the British back to the seas and knock Prussians out of the war.

Napoleon knew that, by being a fugitive and hiding from his enemies, he would get time to recruit men and train them before engaging in the war. The British Commander Arthur Wellesley, the Duke of Wellington, knew that Napoleon was up to something, and they had to counter the threat of a surprise attack and potentially envelop coalition armies. Napoleon was determined to begin by stopping the British to ensure that they would not succeed. To achieve this, Napoleon started by spreading false information about the supply of the Duke of Wellington's chain being cut, hence giving the impression that the Duke of Wellington's deployment would be delayed. When the news reached the Duke of Wellington, he began panicking and could not proceed with his plans of attacking France. It would be a while before he realized that this was false information and that Napoleon was counting on the delay to buy more time and raise an army.

Napoleon raised an army of about 300,000 men by June. He divided his army into three—the right wing (commanded by Marshal Ney), the left wing (commanded by Marshal Grouchy), and the reserve under his own command. The three groups would potentially fight independently, although they were required to remain close and support each other. On June 15, France secured central position between the armies of the Duke of Wellington and Field Marshal Blücher, hoping this would prevent them from coming together and that he would be able to destroy the Prussians army first, then the army of the Duke of Wellington.

The Duke of Wellington got to know about the French's plans late in the night of June 15. On June 16, he received a dispatch from the Prince of Orange, meant to give him reinforcement against Napoleon. At the time, he did not know that Napoleon had already recruited thousands, and he expected any battle with the French to be an easy and effortless win. Napoleon was one who was always unpredictable, and when he advanced, the Duke of Wellington was shocked. Not only was the pace faster than he expected, but he also had a more massive army than the opponents expected. The Duke of Wellington ordered his army to concentrate at the Quatre Bras when the Prince of Orange was holding the tenuous position against the left French wing that was led by Marshal Ney. Napoleon had three divisions in his army and had selected the bravest to lead them. The Duke of Wellington knew Marshal Ney, and he was confident the battle would not be as easy as he anticipated.

Ney's instructions were to protect the crossroads of Quatre Bras, which was close enough to where Napoleon was. Therefore, he could consult Napoleon when necessarily. The crossroads were held lightly by the Prince of Orange, who repelled Ney's initial attack and was driven back by a large number of the French troops. The Duke of Wellington later arrived and drove Ney back, hence securing the crossroads by evening.

Napoleon led his division with vigor and strength, attacking and defeating the Prussians at the Battle of Ligny, using the right wing of his army and without any help from the other divisions.

While Napoleon was celebrating his win, it did not occur to him that this was a trap and the Prussians were just meant to be a distraction. The Prussian withdrawal from Ligny went uninterrupted and unnoticed by the French, and some did not move out until the following morning. Therefore, while Napoleon thought they were still around and the battle would continue, the truth was that they had left to a different location. Most of the Prussians did not participate in the war, a strategy that was meant to ensure they were strong enough for the other upcoming fights. The Prussian withdrawal from Ligny was prior to the Duke of Wellington's position at Quatre

Bras. Napoleon, with his other reserves, joined Ney's at Quarter Bras on June 17 to attack the Duke of Wellington, but they found the location empty. The French army was dismayed and shocked, and they attempted to pursue the Duke of Wellington's withdrawing army into Waterloo. However, they were unable to as the bad weather made it impossible to maneuver the hills. The delay would later have a very negative impact on Napoleon, as it gave the Duke of Wellington the upper hand to prepare for the impending French attack.

Napoleon ordered Grouchy, who led the right wing, to follow the disappearing Prussians with 33,000 men since he was confident that if the Prussians met with the Duke of Wellington, they would fight together. However, Grouchy was too late to prevent the Prussian army from reaching Wavre, as he had started pursuing them late and had been uncertain about the direction of the Prussians because of the vagueness of the orders he was given by Napoleon. The Duke of Wellington arrived at Waterloo with the main Napoleon army following. Blücher was gathering his army in Wavre. The Duke of Wellington was assured by Blücher that the Prussian army would support him. The Duke of Wellington decided to take the ground and battle at Waterloo.

The Armies

There were three armies that participated at Waterloo—Napoleon's army, the Duke of Wellington's army, and a Prussian army under Blücher. Napoleon's army was composed of central veterans who were experienced and devoted to their emperor. There were many units that were guarded by the soldiers they didn't know since the soldiers were assigned units as they presented themselves. The French army was forced to march through rain and coal mud to Waterloo. Little food was available to the soldiers. Nevertheless, the veteran soldiers maintained their loyalty to the emperor.

The Duke of Wellington had very weak, inexperienced, and poorly equipped militia. All the British soldiers were regular soldiers, and some of them were in peninsular war. Most of the troops in the coalition were inexperienced. Many of the professional soldiers in the coalition army had fought with the French military, which made them weak to some extent and worn out. The Duke of Wellington also lacked enough heavy cavalry, which gave Napoleon the upper hand. Despite this lack, the Duke of Wellington was brilliant, and he moved to lead the assault.

The Duke of Wellington stationed a further 17,000 troops at a nearby location who were under the Prince of Orange's younger brother, Prince Fredrick of Netherlands. The role of the forces was to safeguard any possible wide detaching movement by the French forces and to act as a rearguard if the Duke of Wellington was pushed and in case he needed help.

The Prussians were in the process of reorganization in the former reserve regiments, and the volunteers in the war of 1813–1814 were in the process of being absorbed. The Prussian army had the best professional leadership in its organization since they had came from schools that were developed for military purposes. The system contrasted with the vague orders issued by the French army, giving them an upper hand in the war. The system ensured that the three-quarters of the Prussian army was to participate in the field for about twenty-four hours. Although they were defeated in the battle of Ligny, the Prussian army was able to realign its supply and intervene in the Waterloo battlefield within forty-eight hours.

The Battlefield

Waterloo was positioned firmly, having long ridges running east to west and perpendicular to the main road of Brussels. There was an elm tree that was centered near the Duke of Wellington's position and served as his command during the daytime. In front of the ridge, there were three areas that were pivotal to the war. At the right side, there was a house that was described by the British as a *hollow way*. On the left side, there was an orchard of Hougoumont, a house hidden in the middle of trees. And on the extreme of the left side, there was a hamlet of Papelotte.

Hougoumont and Papelotte served as anchors to the Duke of Wellington's army. Prussians used Papelotte to send reinforcement to the Duke of Wellington's position. The French army, on the other side of the slope, could not see the Duke of Wellington's position, which made the position very secure. On the right area of the French location, there was a village of Plancenoit, where Napoleon could see the entire battlefield. Simply put, each and every army had their own position that gave them a competitive advantage, which meant the war would be unlike any other.

The Duke of Wellington wrote a letter to Blücher in Brussels, informing him that he would fight with his enemies at Mont-Saint-Jean and could withdraw to Brussels if Blücher failed to give him at least one force. Blücher persuaded some of his soldiers to join the Duke of Wellington's army. With these preparations, the army was ready to fight Napoleon.

Napoleon, on the other hand, was also making his definite plans, the key of which was to strengthen the main army. He decided that the best strategy was to have Grouchy join the main force reserves, and soon he was ready for the war.

Hougoumont

The primary battle began at Hougoumont, the point where the Duke of Wellington and Napoleon clashed. Both armies believed that holding Hougoumont was cardinal to winning the fight, and a war soon ensued.

Napoleon, undoubtedly, had the upper hand, as his mission of ensuring that the Prussians and the British did not meet succeeded. There was a unit that was engaging the Prussians at the opposite side of the battlefield, and Napoleon ensured the Duke of Wellington did not receive any reinforcements.

The European army had experienced more than twenty years of warfare. Therefore, they had well-equipped weapons and skilled swordsmanship. They were, however, inferior to those of France. According to the Duke of Wellington, although they had superior horsemen, they lacked the tactical ability and were inflexible compared to France. Once again, Napoleon had the upper hand.

The French Disintegration

Napoleon was undoubtedly a fearless and confident leader, considering the manner in which he single-handedly fought the Seventh Coalition. At some point, his army had the upper hand, and they may have relaxed, thinking the battle was over. However, the rest of the Duke of Wellington's army, as well as a few Prussians, arrived just when Napoleon was winning, and a fresh and fiercer war erupted. Understandably, this was too much for Napoleon, considering that he was attacked on all sides. As the war continued, it was clear to Napoleon he would not be able to win the war, and the focus shifted from battling to protecting the emperor. As a considerable number fought around Napoleon, the rest concentrated on keeping the aggressors back, and Napoleon lost thousands of fighters in a single day. Some estimates believe that over 33,000 French militants died while the other armies collectively lost half that number.

The Battle of Waterloo marked the beginning of the downfall of Napoleon as the French emperor. So significant was the defeat that multiple sources affirm that he left the battlefield in tears. He abdicated once more, and he was soon taken into exile on the island of Saint Helena.

Exile on Saint Helena

After the abdication of Napoleon following the defeat during the Battle of Waterloo, Napoleon was forced to renounce his throne once again, and he was sent to exile. The banishment marked one of the toughest times Napoleon had ever experienced, especially soon after he realized he would not be exiled in America as he thought, but rather in the midst of the Atlantic. The location was over 1,000 miles from the nearest land, and the coalition did this to ensure he would not have the opportunity to escape once again. The journey to the island took ten weeks, illustrating how far off the island was.

Upon landing, Napoleon was taken to the Longwood House in December 1815, where he wrote and published a paper implying that the British wanted to kill him before his time. Napoleon complained severally in writing that the room was cold, damp, unhealthy, and poor provision to the governor and his custodian. Further, it was infested with very many rats, and Napoleon was sure the British had arranged for the house specifically so they could teach him a lesson.

Napoleon, with his team of followers, dictated his reminiscences and complained about the conditions in Longwood. However, he still had the role of leading the people, as he was given the title of *governor* upon landing. Life in Helen was very different from Elba. At this point, Napoleon did not even want anyone talking about his previous royal position, and he made a decree that no gifts were allowed if they mentioned his imperial status in the least. The people agreed and even made a promise that they would stay with him for as long as he was on the island.

Napoleon stayed for six years on the island until he developed a serious illness. It was later speculated that his illness was brought about by the deplorable conditions that were there, including instances of arsenic poisoning that was in the wallpaper in Longwood House. The arsenic compound that was prevalent in the Longwood wallpaper could probably be what caused the unknown illness, and most people believe that it could have been cancer.

In the course of his time on the island, the French army had made a number of attempts to rescue their emperor, all of which failed. The British knew the distance was not a hindrance to rescue missions, and they took it upon themselves to take control and totally guard the Atlantic. All the plans failed, and Napoleon stayed on the island until his final days.

Death of Napoleon

Napoleon's personal physician stated that the deteriorating health of Napoleon was attributed to poor provision, cold, and dampness that he experienced in Longwood House. However, the main cause of his death was stomach cancer, which could have been genetic and aggravated by the fact that the diet on the island was extremely salty.

Napoleon died on May 18, 1821. The death mask was created around May by an unknown doctor. Napoleon had requested in his will to be buried in the bank of the Seine, and most people wanted his wishes met. However, the British governors stated that Napoleon was to be laid at Saint Helena, in the valley of the willows.

Later, Louis Philippe obtained permission from the British governor to take the remains of the emperor to France. The hearse progressed from the Arc de Triomphe to St. Jerome's Chapel, where his remains were retained until the tomb prepared by Louis Visconti was to be completed. Napoleon's remains were preserved as stone in 1861 at Les Invalides in Paris, where other France military leaders were preserved.

Napoleon's Legacy

It is evident that Napoleon may not have been appreciated enough while he was alive. It was only after his death that most people, his opponents included, realized that a great man had died. So great was his legacy that news confirming his death circulated all over the world. On July 5, *The Times* affirmed that Napoleon was the most extraordinary life known to political history, with military talent that superseded any other that they might have ever seen.

During the same period, the French publication also confirmed that no conqueror had ever had fame extended as much as Napoleon did. His own will had elevated him and ensured his rise among the ranks. The publication also recognized Napoleon as a man who made a solid impression on the minds and the imagination of humankind with an impartial judgment that changed the governance of France forever.

The London examiner portrayed Napoleon as one of the greatest names that ever lived and one whom no one would ever be able to reach in terms of standards and magnificence. The publication went on to hail him as a fearless man who managed to defeat army after army, making him one of the best leaders that ever lived.

While most of Napoleon's legacy is positive, some people still described him as selfish, wanting to subdue all cities and keep France in a constant state of war. While this may be true, it is evident that Napoleon's good deeds superseded the bad, and he is indeed one of the best militants who ever lived.

References

Connelly, O. (2012). The wars of the French Revolution and Napoleon, 1792–1815. Routledge.

de Bourrienne, L. F. (2012). *Memoirs of Napoleon Bonaparte.*

Shanon Selin, S. (2019). How was Napoleon's death reported? Retrieved 12 August 2019, from https://shannonselin.com/2016/05/napoleons-death-reported/

Thompson, J. M. (2018). *Napoleon Bonaparte: His rise and fall.* Pickle Partners Publishing.

Made in the USA
Monee, IL
28 October 2021